VIRTUS IN ARDUIS

VIRTUS IN ARDUIS

I Did It My Way

PARTHASARATHI SHOME

Orient BlackSwan

VIRTUS IN ARDUIS: I DID IT MY WAY

ORIENT BLACKSWAN PRIVATE LIMITED

Registered Office
3-6-752 Himayatnagar, Hyderabad 500 029, Telangana, India
e-mail: centraloffice@orientblackswan.com

Other Offices
Bengaluru, Bhopal, Chennai, Guwahati, Hyderabad, Jaipur, Kolkata, Lucknow, Mumbai, New Delhi, Noida, Patna, Visakhapatnam,

First published by Orient Blackswan Private Limited 2019

ISBN 978-93-5287-531-3

028707

Typeset in
Minion Pro 10.5/12.6
by Le Studio Graphique, Gurgaon 122 001

Printed in India at
Glorious Printers, Delhi

Published by
Orient Blackswan Private Limited
3-6-752, Himayatnagar, Hyderabad 500 029
e-mail: info@orientblackswan.com

To my teachers

CONTENTS

Preface		*ix*
List of Plates		*xv*
List of Abbreviations		*xix*
ONE	Journey to the United States and into Academia	1
TWO	International Monetary Fund The Initial Years	20
THREE	International Monetary Fund Latin America in the 1990s	34
FOUR	International Monetary Fund Africa, Europe and Asia in the 1980s and 1990s	72
FIVE	Policy Work at the IMF Early Years	104
SIX	Early Involvement with India Back and Forth with the Fund	115
Plates		*between pages 148 and 149*
SEVEN	Government of India North Block	149
EIGHT	Her Majesty's Revenue and Customs	188

NINE India Again 206
Research, Government and Committees

TEN Moving Forward 242

Epilogue 248
Index 256

PREFACE

A memoire is a reflection of past events that are etched in one's memory. It is, therefore, a personal biography. I separate the medieval age from when St Augustine's *Confessions* comes to mind; memoires were terribly revealing then and free-wheeling perhaps. In the current era, if I chose to reveal everything that I know in the contents of a professional memoire such as this, it would lay bare episodes and conversations, actions and thoughts, which would no doubt generate titillation but serve little useful purpose. Therefore, that is not even a remote objective of this volume. Instead, through multiple consultations and explorations with the Orient BlackSwan team, and Mimi Choudhury in particular, and through vacillations and meanderings on my part, I finally seated myself to recount how "Partho Shome came from there to here", as Mimi put her cogent demand on the table. That is my simple and direct objective and intention.

A second dilemma I faced while contemplating this book was the fact that it is almost impossible to remember a person, character or personality as perfect or fully benign or one who is unchangeably vicious or selfish, except for just a few ignoble and, therefore, ignorable, ones perhaps. It is well worth not mentioning the latter since that, in turn, would only reflect one's own recalcitrance to deal with, and confront and battle, the unpleasant individuals who also populate and surround one's life.

It is a relief that so many heart-stopping inter-regional and interpersonal experiences are relatable from one's professional journey. In the final analysis, I admit, they enable one to sit back and ponder life with a sense of satisfaction, and perhaps some amusement as well as heaves of anxiety, an occasional tear even. If such aspects comprise an interesting life, then mine has to be one such. I just hope that my readers experience a sense of involvement as they peruse the lines that follow.

As I reflect, the two most significant moments in my life were when my father and mother left me in 1971 and 2015 respectively. The forty-five years in between represent my adulthood—the period of experience—and events that comprise the thrust of this memoire. However, personality and character, if any, are formative even during childhood and adolescence, what I term the dream period. Thus, I shall occasionally allude to my childhood, generally in the form of flashbacks relevant to subsequent experiences, and the Epilogue also mentions that period.

A noticeable aspect of my life—to me—has been its variety and constant change propelled by an urge to move away from positions and placements even, or particularly, when they have ascended to a high point. I have observed that the changes in my life have been drastic, across continents and into unfamiliar environments of people and surroundings; yet I have embraced change time and again. I have wondered about this personality trait: is it a sense of accomplishment and a search for the next challenge to learn and experience something new? Or is it a fear of conventional success or recognition, perhaps even exasperation with the comfort of familiarity or the stability of surroundings?

Through a passing, ever changing frieze of ephemeral states studded alternately with vicissitudes and elation, I have enjoyed an extraordinary series of life experiences during:

My education in India and abroad, with teachers possessing varying attributes and conveying differing learning approaches and, I must admit, an advantage I enjoyed of steadfast attention, diligence and application, always recognised, if not mollycoddled, by teachers and tutors, thus imparting a sense of confidence in me from early childhood—that is why I have dedicated this professional memoire to my teachers.

My life in academia as a professor, teaching and researching abroad and in India during the early part of my professional life when I recognised and began to fully put in practice a component of travel in my daily life, reminiscent of my father's approach to education when he would take his children across the vast expanse of India, crisscrossing the country, reflecting his belief that travel was the best conveyor of education.

My career at the International Monetary Fund where I worked with colleagues from various corners of the globe, both professionally as an economist, thrust as I was into international economic policy formulation and technical assistance, as well as personally as an individual, imbibing an array of friends from variegated cultures and personal preferences. I experienced the corridors of power and controversy, occasionally with heartrending challenges. I feel that I matured as a person by learning to appreciate orthogonal variations in societal stance and in individual character and worldview that I encountered around myself.

My own views were shaped in the environs of perhaps one of the world's most conservative multilateral organisations, a fact I continue to reminisce about. Its ramifications were crucial in my training, perceptions and convictions regarding human productivity, and in my approach to human interface, especially in circumstances when a challenging, if not controversial, policy goal was to be negotiated with a finance minister or high official, not to exclude the more cordial experience of international social mingling. My reflections lead me to believe that, while conducting myself professionally and adhering to the responsibility of maintaining basic principles for the correction of errant country economic policies, I also dared to question, internally at least, tired and moth-eaten positions taken by multilateral organisations for no other reason than being in a position of power.

My entering the Indian government as the only Adviser to the Finance Minister—at the level of Secretary and then as Minister of State—that comprised the most unique of unique experiences, first, allowing one-on-one exchanges not only with ministers including the Prime Minister, but with leading industrialists, international policy leaders, and government officials of all ranks and, second, enabling me to traverse the length and breadth of India in an official capacity, undertaking fundamental tax reforms and attempting to comprehend my country in its many economic, social and regional aspects. Admittedly, I have formed views regarding the government and its officials, and of the limitations presented by industrialists and the small services sector, all of whom put together point to a deep need to remove the obstructions they pose and, instead, to chart a course to achieve the as-yet-elusive structural reform that India so urgently begs, and yet is capable of.

My being embedded as Chief Economist of Her Majesty's Revenue and Customs (HMRC) of the United Kingdom government, that pushed me onto a professional dais enabled by an exceptional decision taken by the UK cabinet and quite unanticipated by officialdom at large. It was arguably the most challenging period of my professional life since, invited as a "change agent" and hailed as a "thought leader", I had to relentlessly effect change while also attempting not to lose the trust and confidence of officials with and under me. I learnt a lot, including how the UK threw out antediluvian bureaucratic structures that, having inherited, India continues with intact at the cost of her severely constrained growth and development.

Resuscitation of my personal life towards art, culture and reading. Right from the start, my choice of college specialisation was controversial. I had always been clear that I would pursue art or anthropology, while my parents were convinced it would be physics. We ultimately landed on economics which was decided, as a compromise, to lie in-between. Upon leaving government, I am catching up on reading, and writing, in new areas, such as a book on naïve art that I have published, not that economics or taxation has ever left me. After a lifetime, I do not expect to abandon them of course. At this very moment, I am labouring over a textbook at the London School of Economics and Political Science (LSE), something I promised my mother 'to leave for students' after having authored too many professional volumes perhaps. This period thus represents a merry mix of competing yet complementary influences that I have embraced.

In sum, I view my life not as an ascendance but rather as moving through experiences in a continuum of education, resolving to return to my childhood desires, and so to complete the circle. In my life I have visited more than sixty countries, travelling not just to their high and rarefied offices but also their by-lanes and alleys. I have taken the long route, eschewing short cuts. The process has certainly been painstaking on occasion, though the outcome appears to have been a sense of comprehension of subject, society and the individual, and this I wish to convey to an interested readership.

In the Epilogue, I have indicated why I have dedicated this memoire to my teachers from primary school through my doctoral years and after. Though I know I will unwittingly leave out many, I will nevertheless mention a few in the manner and form I knew and remember them, not only for their contribution to my growth but also for the sheer pleasure of putting them on a roll call: Miss Nath and Miss Biswas (Class II), Mrs. Chatterjee (Class III), Shri Sadananda Mukherjee (Class IV), Shri Phani Bhushan and Dwarka Nath (Class V), Mr. Joseph (Class VI), Father Mellon and Mr. Manuel Joseph (Class VII), Mr. Pylee Abraham (Class VIII), Mr. Subba Rao (Class IX), Mr. Miranda and Mr. Lourderaj (Class X), Rev. Fr. Gatti (See Plate 1) and Mr. Ramachandran (Class XI), Professor P. Bagchi (Pre-University), Doctors Mihir Rakshit, Tapas Majumdar, Nabendu Sen, Ajit Dasgupta, Prahlad Jana, and Dipti Bhushan Datta (BA Honours), Professors K. L. Krishna, A. L. Nagar, Manmohan Singh, Meghnad Desai, Elizabeth Krishna, Aman Ullah, Suresh Tendulkar, A. M. Khusro, Dharma Kumar, and Mrinal Datta Chaudhuri (MA, India), Professors Ronald Jones, Rudolph Penner, Joe Kaplan, and Zabel (MA, US), Ravindra Batra, Joseph Hadar, Aman Ullah, and William Russell (PhD) and, Vito Tanzi.

I should thank several persons before I end. Roopa Sharma of Orient BlackSwan managed the project and the cover of the volume, while Moyna Mazumdar edited it. I deeply appreciate the permissions obtained from various print media sources, including from Narasimhan Ravi of *The Hindu*, *The Hindu BusinessLine* and The Hindu Centre for Politics and Public Policy, Shyamal Majumdar of *Business Standard*, Anurag Batra of *BusinessWorld* and Anjuli Bhargava who spearheaded the process, Indrajit Hazra of *The Economic Times*, and Ruben Banerjee of *Outlook*. Rohitash Chaudhary of International Tax Research and Analysis Foundation (ITRAF) lent his technical skills for downloading information, pictures, cropping and improving. A long list of persons stood firm in encouraging a somewhat unwilling author so that I could steel myself to complete the work. I am grateful for their unflinching support.

Partho Shome

www.parthoshome.com London, United Kingdom

PLATES

(*between pages 148 and 149*)

1. Reverend Father P. Gatti SDB, Rector and Principal, Don Bosco, Madras (1965–68).
2. A Western Union telegram, 1 August 1973, informing me that Nuffield College was ready to offer me a full studentship.
3. Letter from the Secretary of the Order, Government of Brazil, 3 February 2000, conferring upon me the 'Commander of the Order of the Southern Cross'.

4a and b. Being presented the award for 'Commander of the Order of the Southern Cross, 2000' by Vera Machado, Ambassador of Brazil to India, at her residence.

5. Giving a speech at a seminar on fiscal policy, Brasilia, Brazil, 25–28 January 1999.
6. Explaining that a minimum alternate tax does not harm investment. *Ambito Financiero*, Buenos Aires, 4 March 1998.

7a, b and c. Goodbyes from the IMF for NIPFP, New Delhi, May 1995.

8. At a seminar on tax policy at Trinity College, Dublin, November 1993.
9. At an international seminar on enterprise income tax, Qingdao, China, 1997.

10. Presenting the final report of the advisory group on tax policy and administration: Tenth Five-Year Plan, to K. C. Pant, Planning Commission Deputy Chairman. First published in *Business Standard*, 22 May 2001.

11. At the investiture ceremony with S. R. Nathan, President of Singapore, 13 June 2002.

12. With Lee Hsien Loong, Deputy Prime Minister of Singapore, 13 June 2002.

13. Letter from the Ministry of Finance, Government of India, 4 October 2006, confirming my reappointment.

14. 'Commander of the Order of the Southern Cross : In his new role, Shome is expected to give tax reforms a big push'. First published in *BusinessWorld*, 22 November 2004.

15. 'VAT: The rollout and the fallout'. First published in *BusinessWorld*, 18 April 2005.

16. 'VAT no fear'. First published in *The Economic Times*, 2 February 2005.

17. Emerging with Finance Minister P. Chidambaram after pre-Budget discussions with Prime Minister Manmohan Singh. First published in *Business Standard*, 10 February 2005.

18. 'Walk on the fringe side'. First published in *Outlook*, 14 March 2005.

19. Non-VAT states hindering CST phase out, ASSOCHAM, 11 June 2005.

20. 'TN, UP may introduce VAT soon'. First published in *The Hindu*, 21 May 2006.

21. With Secretary General, ASSOCHAM, D. S. Rawat. 'Single GST: Centre will share revenue with states'. First published in *The Hindu BusinessLine*, 5 April 2007.

22a and b. GST: 'How it panned out' (1993–2017). First published in *Business Standard*, 5 April 2017.

23. Interview on Budget analysis by Anjuli Bhargava, 'People have not perceived what we've done'. First published in *BusinessWorld*, 14 March 2005.

24. Interview on Union Budget 2006 by Anjuli Bhargava, 'Budget Speak'. First published in *BusinessWorld*, 13 March 2006.

25. Speaking on 'Bank loss due to sub-prime crisis' at a CII conclave. First published in *The Hindu BusinessLine*, 6 October 2007.

26. As head of the first mission on taxation to Myanmar, May 2012.

27. Release of *Tax Shastra: Administrative Reform in India, United Kingdom and Brazil*, February 2012.

28. Letter from Oliver Letwin, UK Cabinet Minister, 2 July 2013, on my paper 'Fiscal Stimuli and Consolidation', in *In the Wake of the Crisis* (2012).

29. With Dr. Manmohan Singh with the GAAR report, New Delhi, 2012.

30. Letter from the Ministry of Finance, Government of India, 13 December 2012, announcing my appointment.

31. At North Block as Adviser to the Finance Minister, Minister of State level, 2013.

32. Release of *Taxation Principles and Applications: A Compendium*, with Daniel Witt, President, International Tax and Investment Center (ITIC), Washington DC, Sudipto Mundle, Emeritus Professor, NIPFP, and K. L. Krishna, Emeritus Professor, DSE, New Delhi, 2014.

33. Release of *Development and Taxation: Sixty Critical Commentaries*, Academic Foundation, New Delhi, with S. Mahalingam, Member, Tax Administration Reform Commission, and Ram Tyagarajan, industrialist, Chennai, 2017.

ABBREVIATIONS

AIIS	American Institute of Indian Studies
AIR	Annual Information Return
ANU	Australian National University
ASEAN	Association of Southeast Asian Nations
BCTT	Banking Cash Transaction Tax
BEPS	base erosion and profit shifting
CBDT	Central Board of Direct Taxation
CBEC	Central Board of Excise and Customs
CENVAT	central VAT
CGE	computable general equilibrium
CGSS	Capital Gains Savings Scheme
CHI	Coefficient of Human Inequality
CIAT	Centre for Inter-American Tax Administrators
CII	Confederation of Indian Industry
CONFAZ	Confederation of state-level Finance Ministers
COS	committee of secretaries
CPC	computer processing centre
CPI	consumer price index
CSR	corporate social responsibility
CST	Central Sales Tax
CTT	Commodities Transaction Tax
DIN	Directorate General of National Taxes
DSE	Delhi School of Economics
DTAAs	double taxation avoidance agreements

DTC	Direct Tax Code
EC	Empowered Committee
ECLAC (or CEPAL)	Economic Commission for Latin America and the Caribbean
EC-VAT	Empowered Committee-VAT
ED	Executive Director
EP	Economist Programme
ERP	European Recovery Programme
ESAF	Enhanced Structural Adjustment Facility
ESRC	Economic and Social Research Council
ExCom	Executive Committee
FAD	Fiscal Affairs Department
FBT	Fringe Benefits Tax
FICCI	Federation of Indian Chambers of Commerce and Industry
FM	Finance Minister
FSU	Former Soviet Union
FTT	Financial Transaction Tax
GAAR	General Anti-Avoidance Rule
GDP	gross domestic product
GST	Goods and Services Tax
HDI	Human Development Index
HMRC	Her Majesty's Revenue and Customs
IAAS	Indian Audit and Accounts Service
IAS	Impact Assessment Statement
IBFD	International Bureau of Fiscal Documentation
ICA	Intensified Collaborative Approach
ICRIER	Indian Council for Research on International Economic Relations
IHDI	Inequality-Adjusted HDI
IMF	International Monetary Fund
IPS	Indian Police Service
IRDAI	Insurance Regulatory and Development Authority of India
IRDP	Integrated Rural Development Programme
IRS	Indian Revenue Service

IT	Information Technology
ITA	Income Tax Act
ITAM	Autonomous Technical University
ITC	input tax credit
ITRAF	International Tax Research and Analysis Foundation
KAI	Knowledge, Analysis and Intelligence
LFP	Long Term Fiscal Policy
LSE	London School of Economics and Political Science
LTU	large taxpayer unit
MAS	Monetary Authority of Singapore
MAT	Minimum Alternate Tax
MC	monitoring cell
MCX	Multi Commodity Exchange of India Ltd.
MD	managing director
MDO	Managing Director's Office
MIT	Massachusetts Institute of Technology
MODVAT	Modified VAT
MoU	memorandum of understanding
NBR	National Board of Revenue
NIC	National Informatics Centre
NIPFP	National Institute of Public Finance and Policy
NPOs	non-profit organisations
NREP	National Rural Employment Programme
NSS	National Sample Survey
OECD	Organisation of Economic Co-operation and Development
OSD	officer on special duty
PFC	Parliamentary Finance Committee
PPP	public-private partnership
PSUs	Public Sector Units
RBI	Reserve Bank of India
RLEGP	Rural Labour Employment Guarantee Programme
RS	Revenue Secretary

RTI Act	Right to Information Act
SAF	Structural Adjustment Facility
SCS	Senior Civil Service
SDA	Social Dimensions of Adjustment
SEZs	Special Economic Zones
SMU	Southern Methodist University
SPVs	special purpose vehicles
STT	Securities Transaction Tax
TARC	Tax Administration Reform Commission
TAU	The American University
TCS	Tata Consultancy Services
TDS	tax deduction at source
TERC	Trade and Economic Relations Committee
TOR	terms of reference
TPL	Tax Policy and Legislation
TRE	Treasury
TRU	Tax Research Unit
UFR	Use of Fund Resources
UNAM	Autonomous National University
VAT	value added tax
VATCOM	Value-Added Tax Committee
WHD	Western Hemisphere Department
WIP	Work in Progress
WTO	World Trade Organization

ONE

JOURNEY TO THE UNITED STATES AND INTO ACADEMIA

I arrived at John F. Kennedy Airport, New York, in September 1972 all ready to go into doctoral studies at the University of Rochester in upstate New York. I had just completed a Master's in Economics at the Delhi School of Economics (DSE), and an undergraduate degree with honours in economics from Presidency College, University of Calcutta. Having matriculated from a Catholic school in Madras, and buttressed prior to that by primary schooling in a culturally Hindu school in Calcutta, there was something ingrained in me right from childhood that resulted in a strong mix of cultures. The switch in emphasis, as my parents moved to Madras with the children, was initially discomforting to my father, his firm conviction being that his children needed a strong grounding in domestic culture in the post-independence era. However, such schools with the right package of subjects were simply unavailable, while the Catholic schools welcomed me and my sisters with open arms. My mother, however, seemed less affected by this eventuality, her view being that we needed to be trained in an all-embracing, perhaps even Western, environment, facing the probability of my father's frequent transfers across India every so many years.

Crisscrossing India by train and sometimes by car from infancy through my teenage years, accompanying my parents and led by my father who had a travel bug in him and a supportive mother, I had emerged adventurous and thoroughly embracing of cultures. Indeed I had preferred to take up anthropology in college, except that my father put an irreversible stop to any such thought, insisting that I go into physics. Those days there was little possibility of opposing parental guidance, nay decisions, all that freely. Hence I first went into physics but, finding it too inanimate, clandestinely took the entrance exams for economics a month late, and subsequently announced economics as my new subject. Being a banker at the Reserve Bank of India (RBI), my father reluctantly agreed though he persisted for some time that I was meant for science. In the meanwhile, my mother, despite being an accomplished and consummate artist, finally relaxed since her fear had been that, stubborn as I was, I would insist on entering Art College.

I remember that September afternoon quite clearly despite the long trans-Atlantic flight—essentially, the shock of seeing McDonald's in what appeared to me like a giant bright red structure set against a clear blue sky as I emerged from the airport, breathing the same air that George Washington, Thomas Jefferson, Abraham Lincoln, Franklin Roosevelt and John F. Kennedy had breathed. For reasons unknown to students, Madras University imposed a full paper on American history apart from twentieth-century Indian history at the school matriculation level, having done away with European and early Indian history in the junior years of schooling. After quick tours of the Statue of Liberty, Empire State Building, the United Nations, the World Trade Centre and the Bronx Zoo—for I have always been inalienably attracted to domestic and wild animals alike—I shot off after a couple of days to Rochester.

The Department of Economics at the University of Rochester had a reputation of being a crucible of mathematics. But I found that that was not the real challenge; rather, it was the use of topology rather than calculus as a mathematical tool; the latter would have been easier to handle. All courses in the theory of the consumer and the firm used topology exclusively. But I was lucky in that I had not been completely untutored in topology, for Meghnad Desai was visiting DSE from LSE during my second year in Delhi and he taught us topology from a text by Apostol. It was an uphill task but I had sat through his lectures, methodical and meticulous, despite the subject being somewhat monotonous. At Rochester, being subjected to placement exams and perhaps being perceived as somewhat advanced in my skills, I was encouraged by Professor Joe Kaplan, the graduate student adviser, to opt out of part of the first level instruction and enter the next.

Accordingly, I got out of macroeconomics and econometrics and took up microeconomics using topology and the specialised field of international trade and finance in my first semester.

What may appear as overconfidence on my part nevertheless had some justification. During my second year at DSE, Prashant Pattanaik, a brilliant young professor, was visiting from abroad and, upon the students' request, had agreed to teach us international trade theory. Pearls of scintillating wisdom passed his lips as they emerged through his markedly regional accent. He used a calculus based, two-sector general equilibrium approach that stuck to my cerebrum, cerebellum and medulla oblongata without the slightest possibility of being dislodged from there in the near future. And we were doubly fortunate that Manmohan Singh instructed us on the international finance portion of the syllabus with studious preparedness and absolute clarity. Thus entering Professor Ronald Jones' trade courses in Rochester did not seem too forbidding despite my classmates all being a year or two ahead of me in the PhD programme. Essentially, Jones used the same techniques of analysis as Pattanaik. I remember when I emerged with one of the two As from Jones' class of over twenty, there was a nod of approval and recognition from the senior Indian student community in the department.

Anjan Mukherjee—Anjanda—was the senior-most among us, being years ahead and close to finishing his doctoral work in a highly esoteric field. I respected him. When he smiled at me in the corridor and counselled me to keep my head high and move forward with my studies—*Bangali* Dada style—I was delighted at the compliment. His ever smiling and helpful wife, Runudi, even had a small dinner get-together though, thankfully, I do not recall that my success was mentioned directly as being the objective of the party. It would have put tremendous pressure on me to guarantee that early success into the future. In the event, I received an A– in the second semester, a notch below a clear A, but still high among peers. Jones was all smiles and called me in.

My shock upon hearing what Jones had to say was genuine since I had not anticipated it. He was moving to LSE, albeit for a couple of years, and he asked me to check if I could go with him to complete my PhD thesis there. Kaplan was clear about university rules. I could not carry over my $2,200 per annum fellowship and tuition waiver across the Atlantic. They were meant exclusively for my stay at Rochester. I had no other financing source. In fact, when I had applied for fellowships, Harvard, Massachusetts Institute of Technology (MIT) and Stanford had said that if I could finance myself for a single semester, I would be funded for the rest of my studies if my first semester results were good. I had not been able to come up with the required amount. I only had a loan of Rs 5000 from Tata Trust for the flight ticket. I had lost my father the previous year during my master's in Delhi. Perhaps if he were alive, he could have assisted me in acquiring a bigger loan. That was not to be. Instead, I was reeling from his sudden absence, as was his entire family.

I went to Rochester, which had agreed to give me a full scholarship and living expenses. On hindsight, I received top quality training that year. It seemed Kaplan was justified in not allowing me to carry the benefit of Rochester's financing to London. I informed Jones that I could not accompany him to LSE. His response and follow-up actions left me astounded. He assured me that Ravindra Batra at the Southern Methodist University (SMU) was also pursuing the same line of research. He offered to call Batra on my behalf. It was sheer serendipity that Aman Ullah, who had been my tutor at DSE and had occupied a room a few doors down from me at the International Students House on Number 1, Mall Road, was now at SMU. I called him and asked him his view. I recall he was excited about the possibility of my moving to SMU and wanted me to begin the process immediately. Batra welcomed the idea as well. I was swept away by SMU's doubling the fellowship I was receiving at Rochester to $5,000. It would take the form of a Merit Fellowship that was pulled out occasionally rather than every year. I felt honoured.

Nevertheless, I had to weigh the offer against exploring Ivy League schools, in one of which I felt I would be able to receive funding, having already spent a year at Rochester. I undertook a due diligence exercise on Ravi Batra. I was floored by his publication record in the top peer-reviewed journals in the area of two sector general equilibrium models. I also learnt that Ravi and Prashant Pattanaik were good friends, having been classmates at DSE and subsequently having published jointly in this field. That clinched it. SMU it was going to be.

When Kaplan learnt about my plans, he strongly encouraged me to complete a master's thesis at Rochester, and I took up the challenge. Amidst the competing tasks around me, I wrote one on the possibility of non-ethical income distribution effects of Pareto optimality in particular circumstances with Rudolph Penner as my guide. His practical bent of inquiry would later lead him to the Congressional Budget Office in Washington DC, and he did a brisk job in reviewing my thesis. I would leave Rochester with a second master's degree.

Indeed, in the midst of the Rochester winter, I had taken a cold bus ride on the Greyhound to MIT and appeared before Nick Stern of Oxford for a Nuffield College studentship. That telegram arrived while I was en route from Rochester to distant Dallas (see Plate 2). Nuffield was ready to offer me a full studentship. I did lose a heartbeat. I had already moved by train and bus up to New Orleans in Louisiana. I was in the miniscule Preservation Hall listening to jazz created by the descendants of American slaves. I had eaten delectable Creole food at the famous *Court of the Two Sisters*. America was beckoning me to stay. The scent of the Rochester lilac had not yet abandoned my sense of smell. I had yet to explore the Wild West. On the other hand, I felt that I knew England well already, having grown up with their cultural reach all through school, learning their social mores, their literature and their poetry, their pronunciation, their idioms, familiarising myself with the shapes of their churches and steeples. Paradoxically, I also felt that had my father been alive, he would have been uncomfortable bidding me goodbye for an education in England when his ancestors, some educated there, had resigned from the Indian Civil Service to join the independence movement, such was the strength of their, and his, views, on India's freedom and future. My mind was made up. I continued to move south to Texas.

There was good and bad news at SMU. The good news was that the credit I had earned for the courses at Rochester would be transferred to SMU so I would not have to repeat the compulsory courses. The bad news was that I would have to take the comprehensive—consolidated—exams on micro and macroeconomics. That would not have posed any problem in the ordinary course, but SMU followed the calculus route eschewing topology. Not that I had not been exposed to calculus in India but, for a whole year, I had not used it in these subjects. Thus, when I opened the advanced texts written by

Joseph Hadar, my new graduate adviser at SMU, I found the exercises tardy, though not daunting. My fortunes shone once again. Jo took a personal interest in me. Twice a week he spent an hour tutoring me, though he had no obligation to do so. Needless to say, I breezed through the comprehensives, aided to no small extent by Hadar's rigorous coaching.

Using the two-sector exposition of Jones and Batra that was used in international trade theory, in which prices were predetermined for any trading country (for it was assumed that every country was small in trade and could not affect relative prices at the international level), I reformulated the model in a domestic economy context and thus had to internalise price determination into the model. Usually in this approach, a so-called 2x2x2 framework was used, that is, two factors of production or inputs, two products or outputs, and two trading countries. It was invariably claimed that the results from this rudimentary approach were generalisable to more inputs and outputs, with an assurance that the outcomes would not change.

My query pertained to the use of this framework when a domestic partial tax is imposed in a closed economy. A tax tends to distort the relation between prices since the tax affects some prices and outputs more strongly than others. Arnold C. Harberger of the University of Chicago had examined this by introducing a corporation income tax exclusively on the capital-intensive sector. He came up with neatly ordered results that determined which economic agents finally bore the burden of the tax. He applied his theory to United States data. He categorised most economic sectors as comprising the corporate sector, leaving only agriculture, real estate and a small miscellaneous repair services sector in the non-corporate sector. Harberger concluded that capital owners in the economy bore more than 100 percent of the tax, reflecting the relative reactive movements in factors and products as an outcome of the tax. This went diametrically opposite to an earlier conclusion proposed by Richard A. Musgrave of Harvard University who, however, had used only an econometric approach that was considered partial, that is, unable to account for what was transpiring in the economy as a whole. The so-called partial equilibrium approach was deemed to be less convincing in an environment in which a newer, general equilibrium approach and framework were being offered.

I noted one lacuna in Harberger's work, for, certainly, land as a factor of production should be important for agriculture and real estate? Yet there was no recognition in his work of land as a factor of production in these sectors. What if I included land as a third factor of production used exclusively in the non-corporate sector? I thus created a model that I termed a third specific factor by two sector model to study the ramifications of a corporation income tax levied exclusively on capital use in the corporate sector. Out poured a series of results quite separable from those of Harberger and Mieszkowski, another economist who had derived some related theorems. I showed that land owners also bore a part of the burden of the corporate tax. The explanation was that the supply of land was fixed in the sector; hence there could be no responsive change in its supply as a consequence of any new tax. With trepidation I gathered the audacity of writing to Harberger and asking what he thought of this. He responded soon thereafter, himself explaining why I had obtained results differentiated from his, and encouraging me to proceed further with my work. I was deeply impressed at his scholarly response, encouraging a distant student whom he had never met.

In parallel, I had been presenting my model, theoretical results and empirical findings to Ravi. When he gave me time, he would usually be sitting cross-legged in his chair with a notebook on his lap, engrossed in his modelling work. While he was guiding my thesis in domestic tax incidence, his own research had been in international trade theory, with paper after paper emanating in peer-reviewed journals. He was always interested in examining my results without expressing overt enthusiasm or optimism, yet ushering me on to the next chapter of my dissertation. It was only from Aman Ullah—they were close friends—that I obtained indications of Ravi's assessment of my work. I felt satisfied but wished he was more open with me. Be that as it may, I could not have had a steadier guide who read my work without delay, with care and a quick grasp of each problem I set out, as well as its outcomes.

I had reached SMU in August 1973. I began working on my PhD thesis immediately even as I was going through course work and comprehensive exams. By the fall of 1974 I was demonstrating my theoretical results to Batra. For my empirical exercises, I spent nights at the computer centre, inputting data in little cards that was the student's wont those days. In early April 1975, at Ravi's urging, I presented the entire thesis to the examining committee, hoping to receive a nod of encouragement and to continue my work. My presentation was interjected by multi-faceted questions from the committee, and detailed explanations from me. At the end of it, I was asked to wait outside.

I expected to be called in shortly and given instructions for further work. Instead, it was a longish wait, leading to some anxiety on my part. When I was called in, Ravi was smiling. This was the first time I had seen him with a full smile on his face. I had no idea what reality I was facing. I recall Ravi congratulating me and informing that the dissertation had been accepted by the committee as it stood though, of course, I would have to get it properly typed and be ready for the forthcoming May graduation. He elaborated on my work in great detail, indicating to the committee in my presence how hard and intensively I had worked to be able to present such a complete piece of work in one go. I was in a daze. I realised that my immediate challenge was that I had not saved money to get my dissertation typed. It used calculus heavily with subscripts and superscripts, which cost much more to be typed than ordinary script. So I learnt typing in three days and typed my dissertation in ten. Basically I hardly slept over that fortnight.

It was a dumbfounding period. I had no job. I had not gone to the job market the previous December as would have been the usual practice. I only had a summer internship lined up at the World Bank that was meant for doctoral students. Even that might now be withdrawn if I already had a doctoral degree. I expressed my reservations in receiving the degree so unexpectedly. But by the time I summoned the courage to express myself along those lines, Ravi already seemed distant behind his usual unsmiling visage. If you could write such a dissertation, you could also get a good teaching position, he seemed to say, and appeared unwilling to hear any further doubts on my part. The meeting was over. Everyone congratulated me. I saw Ravi from a distance, strolling towards his office. Subsequently, the National Tax Association of America granted me the Jeanne S. Mattersdorf Award as "an outstanding student of taxation and public finance" for my doctoral dissertation.

I was no longer a student, however. By the time I joined the World Bank as a summer intern in June 1975, there were few jobs in the market. I was offered two positions, one at the University of Western Ontario, London, Canada, and one at The American University (TAU), Washington DC. I had a tough choice to make. Western Ontario was another seat for research on two sector models, and I felt some friendly pressure from its faculty to take up the job. But when I went there to present my seminar on 19 May 1975, though the sun shone, the ground was still covered in snow. It reminded me of the miserable Rochester winter. And this was across the border, in Canada. TAU, on the other hand, was smack in the middle of the US capital, and I was enjoying the World Bank experience. TAU also had a significant presence of Left economists who nevertheless appeared to appreciate my model outcomes, perhaps because they challenged the Chicagoan Harberger's results, though some of them put me through some rough grinding at the seminar I had been asked to present. Howard Wachtel, chairman of the economics department, assured me that I could continue as a World Bank consultant on a part-time basis as long as I published my research results. I realised that they wanted me there. I too was attracted to the somewhat non-traditional atmosphere pervading the department, often listening to experiences of the Left professors at the hands of the FBI and other agencies. I was young enough to consistently presume that they were imaginary rather than real.

In India I had been a student of brilliant teachers. I tried to emulate their teaching methods at TAU, and it worked. As an undergraduate at Presidency College in Calcutta, I was taught by Tapas Majumdar (utility theory), Mihir Rakshit (macro theory), Dipti Bhushan Datta (theory of the consumer and the firm), Ajit Dasgupta (statistics), Nabendu Sen (Indian economic history), Prahlad Jana (banking), and Deepak Banerjee (remnants of macro). It was the last individual who was instrumental in admitting me into the department more than a month late, and I always remained a bit in awe of him, not the least by his clipped English accent. The legend went that he had absconded to London as a coal hand on a ship and had completed his BSc at LSE, also managing to pick up that unnerving way of speaking that a return to Calcutta had failed to nudge. Amusingly, Tapas babu who had done his PhD at LSE had no accent other than a soft lilt. He lived in the same neighbourhood as ours and was an acquaintance of my father's, the way everyone knew everyone else in those days. Consequently, I made it a point to avoid him, to the extent that sometimes I might have been rude enough not to return a smile. Even so, I remained firm in my resolve almost as if to punish my father and Tapas babu for knowing each other. But the professors were all stalwarts in their own right, and they left us with an unconfused understanding of economics. And the mathematics that was compulsory as a minor subject buttressed the basis of that understanding. Why we had to take astronomy, however, has remained a mystery to me, though I confess it was an interesting subject in itself.

Master's at DSE was also studded with star teachers, A. L. Nagar (statistics), K. L. Krishna (econometrics), Sukhamoy Chakravarty (economic growth), Mrinal Datta Chaudhuri (Indian Five-Year Plans), A. M. Khusro (monetary theory), Vijay Tendulkar (agriculture), the ravishing Dharma Kumar (economic history) and others, and my tutors were Elizabeth Krishna (macro), Aman Ullah (econometrics), K. Sundaram (GDP), and Eva Datta Chaudhury (micro). They were not only great teachers but friendly, beautiful people so that often one could not assess exactly where one stood with them. I must say that Calcutta University exam results were, routinely, announced so late that students from there were first given provisional admission—an arrangement uniquely designed by Sukhamoy Chakravarty and Amartya Sen—during which time no hostel accommodation would be allotted but they could attend class. I rented a *barsati* room in Model Town, made my breakfast comprising bread, egg and tea on a Janta stove, using my skills as a President's scout, and went to attend classes. Below me, in a matching room, lived B. B. Bhattacharya, later Director of the Institute of Economic Growth and Vice Chancellor of Jawaharlal Nehru University. We always maintained a cordial relationship through subsequent years in reflection of the contiguous existence that we endured in those unbearably hot flats, albeit for a short time.

My mother took the train to visit me, and was not impressed by my living conditions. Soon after she returned to Calcutta, Sukhamoyda called me to his spacious bungalow on University Road in the Delhi University campus and told me that I should move in there. Lalitadi, his wife, strolled in, all smiles. I was flabbergasted and quite unwilling to make the move, but soon realised I had no choice. Those days we were not trained to stand our ground to do exactly as we pleased. Interspersed in the one-sided conversation were accounts of their friendship with my parents. Much later I learnt from Lalitadi that my father had been instrumental in resolving a family exigency that I shall refrain from elaborating. The upshot was that I moved in the next day into a comfortable room, perhaps even luxurious by the standards of the era.

I recall the months I stayed there as electric. Sukhamoyda would spend hours in the Ratan Tata Library and arrive late for dinner. Lalitadi and I would wait, spending hours discussing economics and personal matters. Sukhamoyda would never fail to ask me at dinner how my day had gone, whose lectures I had attended and, out of politeness, always refrained from asking what I had learnt. I recall a particular trait of his. I would take the bus to DSE. He would follow much later by taxi. One day he was early for some reason. I was waiting at the bus stop right across the road when he emerged through the gate. Instead of inviting me into a taxi, he crossed the road to stand with me at the bus stop, then got into the bus and chatted with me all the way. He actually seemed to enjoy it. It left a lasting impact on me, and I have attempted to emulate that example and others, strikingly similar to those set by my father, lifelong. It was not just lessons, however. I also witnessed, from a distance, the foibles of that strawberry bunch—Amartya, Nabanita, Eva, Mrinal, Lalita, Sukhamoy, a few others—and learnt with some trepidation the type of personal life I could possibly allow myself to have as a Bengali economist.

When I was allotted a room in both the International Student House and Jubilee Hall, I chose the former, to be close to foreign students and learn from them. They were from Afghanistan, Bhutan, Iran, Iraq, Kenya, Nepal, Palestine, Rhodesia, South Africa, Tanzania, Trinidad and Tobago, and United States among others. I heard students from the Caribbean beat their steel drums to produce a mesmerising, echoing sound, saw students driving flashy sports cars, and an occasional used condom on the corridor floors during weekends, leading the management to ban women from the premises after 8 pm. I made some good friends and also got to know Aman Ullah, one of the few other Indians there. I learnt about Palestine's struggle through an exhibition the students put up. I was delighted to be included in their game of volleyball, poor as I was in that sport. But Sukhamoyda could not easily accept my decision to move out until Lalitadi explained that it was only natural for me to want to be amidst my cohorts. As I was leaving their home, Mouri, their little daughter, looked decidedly forlorn. I bent down to cuddle her. Hearing of Mouri's demise a few years back brought tears to my eyes.

With my learning background, it was natural for me not to easily embrace the American teaching methods of the mid-1970s when I began my teaching career at the American University. As the sun would rise and the cherry blossoms bloom, there would be immense pressure from students to move the class outdoors under the trees. I would half joke and say that I wished I was teaching creative writing. I explained that I needed a green board to write, to ensure that they learnt the building blocks to be able to think and write economics. I would forbid them to read newspapers, eat lunch, drink coke, smoke cigarettes and wear dark glasses in class. As a private university, tuition was not cheap; I would remind them of that just as Tapas babu had reminded absconding students, including me, enjoying the winter sun on the college lawns, that the West Bengal government subsidised each of us by Rs 8000 against a tuition fee of Rs 16 per month. Ashamed, we had trooped back to class. Similarly, I subjected my students to strict and closed exams rather than "open" exams during which they could refer to library books. There was a regimen of cumulative marking over the semester plus a comprehensive one at the end that tested their knowledge accumulated during the course's tenure.

Some of the students seemed in shock, as if in a twilight zone. Howard Wachtel called me in, looking somewhat alarmed, and cautiously informed me that some students had brought to his notice that I was particularly strict. I asked him for a year's time. He agreed possibly with some reluctance. At the end of the year, I had the second highest score in teaching evaluation among all professors, admittedly the first being Jon Wisman who had a congenial personality, taught history of economic thought and occasionally took his class out in the sun amidst the spring flowers. Jon and his French wife Josette were excellent friends, with some of the best French cuisine offered in their home, countering the Indian *khana* in mine. I cannot but mention Josette's chagrin at her mother departing Washington earlier than the planned end of her short visit to escape from a place that had unacceptable bread, married as the French are to their perfect baguette. Those were the mid-1970s. Washington has since changed.

I began teaching at TAU when I was twenty-five. With a quantitative doctorate, I was given to teach four courses in the academic year, only one of which was public finance at the undergraduate level. The others were micro theory and public finance at the master's and PhD levels. My students were largely older and taller than me. As they came out of class, some would not desist from putting their hands on my shoulder. I was surprised but not shocked having already spent three years amidst American cultural practices. I soon realised I could spellbind them in class and hold them to a pattern of devotional learning. I saw with my own eyes a conversion to economics in some of them. Another reason why I was given to teach such senior classes was that I filled a vacancy created by the departure of Vito Tanzi, a senior professor who had taught those courses. He left for the IMF as Chief of Tax Policy. Vito was a gentleman who was willing on occasion to teach a few of my classes on taxation and to continue to participate in some of the PhD dissertations I was guiding. That perhaps lay the foundation of a fraternal friendship that eventually led him to invite me to join the IMF some years later.

My years at TAU were thoroughly enjoyable. Howard Wachtel, Tom Dernburg, Cynthia Morris, other senior professors, the Dean, the President, promoted me to a tenured Associate Professor in four, and to Professor in six years. Of course I had to go through the rigour of external assessments, some anonymous, of my research. They included assessments by Harberger and Musgrave. I became the international student adviser and graduate adviser for master's students many of whom were foreign, thus forming friendships with Indian, Indonesian, Iranian, Malaysian, Mexican, Uruguayan, and students of other nationalities. I served in committees of the Dean, who gave me grants to study during the summer at the Massachusetts Institute of Technology and awarded me teaching relief—based on my publications in peer-reviewed journals—so I could pursue my research intensively. I politely declined a lighter teaching load, reflecting my affinity for it. I became a member of the University Senate, debating issues with the senior-most professors. And I caught the President's attention who asked for assistance on different university-wide matters.

There was an African American student whom I recall. I failed him in a comprehensive micro theory exam. A senior professor, who had never disliked me, approached me and suggested that I pass the student since a teaching position was awaiting him in a southern black college. I remained undaunted, short of accusing the professor of racism. I explained my view. If the student departed with a weak degree, his students would depart thus as well, perpetuating weak learning in their midst. Alarmed at my reaction, the professor sauntered out of my office. I spent the summer coaching the student. He retook the exam and passed with flying colours. The professor came by, all smiles. The student entered his teaching career fully prepared for a bright future. I never believed, or believe, in subsidies that impair the potential of a human being.

Another instance was that of a basketball star in my class, a strikingly tall, attractive African American who resembled Denzel Washington in his early years. While in class he appeared to be listening, but did not often attend. I was never sure if he was practising the game or gallivanting. He fared poorly and received a D. His coach called me and said that he was one of the best sportsmen in the university and that I should give him a C to make him pass; otherwise he would not be able to retain his sports scholarship. I responded by saying that he actually deserved an E or Fail and that I had been in two minds if I was doing the right thing in giving him a D. I told him to ask the student to visit me. He did. I challenged him to undertake intensive learning for a month. He agreed. He bothered me a lot during my office hours. I kept on my smiles. This previously overconfident, disinterested student went through a slam-dunk experience and transformed himself into a person genuinely interested in an education. It took him two months to get a B. He came by to tell me that this was his first B. He had been trudging through Cs, bringing glory to the university at the basketball court without glancing at his grades. I asked him what lesson he had learnt from his experience. He jocularly told me that he now felt prepared to tackle not just a ball, but life as well. He also told me more seriously with glistening, admiring eyes that he now knew how he would bring up his kids when he had a family. Those were some of the best moments of my academic life. It needed no effort for I had witnessed my father assist apparently the most undeserving of candidates throughout his short life.

I utilised the flexibility offered by Howard Wachtel regarding my part-time consulting. The World Bank was glad to retain me as a consultant in their Public Finance Division twice a week. This enabled me to undertake policy-oriented research in different areas. One was the role of contractual savings—life insurance and provident funds—in India, Sri Lanka, Malaysia, the Philippines, and Singapore; did they add to total household savings or substitute other forms? My conclusion was that there was net addition. I studied the role of tax incentives in the same countries and became convinced even at that early stage about their pernicious effects, except in some restricted forms—such as incentives for capital investment—and only in strictly monitored environments of which there were few. The analyses and results of the research were published in national journals of Malaysia, the Philippines, and Indonesia, and the World Bank's own republication programme. I also participated in a strategy review for Africa, surveyed the performance of their non-financial public sector enterprises, and made a series of recommendations on how to turn them around from red to black. There was a complementarity in that I could interest several of my students who had to undertake thesis work for their post-graduate programmes to explore these areas as possible subjects pertaining to their own countries. Those from emerging economies took them up enthusiastically. The American students, some of whom were working in the federal government, were interested in policy research on prevalent American issues. So I helped them to pick current hot topics. This was a fruitful and productive collaboration that I enjoyed while also meeting the course requirements of my students.

An additional attraction of American faculty life was the long annual break from teaching. Essentially the four months between mid-May to mid-September were left free for study, reflection or hibernation. My variation was that I took this time to travel. At SMU I had bought a Chevrolet Vega Hatchback and, in Washington DC, a Chevrolet Monte Carlo, one model lower than the Kingsway which, it may be recalled, had been a popular car in Bollywood films. I selected the Monte Carlo since it looked smarter than the Impala. During those happy years, I drove in and out of some forty of the fifty US states, on occasion wondering if anyone would find me if I were to disappear in the Arizona desert, the New Mexico Indian Reservations, the Dakota

Badlands, the Texas Panhandle, or the Idaho State Park, Yellowstone, Yosemite and other such well-traversed National Parks being easy bait for me. The most exhilarating was when I was nearly stampeded out of existence in my Vega by a herd—the only remaining one—of four hundred bison in the Idaho State Park's plains, the rapidly increasing sound of whose rumbling seemed to indicate that they were charging at my car. My Vega stood still even as they charged and then, quite miraculously, stopped to graze. After an hour, they decided to move on, walking away silently. When I finally saw none on the horizon, I sped up to reach sea green lakes under pristine blue skies on the mountain top.

Another excellent practice of the American system was that after every six years, a faculty member earned a sabbatical or a year of relief from teaching during which the university would pay half the annual salary. Some professors were happy to stay put at home, carrying on with their research. Counting in two summers the total time available during 1981–82 was about sixteen months. I was also active and restless, if not more adventurous, as always. After all I had just crossed thirty. I tapped and obtained two sources of funding. The first was the American Institute of Indian Studies (AIIS) in Chicago that gave me a grant large enough for me to visit DSE as Visiting Fellow for six months and stay during this period at the India International Centre—unbelievable as it may seem at this point in time—and also travel through the length and breadth of India giving seminars at various research institutes and universities. At the DSE, I taught the public finance course that Pulin Nayak had graciously released to me. It was good for my soul to teach at my alma mater. Kaushik Basu was a professor there, and I recall his cordiality. My stay was enjoyable—a good experience. But before I knew it, it was time to leave for England. Sukhamoy most kindly offered me to stay on as full professor but, for a second time, I disappointed him; he had earlier asked me to do my PhD with him at the DSE, but I had then left for the US.

I used the half salary to visit the LSE. I wrote to Amartya Sen who immediately sent me a letter graciously inviting me to an Academic Visitorship there for two terms. At LSE, I mainly attended an immense number of lectures, the most impressive being Tony Atkinson's series on public finance and poverty measurement. Hla Myint, the reputed development economist, took me on and invited me to teach in his intensive MA Economics programme—which was enough for me to feel that I was doing a decent job. In return perhaps I was also invited to the High Chair at a Chatham House retreat, and allowed access to the Senior Common Room—a much more formal affair then than it is today—which I have since often revisited as an LSE Visiting Fellow during 2017–19. I undertook research on labour and its coverage by social insurance institutions. Time for research was constantly challenged by the myriad diversions of London itself. Countless museums—including a small one bulging with the spoils from the conquest of Tipu Sultan—exhibitions: a history of the Sikhs, a remarkable photo collection of the congruent Victorian and Edwardian British and Indian upper class; the theatre: the Greek tragedy *Phaedra*, lasting seven hours with a grand supper with wine in between, were unforgettable; one Shakespeare play after another in Stratford-upon-Avon and London, *Mousetrap*, the *Last of Mrs Cheney*, visiting sundry musicals from Broadway, and retracing the highland trails of Wordsworth and locations made eternal by Charles Dickens and Thomas Hardy.

The second source of funding came from afar. It comprised a fully funded invitation to a Visiting Fellowship from Australian National University (ANU)'s School of Pacific Studies at Canberra, by its then Director, Max Corden. The final four months of my sabbatical at ANU opened my eyes to fundamental institutional research on Indonesia's political economy and economic history that was being undertaken there. For the first time I seriously dove into reading and trying to understand the role of history and institutions in the formation and progress of a modern economy. I also recall the pink cockatoos visiting me and propping themselves on my office window sill, the kangaroos that hopped across my path as I crisscrossed the campus, and the astronomical observatory that, as a student of the subject in my undergraduate mathematics course, raised my curiosity to no insignificant extent. I would climb up the observatory ladder to view the maddening dance of celestial bodies in colours and flows that no mortal can adequately describe.

The travel bug compelled me to fly to Alice Springs and, from there, to take the bus to Ayer's Rock—now called Uluru—the centre of Australia, a mammoth round rock several miles in circumference that changed colour with the rise and ebb of the sun and the moon.

It comprised, and even now represents, the holiest shrine of the Aborigines. I confess I rolled around with them a whole half day, watching them brew their beer right in front of me under dusty trees, and partaking of it, until I was asked to board the bus by an exasperated guide. That detour was compensated by two traditional drives, one through Barossa Valley and its vineyards, in particular for Shiraz, and a drive in New Zealand from Auckland in North Island to Christchurch in South Island. I concluded that nature had blessed the latter country in the distant horizon bountifully, for it had meadows for its three million lambs to graze, volcanoes, snow-peaked mountains, glaciers, fjords, as well as pristine Mediterranean beaches.

Every irrational bone in my body was perilously urging me to stay back, such were my impulses. But I politely declined Max Corden's offer of a full professorship at ANU, just as I had declined Sukhamoy's at the DSE, though I was flattered, if not confounded, by what they saw in me. For personal reasons I knew I had to return to the US, and so I did. That my life would soon take a complete turn from academia I could not possibly have foretold at that point.

As I linger on the early part of my professional career and the years of education even prior to that, two observations emerge. The first is the inexplicable blessing of excellent, compassionate teachers from primary school through junior and high school, college, university and perhaps, to some extent, my particular diligence—*virtus in arduis*—that responded to them. Was it my mother's strict coaching and her methodically following my schooling, or my father's devotion to my academic progress (as long as I did not ask him to teach me anything—that was mother's task) and his interest in discussing politics, cricket, travel and Hindustani classical music with me? Second, was it a confluence of the stars whose flip side should comprise coincidence, chance and serendipity? For my grandmother always lamented that, being born on the 29th of *Ashwin*, my *Rahu* and *Ketu* were apathetic, after knowing which I was forever aware that I needed to make extra effort to subjugate them, much to the discomfiture of her own daughter—my mother—that "your grandmother has eaten your head!". In retaliation, I would jocularly admonish my mother not to compete with her own mother in trying to be my favourite person, in diverting my affection and devotion. That always remained a silent family combat. But the latent confusion of my life's course—led by fate, or effort and perseverance—has never vacated my consciousness or self-assessment despite my rational self-assurance that there can be no matter or energy comprising destiny. Thus it was that I took the next turn in my professional life.

TWO

INTERNATIONAL MONETARY FUND
The Initial Years

Before I departed for my sabbatical in 1981 as a tenured Associate Professor, Vito Tanzi and I had lunch at the IMF, as we did occasionally. In conversation, he mentioned that a regular position—as opposed to that for a consultant—was going to be available in the Tax Policy Division. Those days a regular position in the World Bank was considered lucrative, but one in the IMF was rare. The latter was placed a few notches above the former. Despite my genuine interest, if not some excitement, I was an academician. Through a grinding process of publishing and anonymous assessments of my work, of teaching undergraduate and postgraduate students, and participating in corporate or co-operative work for the university, I had reached the pinnacle at The American University (TAU) through dedication and perseverance. By contrast, I would certainly have to go through another arduous interview process and begin as a rookie at the Fund. I realised that I would have to give myself more time to think about the matter.

I gingerly explained to Vito that I had a forthcoming sixteen-month sabbatical at the Delhi School of Economics, London School of Economics and Australian National University that I did not want to miss, given the effort I had had to put in to earn that time. TAU would pay half my annual salary, and the American Institute of Indian Studies in Chicago had given me a handsome grant covering the other half. Of course Vito knew the sabbatical system well. I recall him smiling and commenting on my adventurous spirit and joking that hopefully I would not be lost somewhere during that time. He concluded the lunch by indicating that I could think about it on my return. I was relieved that I could postpone my decision for quite some time to come but, in the back of my mind, I would nurture some confusion as to what I should do once I returned to Washington.

On the one hand, my father's side of the family was primarily one of bureaucrats. My grandfather had been Advocate General of combined Assam or the most senior judicial official representing a state; of his brothers one was a judge, one an Indian Administrative Service (IAS) officer and one a government head engineer. My father was an officer of RBI, the central bank; his cousins were officials in the IAS, Indian Police Service (IPS), and Indian Audit and Accounts Service (IAAS); another was chief accountant (Chartered Accountant) of a public sector enterprise. My father would possibly have averred at my joining the IMF, fixed as his opinion had been against Western "imperial institutions", but he was no more. The others, alive or those mentioned above, would probably have been impressed if I was 'absorbed' in the IMF, as was the appropriate phrase in use for such an 'elevation'. On the other hand, I knew too well that, to my mother, her son being a tenured academic professor in a good university would remain her primary preference. To her, scholarship was everything. I had to very carefully weigh the pros and cons to which way I should proceed. And, underneath it all, where would *I* be happy? I knew that even if I decided to join the Fund, I could never abandon scholarship as a goal.

On my return, Vito and I met again for lunch. During my travels, I had made up my mind. Passing through academia globally, I felt I had acquired familiarity with that world. I could do with a change in environment. Midway through lunch, I broached the subject and asked Vito if the job was still available. He responded that it was. I skipped a beat because a response would soon be expected of me. I informed Vito that, having taken my sabbatical, I was duty-bound to continue at the university for a year. Vito smiled. During the final semester of the academic year at TAU, the Fund's Administration Department sent me information and an application form. I would have to fill it up and present a seminar and be interviewed by a Fund-wide committee. I went through it all. However, I soon received a shock—and perhaps a fleeting sense of relief—when the Administration called to convey that

I was too young not to enter through the Economist Programme (EP) which was meant for new entrants and required a two-year training and probation period. I called Vito immediately and informed him that, as a tenured Professor, I would not enter as an EP. I felt destiny had intervened to precipitate a decision for me not to join the IMF.

The next thing I knew, I received another call from Fund Administration to indicate that I would not enter as an EP and would not have to go through the two-year training and probation. I was informed that I was the first economist to be extended this courtesy at my age, and that I should now accept the offer. When I called Vito again, he asked me when I would join. Was it fate or my work that had determined my arrival to this point—I do not know, for my grandmother's observation never left me for all impractical purposes. Be that as it may, clearly all obstacles had been removed. I joined the IMF at the end of the 1982–83 academic year. Howard Wachtel and others at the university received the news as a feather in my cap and granted me two years leave. Indeed, I remained fully convinced that, at the end of the two years, I would return to resume my academic life. I had been successfully considered for full professorship on the strength of my publications, student evaluations of my teaching, and in reflection of my global sabbatical experience. Of course the entire external review cycle still had to be completed. I thought it was worth it and initiated the request and process, and completed it successfully. Thus my mind was clear. After two years, after diving into and experiencing what the Fund had to reveal and teach me, I would return to the university as full professor. I looked forward to this presumed dance of events.

Those two years at the Fund were heady in several respects. First, my environment became pervasively international, where I was suddenly encountering colleagues from every continent. I enthusiastically embraced the change, cultural anthropologist that I was in my heart. I realised that the place raised the possibility of an infectious, almost endless mingling in ethnic diversity in professional, social and personal aspects, except for a handful of ethnicities that did not mingle other than among themselves, which was historically consistent. And, later in my Fund career, I realised that it also tended to spur an exclusivist one-way path to career building. However, there are always exceptions as life unfolds for, as I shall relate later,

I also experienced acts of reason, balance, and fairness in our midst. Quickly, therefore, I realised and came to accept that in such a diverse international community, there were bound to be likes and dislikes, not just in professional skills but also based on appearances and perceived abilities based on ethnicity. Having grown up in diverse parts of India as well as the US, I resolved to continue to neutralise differences, find commonalities where I could, and thereby forge ahead with the professional experience the Fund had to offer, thus embracing the very reason why I had come to the Fund.

EARLY MISSIONS

My first mission from the Fund was to Thailand. The mission was headed by Carlos Aguirre, an Uruguayan, who focussed on tax administration aspects. I was lucky in that, despite being several years my senior, Carlos held me in high regard, not hiding his admiration of my quantitative skills. On my part, attending meetings with him with the authorities, I was directly exposed to tax administration concerns. His humorous approach to work allowed me to relax around him, and we made a good team. Subsequently Carlos requested my participation in a mission to Mexico in April 1985.

The work on Mexican value added tax was published in 1988 in the *National Tax Journal*, a top US peer-reviewed journal. I learnt an important lesson. It was possible to publish technical work completed in Fund missions provided one was ready to chart one's course through the complicated process of getting 'clearance'. Keeping this in mind, wherever the work enabled it, I adhered to this approach throughout my subsequent Fund mission work. The outcome was a multiplicity of practical investigative analyses often based on a theoretical foundation. Years later, in 2014, I put together a selection of my publications in *Taxation Principles and Applications: A Compendium* (Lexis Nexis, New Delhi), which resembled a textbook on taxation! It is a collection from four decades of writing, using information and data from continents across the globe, some of it co-authored. This reflected my visits to nearly forty countries, to some many times, to provide technical assistance in the fiscal area or to help negotiate a financial programme with their fiscal authorities with the objective of assisting them to achieve economic viability through fiscal control.

International movement on such a wide scale also helped satiate my penchant for travelling. I realised that each mission lasted for almost three weeks, covering initial consultations with the highest authorities followed by investigations into the statistical vaults, so to speak, of the tax departments to derive the necessary data base, carrying out actual analysis, arriving at conclusions and recommendations and writing the complete draft report. I, with my team, invariably completed and submitted the report to the authorities, usually the country's finance minister, on a Friday, expecting him and his officials to peruse and digest the recommendations in the report during the weekend that followed and have a meeting with my team on the Monday. This allowed me a full weekend to explore the country's heritage in history, geography, anthropology, or art, whichever aspect competed for my attention in the limited time at my disposal. I always looked forward to the exciting escapade before returning to the multiple stages of grinding peer reviews as the report made its way to finalisation at break-neck speed for dispatch to the authorities. Usually the latter were expected to use the report immediately as an integral component of their national economic programme, often guided by the Fund itself. And, of course, I also had the additional objective of carrying out analyses that would eventually prove to be publishable.

During those early years of my Fund life, I recognised particular traits among certain colleagues, strangely, usually from an insular part of the world. They would give reasons not to travel such as back pain or not knowing a requisite foreign language, even though it had been listed among languages they were familiar with, and get away with it so that the heavy burden of travel would become habitually lopsided. I was on the other side of the see-saw, sometimes staying away from Washington DC almost half the year. At least this was my perception and concomitant feeling of unfairness as managing my personal life became increasingly trying and fractured. But I declined to speak up, reflecting my upbringing to maintain a stiff upper lip come what may. However, I began to realise that such persons being at the Fund headquarters for longer—some avoiding travel altogether—allowed them to be near those who would be instrumental in future career progression or promotions. This realisation irked me deeply and I had to make a decision. In school I was quite poor in group sports such as cricket, football and field hockey, though I was definitely more able in individual sports such as swimming, table tennis, badminton and could keep up a game in tennis. Observing this inability, Father Mellon, my Irish school principal, when trying to teach me to cycle, told me, "Never give up, Shome. Keep on trying". And our school motto was 'Virtus in Arduis' or 'Virtue in Perseverance' or hard work. These words were embedded in me like merciless flashlights, forever guiding me to get up and move on without demur. My mother, too, had given me strikingly similar training, as if slapping on a sandwich with me as the filling.

And so it ravelled until my seniors who were responsible for travel allocation used it as an adage, "Partho likes to travel", and then believed in it. The outcome was multi-faceted—a rich experience of meeting and consorting with the highest country officials, travelling sometimes with Vito, a superior who liked to join my missions towards the end, enjoying every aspect of internationalism—great food, culture and art, flora and fauna in the remotest parts of the world, uncommon friendships and genuine appreciation of country authorities who began to trust my judgement and implemented my policy recommendations—one of them, Brazil, even conferring on me their highest civilian honour, 'Commander of the Order of the Southern Cross' in 2000 for my contribution to the country's tax reforms, thus making me the first Indian to receive it since its inception in 1934–35 (see Plate 3). Yes, in the final analysis, my professional life was fulfilling and imparted a genuine sense of accomplishment, though perhaps at the cost of some home–work balance that became more in vogue in later decades. I moved on, and new adventures and experiences never ceased to unfold.

Soon after joining the Fund, my boss informed me that I should learn a Western foreign language. That first suggestion made a strong impression on me in that he himself did not speak any Western language other than English. I grant he must have had my best interests in mind. As a quick learner, as indeed I had been through school, college, university and academic life, I enrolled in Spanish classes. And a whole new world opened up to me. At first I was allotted into a group class. I soon realised, and so did the teacher, that I had an acumen for the language. She recommended that I ask to be allotted an individual instructor in my office but that, in that case, I would have to spend an equal number of hours in the language lab after work every day. I agreed in concept, but a decision had to be postponed.

Within a fortnight of my beginning Spanish, Vito called me in August 1983 and, smiling, informed me that since I was now a Spanish speaker, he was sending me to Venezuela on a mission with the Western Hemisphere Department (WHD) that was negotiating a Use of Fund Resources (UFR)-related economic programme with the Venezuelan authorities. I would be in charge of the fiscal sector of the country programme, and would have to conduct myself in Spanish. Taken aback at the assignment, I informed Vito that I had barely begun to learn Spanish. Still smiling, he said there could be no better place to speed up my learning than in a Spanish-speaking country, and resumed scrutinising the documents on his desk, indicating that the meeting was over. I departed a bit dazed to say the least.

Before moving on, I should explain a little of how the Fund's structure was set up those days, and perhaps even now it is similar, conservative as that institution has been in approach and thrust throughout its existence. The top IMF official, the managing director (MD), is a European by convention. He is the chief executive and also chairs an executive board that seats country authorities from among its members. How much voting power a country possesses is based on a formula reflecting its GDP and other economic indicators, which then roughly determines its 'quota' or contribution to the Fund's coffers. Since it is not a bank, the Fund cannot access private capital and is entirely beholden to its members for capital. How that capital would be lent to member countries in economic distress depends on their quota and the nature of their economic distress, the latter, in turn, determining the rate of interest on the loan and its term.

In order to determine the nature of any loan, the Fund assists countries to construct an economic reform programme made up of macroeconomic corrections and buttressed by structural policies. This is made feasible through professionals under the MD's command, the first being the area departments divided by regions of the globe that look after the macroeconomic components and, second, the functional departments that buttress the programme with structural reform in fiscal, monetary and balance of payments—exchange rate—reform needs. Then there are support departments including statistics, treasurer's, administration and legal, with the former producing some of the most comprehensive global statistics on a regular basis. By and large, the Fund does not charge its members for its services. This overall structure has survived the decades of the Fund's existence, in stark contrast to the World Bank that seems to perennially undergo fundamental structural change with apparently every incoming president, its chief executive. The World Bank president has been an American by convention. Being a bank, it raises private capital from time to time and charges members for its services.

Soon after Venezuela, the Dominican Republic was my second area department mission in February 1984. It turned out to be a satisfying experience for various reasons. David Lipton, the colleague in charge of balance of payments, was cooperative despite hailing from Exchange and Trade Relations, another department perceived to be competitive with Fiscal Affairs, my department. We worked together, exchanging notes on needed fiscal and exchange rate corrections and were soon in the process of building a viable economic programme for the small country. In the evenings we explored the vicinity and found a nice restaurant run by a French couple, discovering the most delectable dessert, *Isla Flotante*, over conversations on how to convey our views to Western Hemisphere Department (WHD), the area department that was in overall charge of constructing and implementing the completed programme as was Fund custom. The mission chief was Colombian, congenial and helpful, leaving us pretty much to ourselves. He called me Paco, an affectionate Latin American diminutive. I corrected him on my name; he promptly agreed and confidently continued to call me Paco, which remained my moniker for the future as well. It was not hard to convince him about my menu of fiscal corrections and associated calculations of the revenue effort needed on the part of the Dominican authorities.

But there was a super boss, Ted Beza, the Director of WHD who monitored the mission from headquarters. Ted was a legend for stirring his fingers in the pot of every WHD country programme. In other words, he carried a reputation for detail and accuracy. He would speak to each mission member regularly as to the nature of recommendations he was contemplating, and the reasons why. By the end of the mission he was convinced, I felt, of my assuredness and he agreed with my menu of options. I confess that the youngster in me allowed me to feel that he was impressed. I knew Vito would be happy too, well aware as he was of Ted's reputation. Once I was sure of Ted's support and Vito's anticipated satisfaction, I relaxed.

I found larimar, a sky blue stone and bought a ring. I wore it for decades linking it with happy events in my life. I enjoyed the delectable seafood of the island nation. I let an ephemeral friend teach me *merengue*, the rapid swirling dance for which the country was famous. And my Spanish improved miraculously, proving Vito correct in his view on language-learning. I visited the place where Christopher Columbus had landed, taken gold and slaves and transported them to Spanish monarchs. I learnt the hard lesson of Columbus's ruthless conduct, much in contrast to what is given in *American History* by C. P. Hill that I had read in my high school in Madras. Back in Washington, it led me to read Howard Zinn's *A People's History of the United States* that appeared to give a more authentic rendition of the history of the American continent.

The pleasantness was, however, followed by a deeply painful experience. I found several government subsidies that could not continue to be financed from government expenditure that had become increasingly dependent on high-interest private bank loans. A high proportion of loans designated in US dollars were from foreign banks, leading to an unsustainably high fiscal deficit as the domestic currency was on a steady depreciation path. I drew up a detailed list of prevailing subsidies and strongly advised that the one on petroleum be slashed, although the one on medicines could be retained. The country subsidised milk highly, which enabled the disproportionate production and consumption of sweets in the consumption basket. I also brought this to the authorities' attention. We stopped at the Presidential Palace prior to the news that would follow. As we left for the airport, news flashed on the radio that the government had removed subsidies on medicines while retaining that on petroleum products, possibly fearing the latter to be more sensitive for urban transport. Riots had begun on the streets and thirteen people had been injured. I had no opportunity to explain that my recommendations had not been followed strictly. I was devastated.

On return to Fund headquarters, I saw Vito immediately to explain what had happened. He listened attentively. I indicated that a job in the Fund would be too unnerving for me if this experience was to be taken as an indicator of what was to be anticipated. I remember

Vito's response as clear as day—that my recommendations should always be honest and based on correct information, data and analysis, devoid of any biases or value judgements. If any country authorities failed to heed them, how could I blame myself? Still doubtful, I left sheepishly. Later, he called to inform me of Ted's satisfaction with my work and that WHD had requested my continuing participation in a repeat mission to Venezuela. Privately, I was unhappy at being assigned to another country in uncertain economic circumstance despite being rich in petroleum resources. I knew beforehand that it would be a trying experience. Thus I went to Venezuela again in June 1984 and again to Dominican Republic in November the same year.

Over the years, as I related some of these tough recommendations (even those I continued to make upon return to India) to my mother, who was a keen listener and a critical reader of my writings, she would half jocularly interject as I spoke with friends that they should be careful what they said to me since I might get a new idea for imposing another tax. One of my close childhood friends once admonished me severely based on his presumption that I had forgotten the small Indian businessman in the design of the value added tax (VAT). I was taken aback, and we never reconnected for two decades. Recently we met when I heard he was not doing well, and it felt good to visit him. In my heart of hearts, I knew he was misinformed about the tax policy then being discussed in the papers. But I had decided not to argue beyond a point and instead chose to retract from him. I have learnt to consider such episodes as hazards of my profession, in particular, taxation policy and administration that are often misunderstood by taxpaying citizens for no other reason than their vulnerability as taxpayers to maintain compliance, or not having a clue as to how public resources they contribute to are spent, whether they are used judiciously or pilfered. I have my own doubts about taxability and the largesse encountered in expenditure on public servants and, increasingly, on politicians including parliamentarians and assembly members. Perhaps, if there were no such largesse or corruption, overall expenditures could be halved for the same outcomes.

When I returned to Venezuela during the tumultuous 1984–85 period—unbelievably similar to its present 2015–18 return of chaos—I found an unsustainably high fiscal deficit, high public sector debt in terms of GDP, and unsustainable short-term borrowing in foreign exchange at extraordinarily high rates of interest. Most remarkably, a whole spectrum of public enterprises were borrowing without any reporting of information to the central government, leave alone control. I had been assigned, prior to leaving Washington, to appropriately consolidate all payments—the intra-sector cross-flows—of the entire non-financial public sector. This meant consolidating the loans and receipts to and from the central government, provincial governments, local governments, and non-financial public enterprises. It was indeed an enormous assignment, the first of its kind for me, far distant from the theoretical two-sector three-factor models I was used to building, analysing and publishing as a professor.

I had little idea of what I was getting into. But Jose Fajgenbaum, an Argentinian economist working in WHD, and co-mission member, who was familiar with Venezuela, was on my side explaining and assisting whenever he could find time to get away from his macroeconomic work. He was also good to observe and learn from his cool, steady and persistent negotiating skills with the authorities. Our software for the job was Lotus that came after Multiplan. So used I was to Lotus that I never became comfortable with Excel that came much later. Those were halcyon days, decades before laptops. On flights each of us carried, by hand, huge and incredibly heavy box computers. Their operational features were slow by standards of current technology. Yet we confidently achieved in technical work whatever was expected at Fund headquarters.

The outcome of the public sector consolidation exercise was to reveal its dire straits and the need to cut back subsidies and sharpen tax policy and administration with the objective of achieving a reasonable consolidated public sector fiscal deficit. This was not an easy task in a country in which the abundance of petroleum revenue had resulted in massive petroleum subsidies and a basically undeveloped system of taxation by Latin American standards. Added to this was the challenge of containing the role of Western commercial banks which had found an easy route and destination to lend at usurious rates. Not all aspects of the job were straightforward. Ted Beza talked to me a couple of times; much of the talking was with his direct officers from WHD. My role as a Fiscal Affairs Department (FAD) economist was to stand guard on fiscal matters and not to let loosen the fiscal criteria in any impending Fund financial programme with Venezuela, while WHD's ultimate job was to put together a viable programme that necessarily required compromises in one sector or another. I learnt in those missions and in headquarters follow-up work how to successfully participate in this give-and-take exercise, realising that, at the end, it was the area department where the onus and responsibility lay.

But, throughout the process, not once did Ted Beza admonish me for my stringency in insisting on fiscal requirements in the programme. I also felt that I had the full support of Vito from FAD. In fact, over the years, I concluded that Vito sometimes admired, and was sometimes amused at, my tenacity regarding the formulation of Fund programmes when the primary interest—and his interest—should be in providing assistance to country authorities in structural fiscal reform such as in the Thailand mission. For me, however, given that I had been assigned the Dominican Republic and Venezuela missions to assist WHD in formulating Fund programmes, it was my job to do that with utmost focus and deliberation. Vito never overruled me in my zealousness. And I came away with Ted Beza's confidence in my work. It was not surprising, therefore, for him to ask for my inclusion in future WHD missions and later, wanting me to move to WHD when positions fell vacant there. But Vito immediately assigned me on additional FAD technical assistance missions and dissuaded me from moving out of FAD at that stage. I felt that I was in a win-win situation, though some well-meaning colleagues informed me that it was also important to have area department embedded experience for a fast-track Fund career. In retrospect, while there was some truth to it, nevertheless Vito's safeguarding my specialisation in the fiscal area had long-term positive ramifications for my reputation as a fiscal economist and, with time, as a global professional in the taxation field.

Strangely, however, the discomfort of a Fund job did not leave my psyche easily. I recall during one of the visits to Caracas, I went out shopping during a weekend with some of my colleagues. I entered a lace shop to buy some for my mother, who was a fantastic embroiderer herself. The elderly lady at the counter was proper and began a friendly conversation. She asked if I was a tourist; I answered in the negative, explaining that I was visiting on business. She pursued the line of questioning to ask what business it was and, without reflecting on the newspapers that had been, as expected, full of news on the Fund mission, I responded that I had come to examine the economy. Her tone abruptly changed, she became withdrawn and I saw her change of poise. I rushed to pick up a few things and as I went to the counter to pay her, she suddenly raised her sombre face and said, not rudely but in a determined fashion, that, in good conscience, she could not sell me anything though she had nothing personal against me. I was truly shocked and hurried out. It was another lesson. When I related this story to my mother over dinner at my sister's New Jersey home on my way to Washington DC, she heard my story silently without proffering any empathy. Looking rather forlorn, she only cautioned me to be careful in uncertain situations. My mother was not in favour of the Fund either, I realised.

This was another rude shock. Despite this, in deference to my mother's heritage, and the strong convictions regarding India's independence struggle in my family, I always had a deep and abiding respect for her views. Yet, interestingly, growing up I had observed and realised that my mother had clearly preferred and consistently ensured that her children received a Western education, while my father only came to accept it later after perceiving that his children were not growing up too steeped in Western culture but in a mix of the east and west that my mother ensured. His first preference had been vernacular education that coincided with my paternal grandfather's view which, somehow, my mother had managed to waylay without confronting, and put us in 'English medium schools'.

Another instance comes to mind. I was visiting Calcutta with an Italian friend and colleague after visiting beaches and other tourist spots across India. My mother expectedly organised a grand dinner. When one of her friends asked where I was employed—which surprised me since there had never been any sustained secret in that community—my mother quickly mentioned the World Bank. My mother was fully aware of the difference between the IMF and the World Bank, though the latter was a common euphemism in India for all multilateral organisations. I looked at my mother but she looked away signifying, in no uncertain terms, that the conversation was closed. Later when I asked her why, her response was quick and direct: it was better for her friends to think that I was employed at the World Bank rather than at the IMF. The pervasive feeling in India that the World Bank was more helpful to developing country interests while the Fund extracted its blood when a country was reeling under impending economic ruin was hard to crack, and emanated from 1966 when India first went to the Fund for consultations after its par value with the pound sterling collapsed. This bias has continued in many a country only because, by its very nature, the Fund arrives to redirect the economy when a country is in dire financial straits. Later, as my mother mellowed, we learnt to live with that difference and even half-joked about it occasionally. But the feeling that she never fundamentally modified her position, despite being happy about my professional successes, remained with me. And I never ceased to fret over it.

As I returned to both the Dominican Republic and Venezuela for ongoing Fund-supported economic programmes, I continued to face extremely challenging tasks, but that initial practical training in the field turned out to be deep and strong, rendering a sense of learning and contribution at the same time. Thus, as the end of the two-year period approached, I felt ready to take on difficult assignments, never declining any assignment, something I found some colleagues quite successful in doing, and I became aware of the good and bad of my acceptances. And, on a Friday evening at the end of the work day, Vito called me to ask if I had made up my mind about continuing at the Fund or returning to TAU, my erstwhile university.

I told him I was in a deep dilemma. He calmly asked me whether I foresaw how my professional life would unfold if I returned to academia. I gave him a list comprising postgraduate and undergraduate teaching, guiding PhD and master's theses, publishing in peer-reviewed journals as well as complete volumes, participating in a corporate role for the university and so on. Vito reminded me that I had already accomplished all those tasks, and whether I felt that I had learnt what there was to learn and deliver at the Fund. I knew I had not. Nevertheless I told him that I needed the weekend to think over. It turned out to be one of the most difficult weekends of my life. I weighed the pros and cons endlessly and finally decided to embrace the location where I would have to face more challenges than where I would feel comfortable and mature. Vito was happy, and possibly not too surprised, when I conveyed my decision to him first thing Monday morning.

THREE

INTERNATIONAL MONETARY FUND

Latin America in the 1990s

As I grew in my role, I acquired a reputation of a "fire-fighter" in Latin America. I enjoyed that term. Indeed, my popularity as a Spanish-speaking Indian economist who could be trusted grew across the continent as I found myself travelling on missions to Argentina, Bolivia, Brazil, Chile, Colombia, Ecuador, Guatemala, Nicaragua, Paraguay, Peru, Uruguay and, time and again, to several of these countries. Commendations from finance ministers landed regularly on Vito's desk who passed them on to me with his inimitable smile or with a hand-written note. I was elevated to Chief of Tax Policy in 1992 until I left for India for my first Indian sojourn beginning 1995.

BRAZIL

Among the countries in which I had the opportunity to provide technical assistance in taxation matters, Brazil was on the forefront. In the 1992–95 period, I visited Brazil four times, heading major missions to mobilise public sector—mainly tax—revenue through a fundamental rationalisation of the entire tax structure and its components. And immediately after my return to the Fund from the National Institute of Public Finance and Policy (NIPFP) in 1997, at the request of the Brazilian authorities, I went back there three times in 1998 alone to continue efforts to reform the VAT and to recommend strategies to control tax evasion as well as to reform the social security administration.

Right from my first mission in February 1992 when I went to Brazil twice, I realised that many areas needed urgent attention. The general government—comprising the centre, states and municipalities—tax revenue collection was between 24 and 25 percent of GDP, certainly very high by Latin American standards. The tax pressure was concentrated on the taxation of goods and services and payroll taxes, while income taxes and customs duties yielded relatively little revenue. Consumption taxes at 11 percent of GDP were based on value added while turnover taxes at 5 percent of GDP were used to fund social security. Individual income tax and corporate income tax yielded 2 percent of GDP each. Thus the revenue composition was skewed compared to other middle income countries. Brazil, being a relatively closed economy with many quantitative restrictions, collected only .5 percent of GDP in customs revenue.

The first visit was to support a 20-month Stand-by Arrangement with the Fund. The tax system included fifteen major taxes that needed urgent attention and had to be redesigned. On the one hand, the tax to GDP ratio of general government comprising all levels was almost 25 percent. But revenue sharing arrangements with lower levels of government made tax policy inflexible. Thus any mission would need to address how to reform a system with a relatively high tax burden combined with an inflexible overall structure.

With the final objective of recommending reform measures I was placed at the head of a large mission comprising Professor Paul Bernd Spahn from Germany who examined the VAT at the central and lower levels of government, together with selective excises that had almost disappeared in scope, Professor Erik Haindl from Chile who analysed the income taxes in particular the financial sector, Lorenzo Figliuoli, a Fund colleague from Italy who studied the social security system, and Arturo Fernandez for tax administration reform. We did not ignore local taxes on property or fees and charges that had important implications for revenue sharing arrangements. Every mission drew up a terms of reference (TOR) in consultation with a peer review committee within FAD which then went to the area department for endorsement. This mission's TOR was long and complex. Vito Tanzi joined us in the mission during its last week as he did in many of my missions.

Reflecting the slew of recommendations that we discussed in our final meeting with the authorities, by April, Ary Oswaldo Mattos Filho, coordinator of an ongoing Presidential Tax Reforms Commission, desired a meeting to discuss their schedule of anticipated tax reform with us. Accordingly a second mission comprising Vito and me went to Brazil to discuss our mutual findings and also to participate in their ongoing national tax commission. We also discussed the contents with Marcilio Marques Moreira, the Minister of Economy, Finance and Planning. I learnt that forthrightness in discussion—whether they could or could not undertake a particular slice of reforms—was the clear approach of the Brazilian authorities.

During all my missions to Brazil to provide technical assistance, attend conferences, or give lectures at seminars and workshops up and down the country, I invariably encountered the same forthrightness that made my professional queries, and their answers, straightforward if not always uncomplicated. How different I found India to be in the years to come! In Brazil, apart from the familiar Rio de Janeiro and Sao Paulo and holding many meetings there, I had the opportunity to visit Fortaleza in the north, Salvador, Bahia in the middle, and sundry other places for analytical work and attending meetings of the Confederation of state-level Finance Ministers (CONFAZ). Convened by a mid-level deputy secretary of revenue at the central government, CONFAZ was a body controlled and guided by powerful state-level finance ministers who met quarterly to discuss modifications in the VAT structure proposed by any state-level finance minister.

I found the Brazilian VAT structure to be complex as one might imagine in a structure that was primarily designed in the 1960s and modified progressively in subsequent decades. To achieve fiscal sustainability, we faced the challenge of not only designing a more rational structure but also for it to be revenue productive since there was limited potential for expenditure compression. This was because there was no major transfer of expenditure responsibilities to the local governments contemplated. There was already a heavy payroll tax comprising a distortionary revenue raising mechanism based on corporate turnover to finance social security. There was little link between financing and benefits. Though the system clearly needed reform, it was a touchy political matter. The individual income tax was also difficult to confront since it was considered to have been just reformed; hence there was at best a limited potential for further gains in that area. Corporate tax reform was certainly needed since exemptions and incentives had eroded its base and yield. At that time, Brazil was also considering a tax on financial transactions as a guaranteed revenue source to close the fiscal gap. But already the cumulative tax rate on financial intermediaries was around 75 percent, and any further burden would exacerbate tax avoidance.

Thus the focus fell inevitably on the Brazilian VAT which needed to be considered in special light. Brazil introduced its VAT comprising all three levels—central, state and local—of government in the mid-1960s. The centre's coverage was, and remained, narrow for it taxed only a short list of industrial products. Local governments taxed selected local services such as laundry, restaurants, parking services and others, though they tended to ignore property taxation and user charges reflecting reduced need precipitated by a new system of enhanced federal transfers from the centre. It was therefore only at the level of states that the VAT was broad-based with a wide array of taxed consumption items. Most countries have, on top of the VAT, a list of selected excises on the turnover of demerit goods such as tobacco and alcohol, and those judged to be depletable resources such as fuels and electricity. In Brazil these were low by international standards and needed to be recalibrated.

Any change in the VAT structure was negotiated through CONFAZ, though discussions actually took place and changes agreed upon prior to a meeting. Only very contentious matters were discussed face to face in CONFAZ meetings. I was invited to many a CONFAZ meeting and I learnt how such complex meetings might be organised, conducted, and results obtained. And, after a hard day of negotiations, the Brazilians moved the chairs out, put on rhumba music and danced away into the wee hours of the morning—a far superior way of ending a formal day than the stodgy manner in which Indians conduct themselves in comparable circumstances.

When I returned to India in June 1995 as Director NIPFP, I spoke to Raja Chelliah, Chairman NIPFP, about CONFAZ. One advantage was that Dr. Chelliah was not disinclined to listening to me on policy issues. He spoke to Manmohan Singh, then Union Finance Minister. Dr. Singh pushed the idea and chaired a meeting of state-level finance ministers that took place in December 1995. He urged the states to reform their terribly depleted sales taxes and work towards a comprehensive state-level VAT instead. Subsequently, the chief ministers of states met and recommended the creation of an Empowered Committee (EC). When India's EC was born it was good that the state finance ministers managed it themselves by electing one of their own as chairman rather than a central minister. In the longer run, it has been beneficial for ushering in indirect tax reform for the nation as a whole.

My Brazilian experience was extremely useful a decade later when, in 2004–07, I participated as Permanent Invitee to India's Empowered Committee (EC) of state-level finance ministers at the EC's invitation. As Finance Minister, P. Chidambaram asked me to represent him in the regular EC meetings, which he would attend only as needed. Thus I could contribute to India's VAT introduction and implementation process imperceptibly, contributing to the understanding of optimal structure as well as drafting important documents and white papers.

A major problem I found in the Brazilian VAT in practical terms was the proclivity of state-level finance ministers to take unilateral decisions when they felt a need to grant incentives, for example, when they perceived fiscal pressure in the state. Thus, in order to encourage investment or economic activity, a minister might declare exemption of capital goods from the VAT if imported at the main port of his state. Or there could be an unanticipated announcement of a temporary lowering of the VAT rate on a selected list of taxable items. Despite its convenorship of CONFAZ, I never saw the Brazilian central government showing interest in, or being able to, lead the way to cohesion. Frankly, state finance ministers considered themselves more senior and more experienced, in particular those of the economically powerful states such as Sao Paulo, Rio de Janeiro and Minas de Rais. This is why India's EC being an entirely state-level entity was a good option. Of course, the Goods and Services Tax (GST) Council, under India's comprehensive centre-state GST introduced in July 2017, necessarily comprises both levels of government, and it is chaired by the union finance minister.

Neither was the centre sanctimonious about restricting tax incentives in Brazil. It provided incentives widely, and an entire free trade zone was established in Manaus, on the Amazon river, roughly at the centre of Brazil whose geographical area is almost three times that of India. I felt compelled to check how it operated and whether any commodity leakage could be gauged, in sum, if the free trade zone comprised good economic policy or was just a drain on tax revenue. Vito had arrived; so we both flew across to Manaus. The free trade zone was similar to any other in the world—tightly controlled on the surface, yet impossible to decipher any underlying machinations. The only ones that appeared to operate as they were designed to operate were those in China, as I later witnessed, with less than twenty in operation in the entire country. By contrast, India's Special Economic Zones (SEZs) number close to a couple of hundred, and the coyest term one could use for them would be 'political'.

The Manaus trip enabled Vito and me to get on a small family boat on the Amazon, land on tiny floating islands inhabited by cheerful indigenous peoples, and gingerly eat some very basic meals, cooked with Amazon water boiled for less than the mandatory twelve minutes, on the boat itself. My prize from the trip was two small piranhas that I brought back, dead of course, to Washington with me. Those were the days when international travel was flexible enough that various forms of inanimate matter regularly travelled back with me to add to my global collection of art and artefacts.

In Brazil, local governments were not unimportant either, in particular the large ones such as the city of Sao Paulo—the New York of the southern hemisphere—that quite independently exercised its taxing powers, not only over selected services but in particular over real estate. The mayoralty was, accordingly, a powerful and influential office. Reflecting Brazil's pioneering and intensive use of information technology (IT) in tax administration at every level, it was impressive to see ordinary citizens using electronic means for tax compliance even in the early 1990s. To no small extent, it reflected the government's use of public-private partnership (PPP) through special purpose vehicles (SPVs) in designing software and for filing tax returns at a time when India would continue to debate for at least another decade, if not longer, the efficacy of bringing in the private sector even in a limited way into the taxation sector that was believed to need protection for reasons of 'confidentiality'. Thankfully, that bias was eventually cast aside, with the private sector coming into PPP set-ups and generally leading IT usage in every function imaginable for ensuring tax compliance. This was enabled at the centre through an Empowered Committee for Information Technology that, in continuation, I took over as chairman when I entered North Block in 2004.

No doubt, my involvement with, and affinity to, Brazil were intense. Through 1993, Jose Fajgenbaum of WHD discussed the fiscal measures being undertaken by Brazil, and that familiarisation and involvement continued in the following years. In 2000, after many a visit to the country and scribing reports on various aspects of tax reform and working with different administrations at central and state levels—for I continued to visit through various changes with the same overall objective of tax reform, and participating in all manner of intellectual discussion on the matter—Brazil recognised my work and awarded me their highest civilian honour for my contributions to Brazilian tax reform. I have appended to this chapter excerpts of statements made at the ceremony by the Ambassador and myself.

In particular, it was a novel experience working with Revenue Minister Everardo Maciel, and the tête-à-tête that did not always result in agreement but added an element of learning new matters on both sides, and also some rambunctious dinners. I learnt about transfer pricing and elements of international taxation that were not in the general purview of the Fund. On my part, I illuminated him about global practices in income tax and the VAT structure and how they were quintessentially different from those of Brazil, pushing for deeper and sharper tax reform there at every opportunity.

It was Vera Machado, Ambassador of Brazil to India, who initiated the proposal for the medal to be conferred on me, being convinced about not only what I had done for Brazil but also what I was doing for India. Since it was impossible for me to travel to Brazil at that time to receive the medal and certificate owing to the heavy burden of my work chairing the Tenth Five-Year Plan taxation committee, acting as adviser to various state governments and conducting research, including on my book *India's Fiscal Matters*, Vera herself affixed the medal on me in an elaborate ceremony in her rambling ambassadorial residence (see Plates 4a and b). Many English newspapers and magazines covered the event, but so did vernacular ones in Bengali such as *Ananda Bazar Patrika* and *Aajkaal*, the latter effusively proclaiming my achievements as, "Brazil gives its highest honour to Parthasarathi", followed by a long article. Vera and her husband Ronald became close friends during their tenure in India.

I visited Vera and Ronald more than once when she was subsequently posted as Ambassador to the Vatican, and lived in an actual palace. The world can be strange. As we sat dining one afternoon at the longest ornate dining table imaginable, a band of tourists passed by, staring through the panelled French windows, much to my discomfiture which must have been obvious from my countenance. Smiling, Vera reassured me that tourists visited only by prior appointment during a limited number of days in the week. When I could not but wonder at this strange arrangement, she explained that, during and immediately after the Second World War, Italy needed its coffee but could not pay Brazil in cash; hence it paid in palaces. However, Brazil had to agree to selected visitors and other accommodating arrangements.

In the final analysis, what I enjoyed most in my Latin American experience was the trust country after country put in me and in my recommendations. In every country I acquired friends and admirers, from Mexico in the north to Argentina and Chile in the south. No less were Bolivia, Costa Rica, Ecuador, Guatemala, Nicaragua, Paraguay or Peru. It is not feasible to describe each experience, but I shall recall some—good or bad. The travel also afforded me visits to many exotic corners, undertaken usually during the short span while the authorities were reading my mission's draft report. As I have said, it was not rare for Vito Tanzi to join my mission over its last leg and be present at the final meeting with the finance minister. It became known in FAD that he and I travelled a lot together, though in reality the common time was intense and crowded into the final phase of my missions.

During travel, I gained from Vito's experience and comportment. It was not just his comfortable way of dealing with the country authorities that I learnt from. It was also his cultural experience. For one thing, though I was already attracted to naïve art, it was Vito who informed me of its global genres and their interpretative foci. This remains my favourite genre of art to this day, culminating in my authoring *Naïve Art: Ode to the Unknown Artist* in 2015, based on my world-wide collection and my mother's paintings, an unknown artist herself. Vito had met my mother, and invited her to view his enormous collection of art and artefacts, including naïve art sourced from all over the world, Latin American terracotta figures, and antique keys housed in a huge basement and stairwell. My mother had enthusiastically appreciated his collection, describing its contents in detail to many a friend, for example, a porcelain tea cup painted with delicate figures that appeared from within the porcelain as the tea receded. She had not seen it since her childhood, and, ever since, had found it impossible to convince those who had never beheld such exquisite magical porcelain of its existence. Vito had shown her the cup, taking great pleasure in reassuring my mother that she had not been suffering from a flight of childhood imagination.

COLOMBIA

Another country in which my involvement with the nation's tax policy and administration continued over two decades, beginning 1991, was Colombia. My experience of a country passing from manual to IT processes was also honed through my visits to Colombia where I led a series of technical assistance missions over this long period. The first was in June 1991. Supported by my mission members, I covered tax policy, tax administration as well as computerisation of the tax department in a comprehensive manner. I had the great opportunity to lead and learn from such missions in which some great professionals and economists participated. They included Arnold C. Harberger from the US who wrote a piece on the direction of future Colombian tax reform. Professor Osvaldo Schenone from Argentina analysed customs duties; Erik Haindl whom I have already mentioned examined income tax; and Senor Pedro Kondratiuk from Argentina examined tax administration.

While I guided the entire process, I also took on the individual responsibility to analyse the VAT structure. At the same time we all looked across and learnt from one another, exchanged notes in the evening and, in the manner of the Fund, in the ultimate analysis, the members reported to me with their analysis and also their draft chapters. I cannot forget Al, the senior professor from the University of Chicago with whom I had corresponded on general equilibrium models as a PhD student, sitting with me with reams of computer output to examine VAT returns. Our objective was to find out how much each economic sector contributed to value added by figuring out the debit and credit of each taxpayer and adding them up to arrive at the outcome for each sector. This I contrasted with the comparable numbers from the country's input-output table to estimate the evasion of the VAT. I have preserved our hand-written calculations and those computer outputs as a memento of those days with Al.

Several papers covered and reported on the entire list of recommendations on the VAT, including *El Tiempo* on 24 November 1991. The comprehensive article appeared to appreciate highly that I had not recommended increasing the tax rate from the prevailing 12 percent but to expand the VAT base comprehensively to include services such as electricity, water, housing, rentals, accounting, legal and judicial services, technical services, publicity, security services, medical services, theatre and cultural services, barbers, spas and so on. And it elaborated on what exactly our report related on how to go about including those services in practical terms. Subsequently on 18 December, a friend wrote tongue-in-cheek to me:

> Your popularity appears to be dropping rapidly in Colombia.

But I never felt any negative vibes there. My continuation with various aspects of Colombian tax reform requiring many subsequent visits—was made easier by my familiarity with Spanish. Indeed, soon after the first June 1991 mission—that the newspapers covered with precision—Finance Minister Rudolf Hommes, in a letter to Vito on 26 June 1991, wrote:

> I congratulate you on the high quality of the mission that just finished analysing the VAT in Colombia.

Subsequently, Hommes requested Vito to send us to Colombia again to study the taxation of international trade. So Vito sent me back in August. I went with Osvaldo, Erik and Emanuel Hife, a Fund research officer from the Philippines. It was a happy group, the kind that forms bonds of hard work and friendship. The studies on income tax, VAT and customs duties were compiled by me and eventually published as, 'Colombia: Fundamental Tax Reform', Fund Occasional Paper 123, in 1995. Of course I had to go through a long clearance process from my own department, WHD which was the area department concerned, the IMF Board's Colombia representative and the Colombian government before it could be published. But as always, it was worth it. And all these trips enabled me to visit, apart from the capital Bogota, other places including Ibague, a provincial taxation hub to check on tax administration, as well as exquisite tourist spots from both colonial and indigenous epochs including Villa de Leyva, Baza and Laguna de Tota in Boyaca, Barichara, Cartagena, Melgar, and a host of other such delightful locations.

At the authorities' request, I made another visit to Bogota in September 1992—on the way back from a mission to Costa Rica—to conduct meetings with Julio Pisa, Director General of Taxes, Mario Aranguren, Deputy Director General, and Jorge Armando Rodriguez, Deputy Director for Tax Policy who was in charge of the technical component of tax policy related calculations, and in whose work I had keen interest. We focussed on the methodologies my 1991 mission had set out for technical tax policy exercises, and the meetings were helpful in clarifying doubts.

Reflecting the Finance Minister's continuing interest and concern with the extent of tax evasion, I followed this up with another mission in March 1993 supported by David Dunn, an American Fund economist, and Victor M. Vallejos, a fiscal panel expert, to delve into the measurement of tax evasion in depth. We focussed on two areas: verifying and advancing research on the measurement of tax evasion that the Directorate General of National Taxes (DIN) was already conducting based on the methodology developed by my earlier mission; and, second, recommending concrete tax administration measures to control tax evasion. Ploughing through stacks of computer printouts of taxpayer returns and the country's input-output tables, we estimated that income tax evasion had declined by 5 percentage points from the late 1980s to the early 1990s. This reflected improvement in the corporate sector, though the individual sector had actually worsened. Typically a tax administration tends to scrutinise large corporate firms while ignoring individuals; our fear was that this had been the case. Accordingly, our recommendations focussed on the administration to improve taxpayer identification, processing of returns, and improving compliance audit. We also recommended that the DIN's computer capacity be increased *pari passu* with streamlining information processed by the computer department.

I was delighted when Salomon Kalmanovitz, an adviser to the Colombian government and professor at the Universidad Nacional where I gave a seminar on the future direction of Colombian tax policy, wrote a comprehensive review in a national daily, *El Espectador*, dated 17 April 1993, covering the details of my analysis and recommendations for Colombia.

Hommes called us back again in 1994 to take an overall review of tax policy and potential for reform. Thus, in June 1994, I went to check on the mechanism for input tax credit for capital goods under the VAT, inflation adjustment in the corporate and individual income taxes—a new area for Fund staff analysis—and assess remaining reform needs. A new system, introduced in 1993 following Chile, adjusted different items of the enterprise balance sheet for inflation, the thrust being to re-evaluate net worth, nonmonetary assets, and nonmonetary liabilities. A special account for monetary correction reflected the increase in assets less the increases in net worth, and liabilities arising as a result of the revaluation. The balance of this special account was brought into profits and losses and treated as regular income for tax purposes. The inflation adjustment affected taxable income through the depreciation allowance which was computed on the basis of the updated value of assets. The main updating index was the consumer price index (CPI) although specific indexes were used for some balance sheet components. Receipts, expenses and final accounts would be required to incorporate inflation adjustment. The question arose as to whether this elaborate calculation method had been correctly configured, or whether a partial application was leading to an unintended loss in revenue.

We went about this complex task step by step. First, the extent of lag for the price index had to be corrected, the correct adjustment method as followed by Chile being with reference to the month preceding the month in which a particular transaction occurred. Second, there should be no inflation adjustment to the cost of an asset for the period for which interest was capitalised. Third, inflation adjustment of net equity should also reflect the capitalisation of interest expense. Fourth, the treatment of dividends, whether paid out or not, should be similar and should not be counted as net equity. Fifth, inventory valuation should allow a smooth inflation adjustment. Sixth, while various assets were adjusted to market value, the adjustment should be included in taxable income. Seventh, inflation adjustment of foreign currency assets should be neutral with domestic assets. Eighth, transition rules needed to assure neutrality between pre- and post-transition. Ninth, there should be no double correction. And, tenth, administrative complications should be minimised. For the first time, I went deep into this aspect of income taxation even as our recommendations were developed keeping in mind that these aspects were realisable. I have, therefore, always reserved a special appreciation for Rudolf Hommes for the extent of confidence he revealed in my work.

Even while I was at ICRIER in New Delhi where I went to do research on Indian fiscal policy for two years from June 1999, I was called back to Colombia by Juan Camilo Restrepo Salazar, the new Minister of Finance, in November that year to revisit the matter of tax evasion. Thus I headed a Fund mission even as I was in India. The report was frank and he sent a letter of appreciation. And the involvement continued. Indeed I felt honoured when on 31 July 2001, Catalina Crane, Colombian Deputy Finance Minister for Technical Matters, wrote me a long letter inviting me to be a member in an international group of experts sanctioned by the Ministry and the Central Bank to analyse and propose fiscal reform. Unfortunately, I could not accept since, by then, I had gone to Singapore as the Fund's Ambassador to Singapore to be Director of the Fund's centre to train finance officials from thirty-five Asian countries, and also to renegotiate the Fund's Memorandum of Understanding on cost sharing with the Singapore government. Nevertheless, I continued to be invited by the Colombians in the following decades in my individual capacity to undertake technical assistance, to deliver lectures at the universities, and generally participate in the Latin life. I harbour a deep affection in every sense of the word for Colombia and Colombians. As recently as 2016, at the invitation of Dr. Soraya Caro, I delivered a lecture on tax reform at Externado University in Bogota, and the involvement continues.

ARGENTINA

In late 1992 I found myself with Vito Tanzi in Buenos Aires on a Fund mission there. The Argentinian Finance Minister, Domingo Cavallo, had requested Vito to visit and assess recent tax reforms, and I accompanied him. Subsequently I paid at least four visits for technical assistance during 1992–99 and shorter visits for conferences, seminars and lectures. The first visit that I made exclusively with Vito, in continuation of a long mission to Ecuador, was a memorable one. Though Cavallo was travelling at the time, we had been invited to review the changes in public finance undertaken by the authorities in the previous two years, and suggest any further changes required. Accordingly we met Messrs. Carlos Sanchez and Carlos Tacchi, the two Deputy Ministers, Ricardo Gutierrez, Secretary of Finance, Roque Fernandez, Governor of the Central Bank, Walter Schulthess, Secretary of Social Security, and others.

The mission turned out to be rather sensitive. Argentina had established a currency board and fixed the exchange rate to the US dollar. Its imports had increased and exports suffered despite inflation—a constant preoccupation—having been controlled. There was a good outlook for investment with an expectation that flight capital would be repatriated. We anticipated that it could lead to an increase in money supply with a deleterious impact on inflation. But the tax to GDP ratio had risen to 25 percent of GDP, an all-time high, reflecting successes in tax administration and policy through policies initiated in 1989. For example, the VAT had registered high revenue productivity through base broadening. Income tax revenue had also climbed. And improvements in customs administration were being undertaken, although I found, and mentioned, that naming customs payment defaulters in a public list was rather draconian. The social security administration was planned to be subsumed within the tax administration, the consolidation expected to result in information synergies across various sources of income and payments.

However, transfers to lower levels of government had also risen by 2 percent of GDP while pensions had grown by almost 4 percent of GDP. Nevertheless, due to the significant growth on the revenue side, the primary fiscal balance—without including interest payments—had improved by 4 percent of GDP. Certainly the non-financial public sector had demonstrated phenomenal improvement in a global comparison. It was obvious, however, that any relaxation could throw Argentina back into economic turmoil. An area of concern was the earmarking of central revenues for local government revenue sharing, thus allowing the latter to spend 11 percent of GDP while collecting only 3 percent of GDP. Any further transfers would result in severe strain in public finances. As I have always maintained, world over, it is the eventual sustainability of consolidated fiscal reform that comes under question. My experience has revealed that, in about five years after reform, tax and expenditure measures begin to crack, sometimes rapidly. Another set of reforms is then needed, often urgently. All these matters, in particular the sustainability of reform, were discussed honestly and in great detail with the authorities. In the evenings Vito would listen to my views intently, and once again I realised his ability to imbibe views. Finally, one lament remained. I was unable to convince the authorities, over the several missions that I undertook, to design and implement a fiscal federal VAT that would include both central and provincial governments. There was too much suspicion and dissension among the provinces and between the provinces and the centre. The Argentinian VAT remained at the central level, with cascading selective excises at the provincial level.

Guided by Vito and his friends, for me it was an immersion into the world of the Argentine pampas, football, tango, icons, *filet minon*, and Malbec, an aromatic wine of which every Argentine is proud. Visits to the colourful La Voca, the palatial mansions of Recoleta, the Sunday antique market of San Telmo, the exquisite buildings along boulevards such as Corrientes and 9 de Julio, all reflective of Argentina's status as the third richest country in the 1930s when its grain exports fed much of the world. Even during the period I visited, its prevailing per capita GDP was over $10,000, highest in Latin America, and the resulting quality of life it had achieved remain ensconced in my memory—as does a visit to the Colon Opera House to lose myself in *Macbeth*, Verdi's opera. Nevertheless, some stories will continue to be set aside, for they should remain in the conjoint memory of friends. Of course, over the decades I made so many friends that such stories are difficult to relate in one go. In 1995 when I was returning to New Delhi, one of my Argentine friends literally wept to say, "Do you not realise that we love you in Latin America?" adding emotionally, "What has India done for you that we have not or cannot do?" I gently explained that heart and actions are sometimes counterpoised, for feelings come from the heart while actions are sometimes propelled from the depth of one's soul. My statement seemed to generate confusion and anguish in my friend in a straightforward Latin American manner. In the event, I returned to India.

By 1999, I had visited Argentina on four missions addressing the possible reform of income taxation and the VAT, and intergovernmental tax design. At the end of my 1998 mission that took a deep look at the tax system as a whole, I was pressed to appear before the media. One interview titled, 'Argentina: Companies pay less to the fisc compared to Brazil', dated 4 March 1998 for *Ambito Financiero*, a highly regarded financial daily of Buenos Aires, was copied to me from the Embassy of Brazil (not Argentina!) (see Plate 6). The unnamed journalist described me as "the Indian economist who emphasized in perfect Spanish that the tax pressure on Argentinian companies was less than in Brazil and that the former should make taxation more revenue buoyant...". Interestingly, on the side, Brazilian Finance Minister Pedro Malan had written to Everardo Maciel, his Revenue Minister, "Is this true?" I knew both of them well, and was a bit amused that the Brazilian authorities had possibly taken my comment as impinging on potential investment there. Of course I had shared that view publicly many a time, for Brazilian companies were burdened with not only the corporation income tax but two major additional taxes based on modified definitions of turnover, the revenues from which were earmarked with socio-economic objectives. This was an example of how sensitive Latin American countries were of one another's economic and tax policies, albeit generally in a friendly way.

On occasion, my visits were reported in a tongue-in-cheek manner. I undertook a visit in 1999 on the behest of Dr. Jorge Alberto Rodriguez, Chief of Cabinet, to examine intergovernmental relations in the context of structural tax reform to be undertaken in association with a Fund programme. After the visit, *El Cronista*, one of Argentina's respected business dailies, reported on 31 May 1999, "... Who was verifying the revenue yield...of the country over and above the tax structure: Indian economist Partho Shome...was here secretly longer than a week in the country." The newspaper went on to say that Economy Minister Roque Fernandez admitted Shome was at work, though not for a fiscal audit. It also revealed that I met Miguel Kiguel, Chief of Cabinet, Pablo Guldotti, Secretary of Finance, Carola Pessino, Secretary for Social Equity, and Guillermo Rodrigo, Deputy Secretary of Tax Policy, who had explained to me that the revenue yield had not been as bad as it could have been. In other words, news of my visits usually made it to the media even though the authorities and I tried to keep it confidential.

That is to say, most of my visits carried a certain sense of negotiation with the country officials who had to be recognised as already doing their best, but nevertheless requiring a soft push to convince them of a need for greater effort on their part. As the 'Indian' economist, over the years, I felt I had been successful in winning their trust for, at the end of the day, a sense of camaraderie and friendship always seemed to permeate the air.

COSTA RICA

My first mission to Costa Rica was in March 1990 and I went with two panel experts, J. M. Beytia and J. C. Gomez-Sabaini, and Vito came in during the last days. In tax policy and administration, Costa Rica faced several challenges. Customs revenue had receded due to exemptions for major items such as high value taxis meant to boost tourism, which was difficult to justify in the face of high customs duties on many regular imports. There was a decline in revenue from coffee as protection was being reduced. The VAT was studded with multiple exemptions. The authorities were on the right track that the VAT base should be expanded before any rate increase. One exemption I recall was for raw materials including bamboo for common housing though not for other purposes. It reminded me of India's exemption for resin used as adhesive in the soles of low value shoes but not for others. Such exemptions tend to result in corruption but are routinely introduced by country authorities as populist gestures. The authorities also favoured a move towards greater income taxation where revenue would respond to inflation. In tax administration, legislation on enforcement was particularly weak, and I perceived that sanctions against tax evasion were imperative. Accordingly, the mission did its work and discussed its findings with the Finance Minister though the final discussions were interrupted by a temblor so that Vito gave me a signal, and we made a hasty retreat from the Minister's chamber. We followed up on the discussion the next day.

Costa Rica was not in a state of devastation, however. Far from it. A small country that had a highly educated population, had eschewed an army, was famous for environmental balance and, consequently, was a tourist paradise and a retirement haven, Costa Rica stood out in all of Latin America as a safe haven for democracy. I must reveal that Costa Ricans, who seem to speak Spanish with a sweet Texan twang and drawl, are some of the most beautiful people in the world. A visit to the country was thus always a pleasure for me. Nevertheless, it also provided an example of how a country's VAT structure could get vitiated over time due to political interests and lobbying, and how long it could take to reform it back. At the same time, a couple of missions revealed how a country could reform if truly serious in its intentions.

In August 1992, I went on a follow-up mission to San Jose, the capital, met the Minister of Finance, the Director General of Taxes, the top tax official, as well as the Head of Tax Policy and Analysis and several tax administrators, the usual panoply of officials that every mission of mine met. But the crux of information, based on which I usually conducted my technical analysis, had to be invariably hunted out from the vaults of the tax statistics division, and the same was the case here. While the authorities had made significant progress in tax administration following a 1990 Fund mission—including consolidation of departments by functional area, decentralising responsibilities to regional tax offices for collection and audit, introducing rational criteria for audit or scrutiny selection such as the ratio of gross or net profits with respect to total sales, and setting up a large taxpayer unit (LTU) and rigorously following up on delinquency—I found tax policy reform was more at a formulation phase through a small panel that had been formed for tax analysis.

The tax policy panel had been formed in response to my recommendations during my earlier mission in March 1990 that had undertaken an intensive survey of the prevailing tax structure and made recommendations for change. Now in 1992, I found that, under the guidance of Roger Munoz, the head of tax policy and analysis, the earlier eroded VAT base had been expanded in various ways: first, by including selected services such as utilities, personal services such as beauty parlours, photography studios, massage parlours, saunas, communication services, and computer software; second, by including construction materials such as cement; and, third, through a 2 percent retention by government from payments to contractors. The number of 600 'selective' consumption taxes that I had found during my 1990 mission had been halved. A scheduler personal income tax that I had found was to be modified to a global income sourcing system. The corporate tax structure was to be simplified from a prevailing system that differentiated rates according to size and sector, leading to confusion and contest in cases of multi-product firms. Finally, reform was contemplated for monetary correction of non-monetary assets including fixed assets, inventories, land and foreign exchange.

While the authorities had indeed begun their work, I encouraged them to pick up speed. For example, while VAT base expansion reflected my earlier recommendations, there were still far too many selective consumption taxes that were applied to both output and input commodities. I also recommended wider use of withholding taxes or tax deduction at source (TDS) for the income tax, especially since the direct tax to indirect tax ratio had declined in recent years. And I advised them to maintain comparability of the corporate tax with the rest of Latin America while keeping revenue protection in mind. I also pointed out that the introduction of monetary correction should not be hastened beyond administration capacity. Last but not least, I recommended a minimum corporate tax based on gross assets, an idea that stood well with the Minister of Finance.

To sum up, when I returned to the capital San Jose in August 1992, I detected a certain maturity in the authorities' approach. Restructuring the tax departments by function was not so common those days, yet they had done so. Decentralising several responsibilities and introducing dynamic criteria for audit, setting up of an LTU for 150 taxpayers with plans to cover the 1,000 who represented 2 percent of taxpayers and accounted for 75 percent of revenue—these kinds of measures usually took years of discussion with the authorities in many countries. Rudolf Mendez, the Finance Minister, and Alan Saborio Soto, the Director General of Taxes, with whom I had several meetings, expressed pride in what they had achieved. It was indeed satisfying to see how some authorities had the confidence to follow the crux of the recommendations being made by this "*indio*"—Indian—economist from the Fund.

OTHER COUNTRIES

Even though I can recall every mission that I undertook for the Fund, those to a few of the smaller Latin American countries fill my mind with academic, professional and personal memories. Among them are Chile, Ecuador, Peru, Nicaragua and Guatemala which I mention here because of the variety of experiences they offered.

Chile

I participated in a tax policy conference at CEPAL or the Economic Commission for Latin America and the Caribbean (ECLAC) based in Santiago de Chile, in which I presented the main findings of a paper co-authored with Vito Tanzi. Vito had expounded on tax evasion, and I had elaborated on how to measure it. The paper was subsequently published in the *IMF Staff Papers*, December 1993 edition. It was also reviewed in *The Economist* of 28 May 1994. The presentation at CEPAL appeared to be an astounding success in a gathering of renowned researchers of the Americas, and my speech was exclusively covered in the daily *La Epoca* of 25 January 1994. Juan Carlos Lerda, head of tax policy in CEPAL, sent an effusive telex on 15 March 1993, indicating that my inaugural speech was much appreciated by all participants, in particular by those who worked on tax evasion, and that my final synthesis of the observations made and points raised during the session brought together the overall thrust. He also expressed a desire to include the paper in CEPAL's fiscal policy series that would ensure its circulation in Latin America's policy circles. Juan Carlos became a good friend, and I continued to participate in subsequent CEPAL conferences and research activity. In one such, there was also Klaus Schmidt-Hebbel who presented Africa, while I presented Asia's performance on managing fiscal deficits. I thus had the opportunity to participate in numerous global conferences that empowered me with in-depth knowledge and insight into global fiscal matters.

Another interesting aspect I found in Chile was that Juan Toro of the Chilean tax administration had initiated calculating VAT evasion every year following the methodology I had developed for Colombia. Juan was later elevated to Commissioner—the highest post—of the tax administration and was finally absorbed as Chief of Tax Administration at the Fund. In those subsequent visits, Erik Haindl took me to his own vineyard to savour the highest quality Chilean wine, famous across the world. By then I had of course learnt not to mention this to my Argentinian friends, who were equally proud of their own Malbec. Erik also took me to the very south of Chile to Patagonia, just across from Antarctica, to explore lost German towns, their quintessential bakeries and salmon farms. It is difficult to describe the beauty of the region, the mountains, and the lakes with floating icebergs mirroring the mountains. My feet were heavy when returning to Washington.

Ecuador

I went to Ecuador at the request of Pablo Lucio Paredes, Secretary of Planning. This was in support of a Fund Stand-by Arrangement to examine and recommend tax reform as well as the collection and processing of tax data. I took along with me Osvaldo and Erik, and also Julio Escolano, an excellent Spanish economist in my division. We also had the luxury of taking along Aida E. Merino, a Fund statistician, to examine data issues. Vito told me he might join my Ecuador mission. The government was making a serious attempt at tax reform, but I found that the new regime was not too keen to retain any significant element introduced by the previous government. Therefore we had to work especially hard to invent a new wheel, though I pointed out that the good elements of the existing tax structure should be retained and the poor ones replaced.

Ecuador added fillip to my consciousness of art, in particular that of Guyasamin and his daughter, Dayuma. Guyasamin's extraordinary, rather brilliant depiction of poverty through tall panels of skeletal figures was astounding. We also visited the point after which the country is named—where the Equator runs across Ecuador. The country is primarily indigenous with 80 percent of its population comprising American Indians, though the Spanish yoke and Catholic Church have a dominant and visible presence, thus imparting interesting colours to Ecuadorian culture and society. It boasts an independent genre of naïve art that is rendered mainly on canvas or leather, while other forms are also highly advanced. In short, to say that a visit to Ecuador is enjoyable would be a great understatement. My only lament is that I could not find time to take off to the Galapagos Islands, which continues to linger in my unfinished global travel agenda.

But there were countries in Latin America that I must mention at least in passing in terms of the economic crisis in which I found them, and working towards their revival posed heavy strains in terms of strategy and time on my part.

Peru

The first was Peru. I visited the capital Lima in October 1990, heading a team of tax experts, Messrs Adolfo Atchabahian and Manuel Beytia from Argentina and Chile respectively, to look into the possibility of overhauling the tax system that had collapsed. The mission's recommendations would feed directly into a Fund-monitored financial programme for 1991 that was being formulated. The Prime Minister of Peru was also the Finance Minister; we met him and worked closely with a few vice ministers of finance and economy. The Peruvian economy was in a devastated state after years of heterodox, demand-propelled policies without the backing of supply, a strategy—or the lack of it—heralded by the previous President, Santos, who, by the time we arrived, had left for Switzerland at a reported cost to the economy of two billion US dollars.

Mainly during Santos's regime, Peru's tax to GDP ratio had fallen steadily during the second half of the 1980s—from 13 percent of GDP in 1985 to 5 percent in 1989—with little expectation of improvement. Added to this was the influence of deep recession and real contraction of the economy during the 1985–89 heterodox period that increasingly forced the economy into the underground. Hyperinflation had ensued, precipitating what was then commonly referred to as a classic 'basket case'. Such an extreme situation was unusual in my experience, though its manifestations in the tax area were numerous. Hyperinflation together with lags in tax collection depleted the real value of revenue. Multiple deductions and allowances reduced income tax revenue to insignificance. Exemptions that pertained to particular regions of the country, to large economic sectors such as construction and mining, as well as those granted by decree wiped out the VAT base and made it impossible to monitor the truncated base. Failure to adjust petroleum prices until late 1990 had eliminated this excise revenue source. An inflexible exchange rate dampened imports and, therefore, customs revenue. Market values failed to be reflected in the property tax base.

I recommended that the authorities concentrate on a limited number of taxes comprising a VAT, a minimum tax based on gross business assets (initially additional to and eventually deductible from the corporate tax), a tax on wages and personal incomes (the top marginal rate equalling the corporate tax rate), a tax on imports through a unification of tariff rates, selective taxes on a few excisable products, and a real estate tax reflecting market prices. Deductions and allowances would need to be scaled back. If designed appropriately—and the transformation to the new structure was spelt out with quantification and associated processes—tax revenue could triple in a year. Vito flew down in the final days of our mission and joined our final meeting with the ministers. I vividly remember the Minister cross-questioning me on several calculations on the proposed tax rates. As I was answering his queries, he abruptly countered that the Fund had not considered how these tax policies would affect the lower income groups.

Vito looked at me uncertainly, as if wondering if I would be able to tackle this final battering. I calmly pointed the Minister to a long footnote where I had addressed his concerns with detailed calculations on the impact on different income groups. I recall Vito looking at me with a sense of relief, perhaps admiringly. That night the entire mission relaxed over an excellent dinner while I went shopping for Peru's famous alpaca sweaters and to order an alpaca overcoat—proud members of my wardrobe to this day. I also accompanied Vito to some private museums of Aztec artefacts in the far reaches of Lima, collections I would otherwise have never encountered. For one, the statuettes were revealing in that, apart from divine subjects and funerary practices, they depicted sexual positions often reminiscent of the *Kama Sutra*, reflecting a penis and vaginal fixation almost, representing deities pertaining to fertility, conception and childbirth. I have always remained curious as to how and why modern societies have consciously eschewed and moved away from such overt depictions quite acceptable to early societies. Is it partly explained by the orthodoxy propagated in the Dark Ages by the declared—rather than evolved—religions that took hold and never went, and later exacerbated by the Victorian colonial era?

Tax administration in Peru had also collapsed. During the previous government, the head of the administration had been replaced every year and even minimal functions were ignored. The mission recommended emergency measures that included elimination of duplication of functions in direct and indirect tax departments, expanding the large taxpayers' unit from the prevailing 1,200 taxpayers, updating the taxpayer register so that cross-checks and administrative control could be instituted. Ironically, three decades later, I pushed for almost identical reform measures in the Indian Tax Administration Reform Commission (TARC) as its chairman during 2013–15, a process that continues to move ahead at its own pace. Subsequently, in the case of Peru, under the technical assistance provided by the tax administration division of the Fund, a completely new and haircut tax administration with younger officers and a salary structure independent of the rest of the public sector was successfully installed. A combination of tax policy and tax administration revolution put Peru firmly on the track of fiscal solvency.

Nicaragua

A country I encountered in economic exigency was Nicaragua, yet another case of the outcomes of heterodox demand-propelled policies, where I went in January 1990 just before the Sandinista regime of Daniel Ortega was to face democratic elections. Nicaragua had experienced a hyperinflation of 33,000 percent in 1988, 1700 percent in 1989, and higher than 100 percent inflation over the previous five years. In February 1988, three digits from the national currency were dropped. The control of hyperinflation had been achieved through slashing public sector expenditure by 20 percent of GDP thus halving public sector deficit from 60 percent of GDP, and the central government deficit from 25 percent to 1 percent of GDP during 1988–89. Given that further reductions in expenditure appeared to be increasingly challenging, urgent action was needed in the tax revenue area.

During 1984–89, central government revenue had decreased from 36 percent to 20 percent of GDP, while the tax/GDP ratio had fallen from 32 percent to 19 percent of GDP, and the real value of revenue had withered away. The causes for the precipitous decline included hyperinflation itself, increasing arrears in tax payment, and tax evasion. A sharp contraction of the industrial sector—a major source of tax revenue—being substituted by a growing informal sector; continuation of specific, rather than ad valorem, tax rates, and the prevalence of a wide variety of tax exemptions, were other causes.

My mission was given a slit of a room in a corner which was literally without light, and electricity was generally absent. As head of mission, I wondered if it was a punishment meant for the Fund. My junior companion was Ildefonso Guajardo, a supportive colleague who became a friend. I am delighted that he has been serving as Mexico's Secretario de Economia or Economy Minister. We decided to work without complaint. The final meeting with the Finance Minister just atop our cave revealed an expansive, luxurious office, and I wondered if he had known about the treatment we had received. It was some satisfaction, however, that Leif Muten, a senior adviser at FAD, who comprised the peer review committee for the mission's report and had a reputation of being a tough nut to crack, commented that it was the best, concise technical assistance report he had read, and that all reports should henceforth follow that model. Many years later after I left the Fund and Leif had retired in Sweden, I met him in Stockholm at a conference, and we nostalgically discussed the process of scribes and reviewers of FAD reports.

In the final analysis, I may be asked what I found to be the central theme of Latin American tax structures and their strategy for reform. At that time when, by and large, many Asian countries were struggling with high income tax rates and distortionary and cascading excise tax systems, Latin America had already installed value added taxes with a credit-debit mechanism and had reformed their income tax systems by leaving out the poor from the bottom with tax brackets starting from as high as three times per capita GDP in some cases. And it must be said that when, from 1995, I returned to India and began pointing out these novelties from the New World, I was sometimes accused of pushing banana republic policies on India by otherwise well-read tax experts. This was just one among many surprises that began to appear on the horizon, or on the forefront, that I had to quickly learn to digest in order to forge ahead in the much more complex Indian policy-making milieu. Today, of course, the world is different and familiarity with Latin America is more prevalent. Indian youth everywhere are selling their wares of information technology and, at the cost of some generalisation, several are dating and marrying Latin spouses and settling down in that continent. I view this as a benign reflection of India's globalisation.

We recommended a drastic simplification of the complex income tax structure in Nicaragua; a simplification and reduction of the corporate tax rates that had varied in the region of 45–60 percent reflecting sectoral differences among agriculture, industry and commerce, and for export crops—coffee, cotton, bananas—multiple exemptions for new investment in selected sectors, and a differential application of a tax surcharge on corporations with high tax liability. These were all recommended to be taxed under a uniform structure. Simplification was also recommended for an existing separate graduated tax on capital, capital formation, capital increases, transfers, dissolution, and mergers. Graduated tax rates were also being applied on real estate and personal property ownership, uncultivated land, real estate transfers, and owner-occupied dwellings. Expectedly, tax collection from these sources was not significant and strong rationalisation was suggested.

On the indirect tax side, selective excises on alcohol, matches, tobacco, sugar, oil, and other products had been reset at ad valorem rates. A VAT was being levied at 6, 10, 15 and 25 percent, reflecting the category of goods. There were exemptions for fuel oil and petroleum by-products. Nevertheless, revenue intake had been quite low. Hence sundry small taxes were being imposed for the sole apparent purpose of generating revenue, including 36 stamp taxes, taxes on rental contracts, commercial and import licences and separate license taxes on factories and distributors, rates ranging from specific to ad valorem. Export products—coffee, cattle, hides and skins, wood, bananas, coconuts, others—were subjected to export duty, thus affecting international competitiveness adversely. At the same time, import duty exemptions were granted to a wide range of commodities.

It was not surprising that tax evasion was rampant in such a complex tax structure, if for no other reason than the impossibility of tax compliance, and the mission set out to recommend a complete restructuring, rationalisation and simplification. What is important to convey is that even small countries may, over the course of years, destroy their tax structures and, instead of correcting the broken systems, impose further miniscule elements merely to generate revenue at the cost of excessive complexity. In such situations, there can be no getting away from drastic and painful action, though that may take years to reinvent and rebuild.

Guatemala

Another Latin American country I encountered in economic crisis in the 1990s was Guatemala where I went in March 1994. An immediate assessment had to be made on the possibilities of short term tax measures to meet the requirements of its economic programme. I arrived to find a country in stall. Ana Ordonez de Molina, the Finance Minister, was resplendent in her presence, sparse in speech, and buttressed by the Deputy Minister Estuardo Mendez. They were surrounded by serious-looking bureaucrats whom I cajoled as best as I could to think out of the box, cautioning them that I and my team would make some challenging recommendations in our report. This reflected the poor state of the economy, tax revenue representing 8 percent of GDP of which a VAT accounted for 2.7 percent and direct taxes not even 2 percent. The consolidated non-financial public sector deficit was 1.5 percent of GDP, but further minimisation of which was required in anticipation of a Fund arrangement from late 1994. Accordingly my mission quantified and recommended demanding measures addressed to simplify and, even eliminate where possible, a slew of unwarranted exemptions. Other recommendations included an expansion of the VAT base, closer correspondence between the market and book values of assets as well as various other business tax measures, and an increase in withholding of individual income tax, the revenue from which was very small.

After submitting our report on the third Friday of the mission—as was my usual practice—I travelled to Tikal, the abandoned Mayan temple from the steeple of which one could see an endless sky and miles of the valley all around. In the forests surrounding the temple there were countless sculptural ruins, of which a few giant, exquisitely carved heads stood out against the dense foliage, staring into the void. Imposing in its raw, forsaken beauty, in sharp contrast with Mexico's well-preserved Teotihuacan and Tula outside Mexico City or Chichen-Itza in the Yucatan peninsula, Tikal embodies a silent ferocity and yet a sadness of abandonment that the others, perhaps more immediately impressive, do not possess. Another poignant discovery I made was its naïve art. Perhaps not as famous as that from Brazil, Colombia, Ecuador or Haiti, Guatemalan naïve art was unique in depicting the arrival of the Spaniards and early American Indian life in meticulous detail, on canvases which were enormous—of which I picked up some.

The final Monday meeting with the authorities lasted long as I tried to convince them about the judiciousness of accepting the enlisted measures, supported by calculations which we explained in detail. From the events that followed, history would bear out the nature of economic measures that Guatemala did introduce. If a country in crisis dithers in undertaking measures in the right direction, an economic adviser has ultimately no alternative except to move on without looking back. With time one also realises that one must patiently accept the limits beyond which many developing countries are unable to traverse, even at a cost to themselves. Nevertheless, one never ceases to hope that one day they will see the light at the end of the tunnel, pick up the old list of reforms and begin to implement them.

Paraguay

Perhaps I should not overlook Paraguay, another crisis-ridden country, where I went in March 1999. The mission was important for three reasons: one, I saw how tax administration could deteriorate and wither even as financial resources are sucked out from it. Yet it was not easy to convince the authorities to undertake meaningful tax reform. The reason was interesting. The executive branch of government had put together a package of tax changes—caustically named the 'Impuestado' to emphasise its heaviness—in which they had included taxing selected rural products among other unpopular aspects. The Senate had great difficulty in swallowing this bitter pill, as Senator Miguel Carrizosa explained to us at a long meeting. He also promised to examine the executive branch's proposals with care. I had no alternative but to inform him that, if a decision on the matter drags on, Paraguay may face difficulty in drawing any credit from the Fund. To my discomfiture, *La Nacion*, an important newspaper, reported all this in detail. Indeed, within days of our departure from Paraguay after the mission, there was an attempted coup, and the finance minister with whom we had the final meeting, and who had reportedly kept a cache of firearms in his office, was removed.

Second, I discovered a strange entity called 'statistical tax' among the revenue entries and was nonchalantly informed that it reflected the foreign exchange revenue earnings from illicit traffic with Paraguay's neighbours. Third, as I crossed the country on the last weekend to see the Iguassu Falls with another friendly Colombian who served as the Fund's resident representative in the country, I was amazed to find that huge chunks of Paraguay were controlled and formally administered by private lords with their own armies. We had no difficulty in driving through, however; if stopped and questioned, an official-sounding explanation would suffice to allow us to pass. At the end, the prize was the Iguassu Falls—a hundred contiguous waterfalls, a marvel of nature that dwarfed other remarkable sights I had been fortunate enough to witness. I also saw what seemed like ten thousand butterflies basking in the sun, and then suddenly take flight, turning the sky into a yellow-orange celeste, perhaps to lead to yet another global butterfly effect!

There were many more missions to Latin America, and I realised at one point that, other than El Salvador and Honduras in the Isthmus of Panama, I had worked in and on every country from Mexico in the north to Chile and Argentina in the south. The experience left an indelible mark on me, like a birthmark as it were, and it has remained so. While Indian business is now exploring that part of the world, I wish more Indians would partake of that continent: the Old and the New would mix very well. In 1991, when I first visited Bogota, and my newly acquired Colombian friends wanted me to cook an Indian meal, I asked if we could get fresh ginger. I was extremely amused when one of them exclaimed if that was not the same spice as used in witchcraft, a 'fact' she had found in a book on the supernatural. During my last visit in 2015, I found several Indian restaurants, a Kerala ayurvedic centre run by specialists from 'god's own country', and the first Durga Puja being organised by the Indian Embassy and Indian corporates. It was fulfilling to find not just Indians but many a Colombian participating in the festivities. The *purohit* was an IT specialist from Bihar. On the following 15 August, a friend sent pictures of the Indian flag being flashed on a skyscraper in resplendent colours. Gone were the scenes that floated in front of me from a quarter century back—Atuk's lonely embassy celebration or visits to the sole Indian restaurant run by a Bogotana enthusiast with mediocre culinary outcomes who had never visited India. Now I felt somehow that my desire to see the Latin American continent and the Indian sub-continent coming together was close, or at least on the way to being fulfilled, though I realised that there were miles left to travel.

A FEW SPECIAL MEMORIES

Having recounted some of my visits to Latin America, I feel I should perhaps explain that honing my Spanish was possible over the decades at the IMF by taking intermittent placement exams to demonstrate that I retained my interest in the language and was capable of taking the familiarity further. For this I had to match every hour of private training with an equivalent number, or more, of hours at the language lab, a task that I nevertheless embraced without much reluctance. I had excellent instructors from Colombia, Ecuador, Guatemala, and Spain, each of whom had a different style and focus, and I remain their beneficiary. I always looked forward to the lessons as they became increasingly complex and advanced into literature, though hours at the lab continued to be demanding. Not only did these language skills enable official conversations at meetings, perusing documents and files, they also laid bare the possibilities of travelling to the interiors, meeting local people, grasping differing accents, embracing local culture, appreciating local food however exotic, and developing friendships that have endured to this day.

Here I recall one mission visit to Bogota when my team and I stayed at an ornate hotel called Casa Medina. It was decorated in meticulously carved teak, ebony and mahogany along the hallways, dining room and bedrooms. Only very high class Bogotanos—old family types—appeared to float in and out of it. Mainly for lack of time, we usually ate in the dining room. But one evening, I exhorted my mission colleagues Osvaldo, Erik and Bernd that we go out to the Swiss Chalet for some *fondue*. To this they readily agreed. As we walked along the corridor towards the lobby, there was a distinct scent of sandalwood incense and, looking askance, Osvaldo indicated that it was emanating from a large hall to our left. He found a door ajar and silently pushed it open, too curious not to. I peeked in too. It was a large, long hall occupied by well-dressed women in strings of pearls and men in formal dark suits, evidently a high society gathering. At the head of the hall was a slightly raised dais on which sat an Indian in a saffron robe, with a flowing beard and long, neatly combed back hair. He was chanting the 'Om' while his rapt audience was repeating softly after him. It was enchanting to find Latin America's interest in India's offerings, in particular yoga and its outward manifestations such as incense and chants.

Osvaldo, a devout Catholic, softly asked me if I would like to join the group, adding that my companions would be glad to wait until I was ready to leave. I spontaneously responded, "Osvaldo, don't worry. This is an exclusive export product of India". They fell into broad smiles, nevertheless respectful, and we moved on for the fondue. My experiences were thus interspersed with cultural influences that criss-crossed the oceans in a free flow of universal understanding. Indeed, in one early mission to Bogota in 1991, Atuk, the Indian Ambassador, had invited me to a function at the Embassy on 2 October. I anticipated long speeches on Mohandas Karamchand Gandhi's role in India's independence. Yes, there was mention of Gandhi, but it was soon followed by an hour of chants and dances by the followers of the Hare Krishna Movement, Satya Sai Baba, Brahmakumaris and others. Obviously enjoying the spectacle, Atuk explained that they were a major source of revenue from visas to India.

On my part, over the three decades during my Bogota visits, I took the family of a close friend, rather irreligious in their practice, to the church of Don Bosco and Dominic Savio on 20 de Julio. I especially liked visiting the small quiet chapel behind the church dedicated to *El Nino*. They were amused at an Indian's greater interest—if not knowledge—of Catholicism, for which as many modern Latin Americans as not seemed to profess a disdain. Later, some of the same family members that I had taken to the church for the first time appeared to have taken up visits to the 20 de Julio area on their own. Indeed, they are now a second family that I have adopted, and have been adopted into.

I found a Salesian run Don Bosco School almost in every Latin American capital. I developed a practice of dropping in to say hello and being welcomed by the curious priests, always appreciative that I too had completed my high school matriculation from a Don Bosco in faraway India. Yet I also found several Latin American colleagues and friends anticipate my sing-song recitation of the *Gayatri mantra* in the early mornings or whenever:

Om bhoor bhuvah svaha
Tatsaviturvarenyam
Bhargo devasyadheemahi
Dhiyo yo nah prachodayat

How can I forget Sergio, a priest in Buenos Aires who would drive up in his Beetle in the evening and take me to see many a soccer game between Argentinian and Brazilian teams—events only the most fortunate could experience. Equally, at my request, he took me to the AIDS hospice run by Mother Teresa's Sisters of Charity in the outskirts of the city. Or the legendary Father Camille Bouche of St. Xavier's, Calcutta, who hailed from western Europe and published in Bengali under the pen name of Kamal Basu, who stayed with me for a few days in Washington DC; out of reverence, I let him sleep in my bedroom, shifting to a guest room myself. It was a learning experience to have him stay. I was later told that he had most commendably recounted that from my bed he could reach out for books from my library since my bedroom was lined with tall book shelves. Then there was Victorino, another young, handsome Argentinian priest who seemed to belong to a different world altogether and was great to meet, chat with and exchange views over global affairs. And my current friends from the priesthood, Jose, Leo and others. But most of all, the priests of Don Bosco, Madras—Mellon, Gatti, Anthony, Salvador, and Christie—who, having landed in India at as early an age as seventeen, from all corners of the world, taught me how to cycle, improve my swimming, appreciate literature, recite meticulously pronounced and cadenced poetry, develop the discipline of scouting, and who were forever unwilling to give up on my flailing attempts at soccer and cricket, perhaps hoping that one day I would rise at least to the standards I had reached in table tennis, badminton or tennis.

Thus it was that my professional visits to Latin America also had the impact of a revelation of sorts—an altogether new and ebullient culture, absence of superstition, infinite geographical and inner beauty full of music and song—the tango, samba, rhumba, merengue, salsa—late night feasting, and hard work and endless creativity during the day. This sense of perpetual newness manifested itself in a state of perennial change. Reflecting the presidential system of government, new governments were installed every four, five or six years with a fresh set of professionals selected by and supporting the president, their main objective seemingly being the introduction of new ideas, concepts and processes. This included the tax structure, so that one witnessed a new set of taxation policies every so many years, one lamentable outcome being the sacrifice of previous, even good, ideas that could have taken years to take hold. Nevertheless, this route was palpably better than systems in prevalence elsewhere that took decades to change and longer to reform, typically where the leadership tends to move out in a horizontal, rather than a vertical, position. This was also true to the extent that I perceived I had won the confidence of many Latin American authorities who described me as "*el economista Hindu quien habla espanol muy bien*", the Indian economist who speaks Spanish very well. I found myself being interviewed by media in newspapers, radio and television—with the authorities' clearance of course—in country after country.

To me, Latin America imparted a sense of vitality, dynamism and excitement—a continent of magic realism. Artists did not recoil from painting trains that moved straight out of the mountains into the open sky, competing with large bells ringing in vacuum, or for fish to be fishing humans just beside postured fishermen, or for farmer families all without eyes to be toiling in the charcoal dark of their meagre homes as if life had given them no opportunity to meaningfully look into the outer world. Painters such as Legarda of Colombia, Bejia and Dayuma of Ecuador, Casimir of Haiti and many nameless artists filled the colourful world of naïve art, though Guyasamin, again of Ecuador, rendered skeletal poverty in the most modernist way, while Botero of Colombia did just the opposite, his family figures being rotund if not obese. The work of these artists has global impact and renown. It was as if quite natural and automatic to cast the arrival of the Conquistadors, the adoration of the lunar eclipse, or the scene of a miracle of the Santa Madonna de Guadalupe in benign, magical tones on the easel.

The dynamism of Latin America flowed over to the negative as well. On the Paraguay border with Argentina and Brazil, I found countless imitations of manufacturers' labels jamming the roads for shipment to the far corners of the earth. When I came across an entry in the balance of payments entitled 'Statistical Tax', as mentioned earlier, I enquired after it and, after some give and take, found that it represented the measured amount of illicit border trade. If I recall right, it was some 10 percent of export earnings.

The impact of the drug trade then centred in Colombia, and now Mexico, converted these societies into violent pockets while, of course, the overwhelming responsibility of those countries that do not strictly control their demand or consumption cannot be overlooked. But even today my admiration for Latin America is not superseded by that for any other region. Despite periodic convulsions of corruption, it is to be observed that once known, it is followed up by punitive action against offenders, and it is not just the party in opposition that is pursued. Its culture is advanced, its people superbly intelligent yet simple by Asian or English standards and full of life, fun and frolic, music and dance, their welcome of foreigners honest and heartfelt. Its intellect, literature, art and sculpture are all recognised at the highest global levels. Its geography, flora and fauna are unique and unparalleled. The indigenous and the Western, the traditional and the modern, the old and the new mingle here as well as has been experienced anywhere else in the world. *Namastute* Latin America!

MY DEPARTURE

Usually division chiefs in the Fiscal Affairs Department (FAD) stayed on for some years in that role as it was considered to be a comfortable, senior management post. However, I undertook considerable travel, mainly at Vito's behest, and possibly reflecting my mission successes, while continuing with research, and my Spanish advancement. Walking away from my relatively short tenure as Chief of Tax Policy did raise an eyebrow or two. Someone put out a note titled, "Who can stop this man!" In an internal circulation called *Cram Notes* dated May 1995, some of my colleagues at the Fund made nostalgic comments, of which jingle:

Howell Zee, my Deputy and expert on the theory of taxation: "... India braces for the return of the IMF Tax Man...."

Yvonne Liem, librarian: "Even though a continent and an ocean will separate us from one of our favourite 'customers', the Fiscal Library would like to keep him informed about new acquisitions by sending him each month....our one and only *List of Recent Additions and Periodical Articles*."

Janet Stotsky, American economist who joined the Fund from the US Treasury: "India is known as a country of many diverse languages and cultures. Partho will be well equipped to deal with his experience with (his) staff from Asia (Hong Kong, New Zealand, Singapore), Africa (Kenya, Ethiopia), Europe (Croatia, Denmark, Germany,

Spain), the Middle East (Egypt, Turkey), North America (Canada, the United States), and South America (Ecuador). However, we have all shared in the hard work and the fun!"

In fact, at the time, the twenty staff in Tax Policy comprised eighteen nationalities. Others from India, Mexico, Thailand and other countries had worked under me and moved on elsewhere in the Fund. I have kept that edition of *Cram Notes* simply as proof that tax professionals can and do have a sense of humour. Susan Otero wrote a little poem in Spanish which went:

Partho es un excelente jefe de mision!
A pesar de la presion que tiene toda mision siempre guardo consideracion.
Por su buena organizacion ni la altura de La Paz (Bolivia) lo vencio
Y hasta a los ministros con su informe convencio.

Partho is an excellent mission chief!
Despite the pressures that every mission experiences
He is always considerate.
Neither his adherence to organisation nor the altitude of La Paz
Defeated him.
And he convinced even the ministers with his reports.

Alas, my research officer and good friend Assi Woldemariam's statement in Ethiopian remains a mystery, until I make that promised visit to her country.

The send-off was held at the Georgetown home of John Norregaard from Denmark, who had done excellent work on alternate definitions of the progressivity of income taxation in his prior location at the Organisation for Economic Co-operation and Development (OECD). But the main architect of the party was Lyndsey Livingstone from New Zealand, my administrative assistant, whose typing and work were so meticulous that I never encountered the same standard anywhere else where I was posted. My departure was nostalgic. I received a large send-off card with more comments, some funny, some sad, their love evident in all (see Plates 7a, b and c). I like to believe that I had guided all of them through a grinding, exacting and hopefully inspiring exercise of writing a *Tax Policy Handbook* (IMF, 1995), in which individual chapters appeared under their own names. The *Handbook* is taught in universities and governments in many countries even today. Almost two decades later, when I led the first tax reform mission to Myanmar in May 2012 (see Plate 26), a senior tax official approached me with a threadbare copy of the volume, saying it had been his gospel over the years, and requested me to sign it. I was truly astounded though not entirely surprised.

It remains difficult for me to explain my departure in 1995; it was almost as if some internal force was pulling me back to India. I recall two and a half decades earlier, in June 1971, as my father lay in hospital, he asked me if my university results for the first year master's course had arrived. I told him I had been ranked first in Delhi University in MA Previous, just as I had for my BA Honours degree at Calcutta University the year before. I knew that my father was proud of me, though he never showed it. He fell silent, then softly said that I was likely to win a scholarship and go abroad for my doctorate degree. He added that I must return to India later, because India would need my generation for her growth and development. He fell into a coma thereafter and passed on days later, leaving us transfixed over the last breath he took in front of us. My father's last words to me together with the patriotism and love for the country embedded right from childhood by my mother, my grandparents, relatives and teachers have always had a certain power over me. And somewhere that year, they propelled me back to India. I joined the National Institute of Public Finance and Policy, New Delhi, as its Director in June 1995.

ANNEXE

Statements at the Ceremony admitting Dr. Parthasarathi Shome as Commander of the Order of the Southern Cross

"It is with great pride, that, in the presence of such a distinguished audience, I bestow the decoration of the Order of the Southern Cross at the grade of Commander to Dr. Parthasarathi Shome.

"This is the most significant medal of the Brazilian Government created in 1932, as a symbol of recognition of relevant contributions of foreign citizens to my country.

"Dr. Shome highly deserves this decoration. A respected economist with a strong academic background, he has been indefatigable in the accomplishment of his tasks of advising authorities in Brazil in fiscal matters during the IMF missions. In performing this task, he was able to combine the IMF austerity to the sensitivity for the social aspects in Brazil. I attribute these qualities to the fact that Professor Shome is a native of India, and has inherent in his mindset the clear awareness of the social needs of developing countries. This is probably why he has made so many friends in Brazil, and in other Latin American countries as well. As far as Brazil is concerned, the Revenue Secretary Everardo Maciel, the Social Security Minister, Waldeck Ornelas, the high officials from the Finance Ministry, including Mr. Pedro Malan, are among those with whom Dr. Shome has established a working relationship of mutual respect and, with some of them, personal friendship.

"....I am sure that Dr. Shome's participation in many training programs for Brazilian fiscal specialists in the last decade might have represented a long lasting contribution to the acquisition of the right tools by those he trained and who might have been involved in the decision-making process regarding the fiscal policy changes.

"The recognition of his professional qualities was demonstrated by the quick acceptance of my recommendation to include the name of Dr. Parthasarathi Shome as a member of the Order of the Southern Cross.

"It is therefore my great honour to read the diploma of admission of Dr. Shome in the Order, in a non-official English version:

> *The President of the Federative Republic of Brazil, Great Master of the National Order of the Southern Cross, decided to bestow to Mr. Parthasarathi Shome, Economist, a national of India, the degree of said Order, by Decree of February 2nd, 2000.*
>
> *And to keep this on record, by instructions of the President of the Republic, I sign this diploma which bears the seal of the Order.*
>
> *Brasilia, on the third day of February 2000, year 179 of the Independence and year 112 of the Republic.*
>
> *Frederico Araujo, Secretary of the Order.*

"Congratulations, Partho.

"New Delhi, 20 April, 2000."

I too gave a speech comparing Brazil and India and, in my style, providing voluminous cross-section statistics on economic and socio-economic indicators. A close friend later said he heaved a sigh of relief when I desisted from reading it out in all its minute detail! I confess, this Brazilian recognition was for me a great achievement reflecting the multi-faceted approaches and ever expanding scope that I had to employ and the dexterity and persistence with which I had assisted in modifying Brazil's tax structure over the previous decade. Vera informed me that I was the first Indian to have received the title.

The media coverage—television, magazines and newspapers—was wide and instantaneous. There seemed to be countless interviews and reports even in vernacular—I saw Bengali and Tamil ones—amazed as I was to see how they could extol someone when in the right mood. Jokes apart, I was truly humbled, constantly recalling the benefits and advantage derived from a long list of ancestors and teachers every step of the way whose unwavering goodwill and blessings had ushered me along. I look up to them rather than to the pantheon of gods and goddesses to whom I have the advantage of access, not that the cultural anthropologist in me is not drawn to their exquisite repositories across the world.

FOUR

INTERNATIONAL MONETARY FUND

Africa, Europe and Asia in the 1980s and 1990s

Apart from Latin America, I was fortunate to experience the tax systems of selected African states, East and Southern Europe, the Former Soviet Union (FSU), as well as Asia. These experiences were unique and challenging in their own right, and many of them were delightful. Today, in retrospect, I seem to have only beautiful memories of them and, though realistically I must have had a few close calls, I shall try to jot them down to the best of my recollection.

AFRICA

Botswana

The first technical assistance mission that I headed was to Botswana in Southern Africa in September 1985 where we conducted a complete survey of the tax system and its administration. A country as large as Texas, yet with a population of a mere one million, it possessed a rudimentary tax structure. The bulk of its revenue came from the beef industry from which revenue was extracted directly from a couple of government abattoirs, and from uncut diamonds mined in Botswana but managed entirely by De Beers from South Africa that paid Botswana in pre-determined royalty.

To change the mindset of local officials towards a conventionally structured tax system was no easy task. Frankly, I did not see the need for a switch, except in case of a possible future rupture with De

Beers or an unanticipated capricious reaction from the European Union regarding beef imports from the country. An odd matter that I noticed was the presence and considerable power exercised by expatriate advisers in government even though the top ranks were expectedly occupied by Botswana nationals. To some extent this was obvious since high officials were often found to spend long periods at their cattle ranches which, in response to my question, was explained by their natural affinity towards land and cattle.

Be that as it may, we developed a system of simple improvements in both tax structure and administration, which the Permanent Secretary of Finance, a young, dashing yet thoughtful man, quietly welcomed despite my caution that the proposed changes would require steadfast movements in a new direction. I recall that, among other analyses, I carried out an exercise demonstrating *bracket creep* (revenue increase due to inflation) in the income tax, and he agreed to change the structure to correct the problem. Later, I published the findings from the exercise in a research journal, subsequently reprinted in my *Tax Compendium*.

What made the most striking impact on me in that country was the breathtaking beauty of the Botswana wilderness. Until that time, my favourites were the flashing aurora borealis of the northern skies, the Norwegian glaciers, and New Zealand's ever changing panorama of volcanoes erupting from snow-capped peaks, its sandy beaches and blue-green seas. Now, Botswana replaced them as my top favourite.

As always, I picked the last weekend to take a long flight from the capital Gaberone to Maun in the north and at the edge of the Kalahari Desert. Soon after the plane glided onto a runway of sand, I found myself in an old colonial hotel complete with liveried butlers and a full English breakfast. The hotel was on the bank of the Okavango River that flows untroubled until it inexplicably disappears into the desert. After breakfast, as I emerged from the hotel, I was struck both by the natural beauty of my immediate surroundings as well as a one-storey high anthill in the hotel lawns, and an anteater poking its long nose into it. For a moment I was transfixed, but soon realised that the animal bothered no one even as hotel staff flitted past carrying on with their daily chores. Reassured, I proceeded to board a canoe which was being held in place by its owner at the steps leading to the river.

As I seated myself gingerly in the narrow canoe, I realised that I barely fitted on the bench, and that any crocodile, which the river was full of, could raise its head and take an easy bite out of my buttock. Bracing myself, I asked the boatman to proceed, and was soon lost in the spectacular, if terrifying, sights that surrounded me. I saw a crocodile devouring an antelope on the banks from uncomfortably close quarters, and half-eaten, abandoned cattle. I saw crocodiles swimming past us along the length of the canoe several times, causing me to lose a breath or two. After about one and a half hours of floating along, quite suddenly the river opened out, and I found myself in the Okavango River Delta.

To this day that spot remains the one that I associate with paradise, if there should be one, and my first moment there was epiphanic. The river stretched out into the horizon before me as far as the eyes could see, with the delta forming an island of beauty. From it rose tall shady trees. White-plumed, long-tailed birds flew gracefully from one tree top to another as others sat on their perches humming and, strangely, not screeching. The water was covered with red, pink and white lilies, and my Indian eyes spotted some lotuses as well. As we entered the lily-covered water, I asked my English-speaking rower to stop ... *stop here, or gently pass...* as William Wordsworth wrote more than a century ago. As I beheld the scene, a great calm overwhelmed me. I am not sure how long we stood still. The silence was broken only when he nudged me gently, indicating that we would soon have to turn back, and whether I would like him to row us further on. I reluctantly agreed, for what further revelation could come upon me with more movement? We moved on deeper into the delta.

That night the dinner, over a glass of decent wine and English roast, was contemplative. When alone, my mind and heart were so overwhelmed with thoughts of Creation and its myriad multi-dimensional possibilities that the following morning I realised I was being irrational, for I did not want to move from there; I wanted to settle down not just in Botswana but at that very spot so that I could visit the Delta every day for the rest of my life. Eventually, I thought of my ageing mother and my worldly responsibilities and dragged myself to bed, for the rest of the weekend also promised to be eventful.

The next morning was glorious, and there was a SUV waiting for me along with David, a robust fellow with a polite smile who would be my driver and guide for two days in the Moremi National Forest. Evaluating him mentally, I felt I could safely repose my confidence in him. I sat at the back under a clear, open sky. I must have been so excited that the journey to the edge of the forest seemed rather short. On entering barely a few yards into the forest, David stopped short and, through the rear glass window, indicated to me to be silent. I obeyed. Soon, a short distance away on my left I saw an elephant suddenly appear, steadily moving in our direction. I almost panicked. David again gestured that I be quiet. As the elephant got closer, David moved forward slightly but stopped again. Now the elephant sped up and charged straight at us, with its herd of nine or ten following suit. David continued to stand absolutely still until the leader of the herd came to about six feet of our vehicle, by which time my heart was in my mouth. Only then did David speed away. Once I felt safe, I asked him to stop. He got out of the SUV, smiling broadly, until I asked him exactly what his intentions had been in exposing me to such certain and grave danger. He retrieved his smile to explain that I had been really lucky to encounter an entire elephant herd in the wild, and had he not blocked their path momentarily, I would not have been able to see the lot of them together in action. I was speechless, but for some reason, at that moment I decided to trust David completely with whatever would happen in that forest.

As hundreds of wildebeest took flight in their annual migration and prides of lions roared past, bloats of hippopotami bobbed in and out of shallow water bodies, I finally gave up clicking my complex camera, so mesmerised I was by what was going on around me. That such fundamentally natural scenes were unfolding right in front of my eyes had a profound impact on my assessment of life and death. It was as if the latter did not matter anymore.

As we crossed a handmade wooden bridge over a rivulet, I bent over to view its crystal clear waters and could see right through to the sand at the bottom and the shoots of tall grass that stood up from it. It was extremely inviting for a quiet swim, my favourite activity. I used to in fact stop by the Young Men's Christian Association (YMCA) in Washington every evening for a forty-five minute swim on my way home. As I pondered the idea, I assessed the possibility of crocodiles making an easy meal out of me. I broached the idea to David, fully expecting, if not hoping, that he would annul it on the spot. Instead,

I was surprised at his conditional response: he indicated that he would beat the water with a long thin stick at a steady pace which, he guaranteed, would keep the crocs away. It seemed dubious to me, but I had already decided to put my faith in him. And so I disrobed and entered the water and swam the best, most serene swim of my life for forty-five minutes in the cool, clear water under a bright sun, as David, the devoted yet always professional driver, kept dutifully beating the water with his stick. And I forgot all about danger. When I got out of the water, I was contemplative, nay meditative, and ignored the smile on David's face, though I did thank him for making the swim possible.

Later, when I tried to recount the incident over the phone to my mother, she stopped me short, asking me why on earth I should put her through the suffering of hearing stories of her son's impending dangers across the world. When we met, however, she wanted to hear every detail as she always did of every adventure of mine. I must conclude by saying that comparable visits in Kenya to wildlife parks did not inspire or move me in the same way as the Moremi did, for they were more formal, organised and structured, although I did see a rhinoceros being born on one such trip.

South Africa

Another country that astounded me in the African continent was South Africa. During the apartheid regime, South Africa was located in the European Department in the Fund, certainly an oddity. While I was never silent about such anomalies in the Fund even with senior colleagues in private conversations, I kept out such eruptions during my work day. While I was on another mission, I was assigned to accompany Ved Prakash Gandhi to South Africa. I had worked with him in Thailand earlier, and he had appreciated my work. Hence that was not an issue. But on my return to headquarters, I took umbrage at having to visit South Africa before regime change. Ved explained somewhat apologetically that he had thus far not assigned me any country without my consent—a bit of an exaggeration in itself—but that I was the staff member found to be most suitable to study the VAT under preparation in South Africa. I had little choice after that.

The country's Value-Added Tax Committee (VATCOM) had recommended that maize products, rice, bread and milk powder be zero-rated. In light of this, our mission was one of the first technical assistance missions to devote considerable attention to the proposed VAT's impact on the social safety net. That specific task was given to me. I took it upon myself to visit the Homelands, the unfertile enclaves relegated to black Africans. I found there was little agriculture there and that inhabitants had to depend primarily on canned food for their subsistence. Corner shops made these available to them at remarkably high prices. I also went to some primary schools run by Catholic nuns and found that the little students were fed 'miley meal', which was a mix of various cereals sold in big packets and was vital for their daily intake of protein. I also made a price check in grocery stores in Soweto, the segregated city for blacks from where, I noticed, they could not drive into the highway built for the whites.

In analytical terms, in the excellent research being conducted at the University of Johannesburg, I found that the professors had nonetheless missed out considering the actual consumption patterns in the proposed VAT structure, thus taxing canned and packet food while exempting luxury bread and the like available in exclusive bakeries. I brought this and other such anomalies to their attention, which was appreciated. My work also assessed the extent to which existing institutions and mix of instruments could be used for social assistance distribution to the most vulnerable groups after the VAT was introduced, and proposed possible options. Needless to say, these recommendations fell a bit out of the usually accepted conservative VAT structure.

Perhaps more controversial within the Fund itself was the mission's finding that the aggregate price level would decline with the introduction of the VAT despite its being structured on a revenue neutral basis with respect to the prevailing 13 percent General Sales Tax. The explanation lay in the cascading elements of the GST that the VAT would eradicate. Elimination of cascading would generate a significant supply response from the same quantum of economic resources that should be observable in the medium term. With the same revenue against a higher GDP, the immediate tax/GDP was expected to decline, ushering in a positive supply response. It would not be an exaggeration to say that this finding raised a hue and cry internally, but my colleague who carried out the technical elements of the exercise could not be faulted. Coming to his juniors' rescue,

Vito, as head of FAD, provided eloquent justification of both the price and supply elements on the one hand, and the VAT's assessed social impact on the other.

A year later, on 23 January 1992, Lesley Lambert of *Business Day* of South Africa reported in 'VAT': "Prices of goods and services declined by an average 0.27% in December, VAT Watch announced yesterday. This was the second price decline recorded since VAT was introduced in October, the watchdog organisation said..." Of course some elements of the food basket experienced price increases, but there were compensating effects from others.

This experience left me with a conviction that a monitoring cell (MC) needs to be installed when a VAT or GST is introduced or improved. In India, too, a fiscal federal GST comprising both the central and state governments was introduced on a revenue neutral basis on 1 July 2017. There are bound to be winners and losers among the various players, for example, among various state revenue authorities, among producers and dealers, and among consumers. So there is bound to be some dissatisfaction associated with redistribution among different players. What is important, however, is to install mechanisms to monitor egregious anomalies and malpractices that could occur, in particular during the early implementation period. Thus it is important to put in place an MC to check if retailers are charging excessive prices and other such challenges that are not unlikely to appear. In South Africa, an MC played a crucial role in checking the immediate ramifications of the new tax, bringing to notice the actual decline in the overall price level that would otherwise have certainly gone unnoticed. In India, too, monitoring during the first year post GST was comprehensive, but the absence of a specific MC did not allow exact calculations of price effects to be made.

Before I move on I must, however, relate how uncomfortable I was working in South Africa for three weeks. To begin with, we were housed in a luxury hotel where the only non-whites were our three mission members. It seemed almost as if we were on an island. After days of continental roasts and the like, Ved took it upon himself to lead us to a pizza joint half an hour's walk away. That was a relief, and he repeated the exercise almost every night. South Africans of Indian descent invited us occasionally to their segregated club or restaurant, though that too fed a deep discomfort within me since I did not find a single black South African in the vicinity.

However, it would be wrong not to recognise the authorities' anticipation of the impending regime change, and their sincere and fundamental work towards a peaceful and technically well-prepared transition. They also insisted on our seeing South Africa, apart from the main cities, through the wine country, the Cape of Good Hope, a gaudy entertainment complex whose name I have thankfully forgotten, and other tourist spots. Since I had already visited the Homelands and Soweto, when I left the country I knew that my visit to South Africa had been holistically instructive, for where else could I have witnessed the ramifications of such enforced ethnic separation. I realised that I would not have missed it at any cost, if only to strengthen the convictions that I already possessed.

Rwanda

Hatred of compatriots is incomprehensible and loathsome; yet it has been known and witnessed throughout human history time and again, including in my own lifetime, and perhaps it may even be on the rise. In my visit to Rwanda for a conference to seek aid from Western donors in the post-genocide reconstruction, I found any number of limbless people on the roads, victims of a common form of revenge between the Hutus and Tutsis. It was claimed that German colonists had used one group against the other, giving birth to the blood feud. During my visit to Eritrea with the same objective, I found similar animosity between Eritrea and Ethiopia, countrymen who had fought a war, separated, and were now enemies. Were the Italians to blame for this? The India-Pakistan divide is no better. Are the English solely to blame? Siblings quarrel even within families; but it is those who make up who win. In the same way, despite the incidence of history, the lesson that emerges is that it remains the responsibility of the newly emerged nations to bridge the gap with their cousins, for they are now neighbours and the colonial occupiers have gone. Of course this is easier said than done for hatred, when it takes root, is difficult indeed to uproot.

TEACHING TAX

Before I end this section, let me digress a bit. Over the years, I went to several countries to teach tax policy including Kenya, Abu Dhabi, Indonesia, Hungary, and China. I did the same in Singapore where I went as Director of the Fund's training institute located there. Teaching at the Central Bank of Kenya was not challenging in that the students, who were mainly African economic officials, were intelligent and well prepared. But what lingers in my memory was the deep social divide between Indians and Kenyans, making me wonder why Indians had such difficulty in mingling with any local population. I found the same to be true in Guyana, Fiji, Myanmar and South Africa, the latter of course encouraged by past governmental policy. Another explanation could be that the main sites in India from where such emigration had taken place were replete with their own history of exclusion by caste and creed. An exception to this type of segregation was Singapore where cultural mixing seemed to be actually encouraged, if not effectively mandated, even for climbing up socially.

Today, Britain boasts of having the most mixed society. This may be seen to be true just from the commercials portraying mixed couples of different colours, ethnicities and sexual preferences—a matter still *verboten* in the US and much of Europe. However, at the very top, even British society appears reflective of a non-mix hierarchy, and various recent academic studies have established a continuance of racism. Prince Harry's recent marriage with Meghan Markle, who is of mixed parentage, added excitement, albeit after some untoward reactions. Colour and caste differences that have lost all rationality and legitimacy in today's modern world continue most primitively, prominently and perniciously in India with tacit encouragement for narrow political goals, with oft-repeated painful consequences.

EUROPE AND THE FORMER SOVIET UNION

One set of countries I had to visit included those of the Former Soviet Union (FSU) and Eastern Europe as this entire region was emerging from the Second World. I recount some of them here.

Kazakhstan

I recall Kazakhstan as it stood out with its challenging tax matters in a backdrop of near complete darkness about the non-Soviet world, thus offering unique and unexpected cultural insights. I went to Alma Ata (now Almaty), which was then the capital of Kazakhstan for a three-week period in December 1991; the capital has now shifted to Astana. I went at the head of an eleven-member team, the largest I had led and rather unusual for the Fund, to study and recommend fundamental reform in Kazakhstan's tax structure. We were the first Western visitors for the government which, it appeared, was enamoured by us. As usual we met with the Minister of Finance but worked closely with the Central State Tax Inspectorate that was independent of the Ministry. The warm welcome by the authorities stood out against the cold, stark, snowy winter. The warmth was shared at the Ministries of Labour, Social Security and Health, as well as at the central statistical agency which we consulted, for the scope of the mission was wide-ranging. It had been asked to go beyond the usual fiscal concerns and issues. Thus the mission not only analysed tax policy legislation and assessed tax administration capacity, it also identified measures for social insurance and the process of market reform with a view to their budgetary ramifications.

From political, economic and social autarky, Kazakhstan—an area comparable to India with a sparse population of 17 million inhabitants—was undergoing rapid change. On the political front, during the mission's stay, the name of the republic was changed from Kazakh SSR to Kazakhstan; President Nazarbayev consolidated his position through a single-candidate election; it was noteworthy that senior officials invariably toasted the President as "popularly elected". There was a satisfaction that now orders did not have to be taken from Moscow. And the Supreme Soviet began debating at great speed the population's own future through draft laws.

On the economic front, there was concern among the authorities that the close links with other ex-Soviet republics, with which Kazakhstan mainly traded raw materials in exchange of finished products, might be irrevocably broken in the near future. This was associated with an inflation rate of 100 percent in 1991 and an anticipation of 200–300 percent in 1992. Revenue needs posed another challenge. The Union revenue-sharing arrangements—in which Kazakhstan was a net gainer—having broken down, had led to interest in new revenue sources. This was in the background of Russia modifying its tax laws unilaterally—despite having earlier agreed to coordinate them with the other republics—even in the areas where inter-republic relations had important ramifications. In 1991, Kazakhstan's state budget deficit—including central and local level governments—was projected at 20 percent of government expenditure and, without appropriate revenue measures, was feared would rise to 30 percent in 1992.

On the socio-cultural and demographic front, Kazakhstan's tapestry of multiple nationalities—including two-fifths Kazakh and one-third Russian—appeared to be cohesively integrated, minimising the chances of future social strife. Perhaps this was an important reason—apart from the overwhelming attraction of an infinite supply of natural gas—why foreign business interests were already expressing interest in Kazakhstan's welfare. The IMF mission arrived in this socio-economic milieu.

We examined the draft income tax law and found that the individual income tax, despite its many exemptions, was being reformed with a top marginal rate of 30 percent. The corporate income tax was being correctly based on profits with a rate of 35 percent. Two exceptional rates of 40 and 50 percent were to be applied on royalty incomes from the republic's rich natural resource endowment (mainly oil, natural gas, coal, iron ore, and nonferrous metals including gold). Nevertheless, various special incentives were being offered for foreign investment and joint ventures. Examination of the draft VAT law revealed that the base was broad and coordinated with other republics, though with a rate between 27–28 percent, among the highest in the world.

We recommended to the authorities a tax structure with low tax rates for the FSU was typically burdened with high rates, for example, near 30 percent rates for the VAT. Instead we strongly suggested broadening the tax base by minimising special privileges and allowances, and equal treatment of all forms of organisation, whether public, private, joint ventures or foreign enterprises, while introducing withholding taxes on interest and dividends. We suggested that the corporate and top individual income tax rates be equalised at 35 percent. On tax administration, we recommended a menu of modernising measures. In the area of social safety net, we suggested methods to streamline broad-based social insurance schemes that could have direct or indirect budgetary ramifications, and the construction of custom-tailored programmes targeted at the most vulnerable sections during the process of price and tax reform—rather than old-style programmes that covered the entire population.

We did not confine ourselves to the cold of Alma Ata but went westwards, some 600 kilometres, to Jumbool, after passing through Kyrgyzstan and its capital Bishkek. We assessed the prevailing status of tax administration capacity and apprised the authorities, not only of broad directions for reform of smaller administration offices, but also of the need for redoubled efforts in preparation for VAT implementation—though to be levied only up to the manufacturer stage—in areas away from Alma Ata.

Surprisingly, the authorities seemed to welcome our recommendations and requested me to carry back their request to Fund headquarters for more technical assistance. On the way back, I first briefed Vito who was anchored in Moscow and seemed happy with the outcome of the mission. I also stopped at the European Community in Brussels to coordinate future fiscal technical assistance work on the FSU as a whole, in coordination with various multilateral agencies. It was a great relief to return to the regular world, walk into the Magritte Museum, always one of my favourites for the artist's surreal imagination, and heave a sigh.

I should also touch upon the personal and cultural aspects of the mission's experience in Kazakhstan since they were indeed unique. The mission had arrived in Alma Ata in an environment of rapid political, economic and social change. The mission members comprised a wide range of nationalities including those from Bolivia, India, Japan, the Netherlands, New Zealand, Turkey, the United Kingdom and the United States, and each seemed to face a different set of challenges. Breakfast was a type of cereal with a blob of cream made from lamb's milk, and uniform tea. Everyone was served the same tea, one morning without additions, sometimes with sugar, occasionally with milk, sometimes both. There was no choice. Lunch was boiled cabbage and steamed lamb. Reflecting some unknown intuition I had declared myself to be vegetarian; hence I received an apple or orange instead of the meat. Soon my colleagues would pay anything to exchange meat for my fruit!

At the official dinner, a huge roasted lamb—what else—was brought in and, as head of mission, I was given the task of carving it. I managed and, for the same reason, could not get away from eating an eye, which was inserted into my mouth by the Minister. I was genuinely relieved when my Turkish colleague bent over to ask me if he could have the other eye, his congruent ethnicity coming to my timely rescue! When we returned to our guesthouse after such dinners at the 'long table', we would have to open the windows to be relieved of overheated rooms. While it was much below freezing outside, the inefficient temperature control systems rendered the rooms unbearable inside.

A major experience in Jumbool was a yak ride, which seemed obligatory from the authorities' point of view. At Bishkek, we encountered an expansive open market and I felt a bit like what Marco Polo might have felt in the late thirteenth century when I saw the head of a horse staring at me from a display at a meat shop. It was good preparation, however, for horse meat would soon be literally fed to me for lunch by the Minister; when I balked, he assured me that it was a special breed for human consumption, and a matter of national pride besides. I remember it had started to snow as I looked out and tried not to think too much, but my attention was soon diverted as news arrived that President Nazarbayev had been re-elected, and that more than 95 percent voters had voted. When I asked who the other candidates were, I was stonily informed that he was such a popular leader that there had been no contender. I felt a bit foolish for having asked the question. Given the prevailing trends in several global democracies, that does not seem so unusual today.

Several of our Kazakh counterparts invited us home and offered us their choicest delicacies, which touched me deeply for there were hardly any consumables in the country. I had noted the lack of variation in that society, everyone with the same heavy black-rimmed glasses and gold-lined dental fillings (the Soviet Union was rich in gold). Stalin had infused Russians into Kazakhstan so that one-third of the population was Russian. We found no animosity across the ethnicities; indeed officers represented a good mix of the two. Some Koreans had also been planted there during Stalin's massive programme of shifting and mixing populations. Paradoxically, one benefit we enjoyed was that the only private restaurant we could find was a Korean one, though the food there was strange compared to the Korean cuisine I was familiar with in Seoul or Washington.

There were a few available items such as attractive hand-knit and locally designed carpets that were cheap, and several of us acquired at least one. Word went around that the mission head was from India—though at the beginning they had thought we were all from the US, reflecting their interpretation of the world—themselves, and the US—until I had disabused them of their erroneous understanding. The outcome was that we were all invited to a specially organised show at the Museum of Musical Instruments, and, lo and behold, a dancing troupe entered the stage and danced to the tune of '*ichak dana bichak dana*'. The entire country seemed to be fans of Raj Kapoor, the Indian matinee idol from days of yore. It appeared that here time had stood still.

But the day of departure tested to the core my managerial and diplomatic alertness as mission head. As we approached the airport in the morning, a short wave radio that a mission member was carrying announced that there was no aviation fuel in the FSU and that the region was in chaos. I realised that we were taken to a separate house that served as the waiting lounge for official foreign visitors. There was no heating. We waited patiently after I argued with the person at the counter who was preparing to extract an exorbitant excess luggage fee. Having been cautioned that such a thing might happen, I had taken with me the printed rules from the Aeroflot rulebook, which eventually nipped the problem.

During our stay in Alma Ata, there had been no phone connection. I could not keep in touch with headquarters, leave alone mission members with their families. While my Japanese colleague, whose wife had brought their new-born baby to see him off at Dulles airport, sat meditatively in the lotus position through the day and evening, my heart ached. The Kiwi had been pacing the floor for what seemed like hours. Time and again I had asked the Kazakh Deputy Minister, who had accompanied us and stayed on, when our flight would materialise. Then I found out from the short wave radio that there was a flight that would fly through Tashkent to Moscow. I approached the Minister and, in sum, said that we were the first multilateral mission to visit

Kazakhstan, and that it was the authorities' responsibility to address our comfort and safety until the last minute. Otherwise, future co-operation was likely to be jeopardised.

The Minister got to work. Phone calls were made. The flight to Tashkent was diverted to Alma Ata. We were picked up. We went up through the back stairs past the luggage and sacks of potatoes and chicken. We were seated at any which seat in the plane. But we were on our way to Moscow. On landing, we found ourselves in the midst of a hue and cry being raised by the Fund staff in Moscow. Alarm bells were ringing at headquarters as to whether we had gone missing. No wonder. That was the frontier era of the FSU breaking up brick by brick. The rouble was devaluing by the minute unbeknownst to the citizen. When it was rouble 100 to $1 inside the hotel, outside they were still exchanging at par. Foreigners were buying antique icons at 1/100th of their market value. I could not do it. I bought a naïve painting after informing the dealer of the correct exchange rate, though he could not fathom what I was trying to explain; no ordinary citizen had any concept of exchange rates. When I gave him too many roubles, he politely returned them to me, until I pressed him that it was a gift from me to his family.

I recall that prior to the Kazakhstan mission, at Moscow we had to walk miles to the Kazakh House to obtain our visas there. And on the way, I had seen several elderly people lining the plazas, holding a toothbrush or comb or utensil each, presumably hoping to barter them for food. I had walked into a supermarket to find only bottle caps on the shelf. I could not rob these people, not those who had signed the 13-year Friendship Treaty with India in 1971 when the US's Sixth Fleet threatened to enter the Bay of Bengal—the handiwork of Nixon and Kissinger—as India was poised to liberate East Pakistan. I could not forget the faces of Krushchev and Bulganin, whom we had gone to see and wave flags for as children in Calcutta. The upshot of my mission's trials was that members of subsequent Fund missions to the FSU, of which there were many, were allotted chartered flights from Switzerland. I was glad for them, though my mission members acquired star status at Fund headquarters, albeit ephemerally. I did not return to Kazakhstan when it became rich and modern through its perennial supply of natural gas, open for exploitation by Western companies that soon invaded the country. China was another story that I shall recount later.

Romania

Perhaps I should quickly pass through Romania, a Second World nation so to speak, which I visited in August 1993 as mission head. It had just survived a revolution and was poised for change. We visited not only Bucharest, the capital, but also Vilcea, about 250 kilometres away, to assess tax administration capability to implement what we would recommend. Some colleagues also managed to visit Dracula's castle in Transylvania, though I stayed away from that trip! Many of Romania's immediate neighbours had also experienced revolutions. But I had seen President Ceaucescu and his wife Elena being shot dead, disbelief written on their faces, on a global television channel. It was shocking to see this darling of the West—for standing up to the Soviet Union—being subjected to the ultimate solution by his own people.

Nevertheless, it became apparent to me why a society could turn violent towards an earlier revered leader. Ceaucescu had been spending almost a third of the country's GDP annually on building a huge palace for himself. Since he did not comprehend architectural plans, he would describe what he wanted and, if the outcome did not please him, he would have it torn down, including stairways made of Carrara marble, halls and hallways. He built almost a mini palace within the palace for his role as president, and another for his role as head of the country's Communist Party. The dimensions of the intricately carved doors were so huge that the walls of factories had to be opened up to take them out. The palace looked out on a replica of the Saint je Elise—Ceaucescu so craved to build another Paris. Indeed, the Romanians have always felt an affinity towards French culture and pointed out that theirs was the only romance language in the region. The art museum was filled with medium quality Impressionist paintings.

Ceaucescu moved ancient churches to build boulevards for the palace to overlook. When ordinary labourers refused to cooperate, despite fears of losing their life, he used prisoners to accomplish the task. Romania, a seat of the Eastern Orthodox Church, was traumatised even as nuns of the numerous convents were put to weave complex tapestries for the vast palace windows and walls. His wife wore sandals studded with diamonds, while his dog was fed after the food was weighed on a solid gold machine. The country seemed relieved that they were gone.

The palace had been only partly completed. At the time I visited, only 10 percent of it was being used as service areas—including dining—for new parliament members. Most of it was already dilapidated. Capital and services had fled the country. The only restaurant we found in the market was a Chinese one run by an elderly couple. It was a homespun affair. A notice declared on the pavement that it offered fish, chicken and meat, though inside, only one dish was on offer. There was a high-class new restaurant that, we were informed, had opened recently; curious, one evening we invited the mission's interpreter there. When we finished dinner, we had emptied ourselves of more than hundred times what we spent every night at the Intercontinental Hotel where we were staying. In other words, the satisfaction we had derived until then over the minimal cost of a bottle of wine every evening, which came to exactly $1 a person, was gone in that one dinner. We left dumbfounded, but sometimes in life, one learns to simply accept rather than to challenge reality.

The new regime was open to ideas and the mission received strong encouragement from the Deputy Prime Minister Florin Georgescu and Finance Minister Eugeniu C. Gorcea, the State Secretary of Finance, and their various officials. We were also welcomed by officials of the National Bank and National Statistics Commission based on whose information we constructed quantitative estimates of revenue potential for the authorities. The authorities not only cooperated but utilised the mission's presence to their maximum benefit—holding long, intensive meetings, clarifying aspects of various taxation areas and providing necessary information. It was amusing to find in the income tax law depreciation for cattle, sheep, etc., apparently reflecting ownership patterns of farmers from an early epoch, and having to convince the authorities to do away with archaic provisions.

The VAT base was narrow and the tax rate touched 25 percent while revenue collection was barely 50 percent of the theoretically calculated potential. Luckily, in my early meeting with the Finance Minister I had informed him that the Fund mission was likely to recommend a complete overhaul of the tax system. Those were early days when the Second World and FSU were open to almost any idea emanating from the West; so one had to proceed with responsibility and caution to ensure that no country was led astray.

If revenue were needed, the mission's analysis revealed several options. On the indirect tax side, broadening the VAT base, increasing excises on gasoline and natural gas to international standards, introduction of excises on luxuries including cars and an airport departure tax, could comprise a realistic menu. On the direct tax side, inflation adjustment of company assets, scaling back of tax holidays, a minimum gross assets tax as well as withholding and presumptive features in the individual tax could be considered. We found a peculiar element in the company tax design in that it allowed receipts to be calculated on a cash basis and expenditure to be calculated on an accrual basis; that would need to be set right. On finding a detailed list of depreciation rates for animals—cattle, sheep and others—Osvaldo Schenone, a mission member, burst out in exasperation as we trawled the code with a fine tooth comb, "And why are lions and tigers missing?"

Ultimately, the mission reiterated something important, however. Even though the highest authority of a country may be on the same page as you, they may find it difficult to take corrective economic measures due to political constraints. The Minister was concerned about VAT base expansion while being comfortable with the income tax and excises that were in the nature of adjustments. Primarily, the anticipation that parliament could reject a packet of measures had a softening influence on the Minister.

Andorra

A unique bit of a country to which I led a mission in May 1994 was Andorra. A pinhead tucked between Spain and France, its dimensions were some 400 square kilometres, though it was possible to go up and down snow-peaked hills giving the illusion of larger space. After the occupation of France by Nazi Germany, the SS had proceeded to the boundary of the small principality which would certainly have been occupied. But the Pope intervened, and an agreement between him and the Spanish monarch ensured Andorra's continuing existence on the map as an independent entity. After the war, the French

President replaced the Pope; so, when we visited, the Spanish king and the French president were the joint managers of state. Andorra was a tourist haven, tourists far outnumbering the local population at any given time. It also survived on financial intermediation for intra-European transactions.

The chef de cabinet had developed an interest in the revenue potential from regular sources of taxation, which was the genesis of my mission. There was a high and growing budget deficit to the extent of 4 percent of GDP that was financed by the banking system. Yet there were growing expenditure needs for education, health and infrastructure, reflecting population growth. Two-thirds of tax revenue came from the usual selective excises on tobacco, alcohol and energy products and a small amount of customs duties, and there were some charges on business registration, telephone and electricity. However, when we arrived, we found that there were no national accounts or tax administration. Hence Erik Haindl went about creating a GDP series. Bernd Spahn, a Europe specialist, and I went about working out a rationalisation of the selective excises in the short run. In the medium term, we asked if a VAT could be introduced including a simple system for small taxpayers.

I contemplated recommending a property tax in particular since a large portion of foreign and Andorran savings were invested in real estate. But I also found that, in that minute country, there were upwards of ten municipalities competing for electoral votes; hence there was little possibility of any one of them introducing a property tax if there was even one that failed to do so. I also examined the possibility of income-based scheduler taxes and a limited corporation income tax. At the final meeting the cabinet thanked us profusely for generating the GDP series but informed us, somewhat unexpectedly, that they had decided not to introduce any tax after all. We had worked hard ignoring the beautiful natural surroundings and the shopping for which Andorra was famous. In retrospect, Andorra remains a unique experience in how to address economic and taxation issues in a sovereign state with a miniscule dimension.

The Basque Region

Soon, I was told by Vito that Messrs. Carlos Lambarri Gomez, Vice Minister of Finance, and Juan Miguel Bilbao Garai, Director of Tax

Administration of the Basque Government—an autonomous region of Spain—would visit us. They visited Fund headquarters on 18 May 1993, and Vito, as Director of Fiscal Affairs and I, as Chief of Tax Policy, met them for long technical meetings. They requested that I visit the Basque to lead a mission on tax policy reform since their fiscal and tax structures were autonomously determined from Spain. Vito politely explained that that would not be feasible since the Fund did not send missions directly to regions administered by sub-national governments.

But Vito did agree that I would write a paper on tax reform that could guide their tax policy. Eventually, Bernd Spahn and I wrote an article in 1994, delineating the nuances of tax reform for *Zergak*, their central bank journal. The Minister gave us a beautiful coffee table book on the Basque region. I recall this small event in the background of the strife currently occurring in Barcelona, the capital of the Catalan region. Having visited Barcelona and partaken of the creativity of that society in its ongoing construction of the surreal church, *La Sagrada Familia*, or The Sacred Family, and having enjoyed the walks through its broad beaches and boulevards built in absolute urban equilibrium, I can only hope that a via media will be found before further upheavals and reprisals destroy the peace and life of the region.

Ireland

While I will have to miss out some others, I feel compelled to mention my November 1993 visit to Dublin, Ireland, to participate in a conference at Trinity College on Irish concerns over income taxation (see Plate 8). It was organised by Ireland's Institute of Fiscal Studies, the premier research organisation on tax matters. My paper, subsequently included in the Fund's policy series, argued that at least in advanced countries taxpayers should not be excluded from below since the revenue potential from lower deciles could reach 10–20 percent of potential revenue collection. I remember this as being quite controversial. I admitted that in developing countries, such a strategy would not make sense since little revenue would emerge from much effort. I recall the hospitality of the Irish professors, in particular, Professor Kuane who, with her colleagues, had organised an evening of theatre and dinner. In the event, I did not understand much of the Irish dialogue, though with food and drinks flowing, the evening was a typical fun-filled Irish hallmark.

At the conference lunch, I was seated next to Mr. Ahern, then Finance Minister. I recall an interesting point he made. When I complimented him on Ireland's use of European Union funds for her economic growth, he said he was not concerned about Europe as much as he was about countries such as Bangladesh that were increasingly competing in international export markets in goods like textiles and tailored clothes. Bangladesh has continued to remain a formidable textiles exporter, though it must be recognised that the physical conditions in selected textile factories have been below acceptable international standards.

I was put up for two nights at the Trinity College senior guest house, which was a delight. In the morning a buxom woman came to prepare a sumptuous Irish breakfast, which more than filled me. Looking out from my corner room, I could see two orthogonal fields with students playing rugby and hurling, a game of ancient Gaelic and Irish origin. The meticulously maintained college campus and grounds, originally built by the English and very similar to Calcutta's Presidency College, made me both nostalgic and sad when I thought of the present-day condition of my alma mater. The one matter that irked me greatly, not that I had been unaware of it before, was the treatment, historically speaking, of one island by the other. Students were barred from entering Trinity unless they converted from Catholicism to the Church of England and, going back further in time, the atrocities wrought were more extreme. One had to constantly remind oneself that the Irish had fought hard for their independence, just as so many lives were lost for India's own freedom from colonial rule. It is indeed ironic then that in modern times we continue to witness appalling inequities wrought by policymakers over the blood and tears of their own compatriots.

Italy

My last European mission was to Italy where I was assigned to study and recommend fiscal federal reform at the head of an excellent team. From my readings I concluded that Italy's centre-province relations were extraordinarily complex, a reflection of its history and its final consolidation of various independent and semi-independent regions into one federal state—usually associated with the name of Giuseppe Garibaldi in the mid-nineteenth century. But that mission was truncated at the preparation stage since in late August 2004 I was suddenly called by Palaniappan Chidambaram, the new Indian Finance Minister, to ask if I would return to India as his sole adviser at the level of Secretary.

My mind was preoccupied since I was in the thick of a negotiation with visiting Venezuelans who had returned to a near crisis state. When I demurred, the Finance Minister informed me that the Prime Minister Dr. Manmohan Singh was also keen that I should go to India as his adviser. He was so persuasive that I agreed to go lock, stock and barrel, and entered North Block on 1 October 2004. Vito was delighted, for he had by now become used to my taking leave twice before to flit off to India. But the Deputy Managing Director of the Fund called me up to say that I was needed at the Fund, in particular in Latin America, and that I should make sure to return to IMF at the end of two years. She also informed me that in that time the new Indian government, if seriously interested, should be able to carry out the necessary fiscal reform in which I would be involved. I felt that, despite her familiarity with India, she was overly optimistic about the probable time frame for Indian tax reform.

ASIA

Thailand

Even before I joined the Fund, a mission to Thailand had been assigned to me to accompany Carlos Aguirre, an Adviser in the Fiscal Affairs Department. While he would concentrate on tax administration, my job was to work out the feasibility of converting their indirect tax system—poorly constructed turnover taxes that cascaded over a wide range of goods, as well as selective excises that also cascaded—to a well-designed VAT that would distort less the demands by consumers of various goods and services. It was no easy task. The turnover tax was old and its structure had become gnarled like an old, dying tree. The excise taxes were controlled by a powerful, retired—and explicably hospitable—general with political connections who would hear nothing of, first, including the excisable items under a VAT, and second, imposing a selective, turnover-based excise on some of them. If a commodity such as tobacco, alcohol or petroleum was taxed exclusively as an excise and excluded from the VAT, information on it would be minimal and its administration would be easy to obfuscate and, therefore, subject to diversion of revenue from government to officials.

I decided to undertake two detailed statistical analyses. The first was an analysis of the distribution across deciles of expenditure groups of replacing the prevailing tax system. The second was to calculate if there would be additional collectible revenue from a new VAT. For this, I calculated potential VAT revenue by attempting to construct a rudimentary input-output table for the taxable goods and services and, based on that, calculated potential revenue. I then compared that with what was being collected using the tax returns. Indeed, the exercises also yielded a good idea of how much tax was being evaded. I developed and fine-tuned this method in future missions to other countries such as Mexico and Colombia, and witnessed its growing and widespread use in Latin America. A part of my technical work on Thailand was published in the *Singapore Economic Review* after a long, complicated process of obtaining internal clearances from concerned Fund departments as well as the country authorities, a rigorous process that I have already elaborated.

Before long I returned to Thailand with Ved P. Gandhi, who was then Chief of Tax Policy, to continue with further analysis and implementation of a new VAT, and several times thereafter to oversee a modernised data generation and data mining system. In the late 1980s, I was lent to the World Bank, which was negotiating a structural adjustment loan with the authorities. My task was to study and recommend tax policy reform. The World Bank worked at a much more relaxed pace than what I had been used to at the Fund; hence I realised that bulk of the work in public finance fell on me. But I did not mind since the authorities were already familiar with me and my approach so that I was able to readily access information and data from the various data vaults.

Turkey

A similar experience occurred in Turkey where I went with the World Bank in 1986 to analyse and suggest reforms for the Kathma

Diyar Vergisi, the Turkish VAT that had fallen into disrepair with an emaciated base and unsustainably complex and high rate structure. I soon found that I was not only examining the VAT but other aspects of the tax structure as well and, in the final meeting with the authorities, it became apparent that I had their exclusive attention on the taxation aspects of the mission. Subsequently, they undertook fundamental tax reform along the lines of my recommendations.

It is difficult to describe Turkey in any other terms than with unflinching admiration. Colossal in their hearts, perhaps reflecting the excesses of the Ottomans, combined with the modern sensibility that Kemal Ataturk ushered in the early twentieth century, they are terribly classical in their music, opera and social dance habits. They are beautiful people and look fit to live in the grand palaces of Istanbul, San Sofia and the other magnificent edifices that reflect their rich and complex history. Their eclecticism restrained them from destroying the churches from the Christian epoch of Constantinople. The Turkish sultans had only covered the icons and frescoes inside the churches with lime; and I found that a public project was ongoing to dextrously remove the lime for the benefit of the modern tourist. In Istanbul I saw the largest ever carpets covering the mosque and palace floors, and huge chandeliers hanging from their vast ceilings. Beautiful jewels adorned their museums. Yet the covered market of Istanbul was quaint, traditional and full of antiquities, and joyful people ready to overcharge unless one was very careful and knew the value of what they were about to buy.

I found the Turkish to be friendly, the Deputy Minister inviting me to accompany him and his family to his club for a weekend lunch and tea. One matter which, however, remained a mystery to them was how Indians and Pakistanis could consume such hot spicy food. I did not of course reveal that I found Turkish fare rather mild. My interpreter, herself a Finance Ministry official, invited me for some homemade Turkish coffee so that I could see the exact method of making it, took me to a Western classical soiree in the concert hall of Ankara, the capital, and I was amazed at the high quality of the performance. There was standing room only, but as luck would have it, we had good seats. On parting, a special friend gave me a gift that I still possess. It was a cassette containing songs by a Turk and a Greek and the lyrics of the main song describes parted lovers, distance apart, seeing the same moon on a lonely moonlit night. Later I ordered and bought a CD of the same. How can one forget such experiences?

Bangladesh

During the years 1988–90, one country I visited several times to study the possibility of introducing a VAT and set up a structure for it was Bangladesh. This country stole my emotional interest and curiosity for my paternal grandfather Paresh Lal Shome hailed from Maulabi Bazar in Sylhet district of undivided Bengal, now in Bangladesh. Though Bengali-speaking, Sylhet was conjoined with the belly of Assam, which was administered mainly by the Bengali upper class. My grandfather had come to Calcutta to study in Presidency College where, I am told, he was a housemate of Rajendra Prasad, India's first President, at the Hindu Hostel. Subsequently, by the time of my parents' marriage in 1944, my grandfather had become Advocate General of Assam. After a week of the lavish wedding, representative of the urban Calcutta from where my mother's family hailed, my mother was sent to serve her widower father-in-law while my father remained to serve as General Manager, Bank of Tripura.

My mother had often recalled that her father-in-law lived alone in a gargantuan bungalow atop an entire hill that provided her with a plethora of wild and cultured orchids, colourful birds and beasts as live subjects for her canvas. An artist from an early age, she did not rest from painting, in particular because there was such a large number of butlers and liveries that the young woman's attempts at helping would be viewed as interference and meddlesome. Her artistic abilities were duly observed and appreciated by my grandfather—much more so than my father—and whichever paintings were not given away were duly framed and hung. My parents' match was a marriage of East and West Bengal, for their cultures were distinct and the dialect spoken in Sylhet was incomprehensible to my mother. But my grandfather, despite his Gandhian lifestyle, especially during the Indian independence struggle, had apparently been an admirer of the urban Bengali culture for he himself had married Nilima, a quintessential Calcuttan and Netaji Subhas Chandra Bose's first cousin. My grandmother died in her early thirties, leaving behind four children all below ten years.

This antecedent is terribly important to assess my frame of mind when I first touched Bangladesh soil. My grandfather chaired the Sylhet referendum to determine its accession to India or Pakistan. Sylhet had been the only Hindu majority Bengal district that went to East Pakistan. However, the fear of the Assamese leaders that Bengalis would remain contiguous to their soil and thus continue to call the shots propelled Nehru to rush there before completion of the referendum to declare Sylhet as having acceded to Pakistan. At least this was the story I had heard in the Shome family from time immemorial, including from relatives in the wider reaches of the large family who were the narrators of family legends.

After that incident, my conclusion had been that Paresh Lal Shome had become a somewhat subdued and reserved man, stoic and upright, caring, though somewhat distant. Note that following the practice common in the 1950s, my great grandmother with her five sons and their sons, of whom my father was the eldest, all lived in the same house constructed by my grandfather in south Calcutta—away from the hustle bustle of central and north Calcutta. Subsequently, my grandfather served the government in various capacities, including chairing the Language Enquiry Commission in the 1950s that concluded with Hindi as the national language—though he knew little of the language—and my father became an official of the Reserve Bank of India. The Commission sat at the Khasa Kothi in Jaipur, where we visited grandfather for long holidays. My memories take me back to the hundreds of flying peacocks, and of Britishers thronging the formal dining room that served only continental food.

Among my visits to Bangladesh, the one in June–July 1990 stands out most. Apart from technical officials, I met the Chairman of the National Board of Revenue (NBR) as well as Mr. Chaudhury, the Governor of Bangladesh Bank who had been NBR Chairman during my earlier missions. My investigations on the VAT structure together with two consultants focussed on whether the proposed system would be based on solid principles of taxation. It would comprise the principal structural reform measure in a possible three-year Enhanced Structural Adjustment Facility (ESAF) with the Fund. ESAF loans were designed with somewhat lenient financing and repayment conditions; hence the economic programmes buttressing an ESAF were subject to strict scrutiny. We looked extensively at the draft VAT legislation, and I had to do it in formal Bengali, my mother tongue that I had learnt in school up to fifth grade in Calcutta after which I had changed to Hindi in Madras. I also helped design publicity and training materials. I examined closely to what extent the authorities' proposals matched our recommendations in an earlier 1987 mission regarding domestic consumption taxation. That mission had been undertaken in the context of a Structural Adjustment Facility (SAF) whose extension comprised the ESAF currently under discussion.

I found the proposed VAT to be a rudimentary mechanism that would convert the prevailing multi-rated excises into a single tax rate, provide credit for taxes paid on inputs, be applicable only up to the manufacturer-importer stage at least initially, and include services selectively in the tax base. While the authorities were rushing to introduce the VAT on 1 January 1991, I persuaded them to delay it until 1 April 1991 considering the many administrative functions that still remained to be completed. I also recommended an initial single rate between 12–15 percent depending on the calculation of the outgo of input tax credit and an estimation of tax evasion in the future, even if reduced. I strongly suggested a rapid increase of the taxpayer base from the initial 5,000 excise registrants. For a modern tax, audit should be accounts-based rather than using physical control or search and seizure. And for this, decentralisation was essential. I pointed out that basic personal computers (PCs) should suffice instead of costly hardware that the authorities were contemplating importing, and that I found some aid agencies were pushing attached with high price tags. I also insisted that the PCs be located at the decentralised level or collectorates rather than only at the head office or the VAT Cell in Dhaka.

Sometimes praise came not just from the authorities but also at headquarters. Christopher Browne of the Asian Department, who reviewed my report from the area department concerned, wrote to FAD on 26 July 1990:

> Thank you for sending Mr. Shome's report to the Asian Department. I am impressed with the quality of the report and the speed of its production.

It was such appreciation and praise that were fulfilling, and certainly had something to do with my quick accession to Deputy and then Chief of Tax Policy.

During the June–July 1990 mission, Mr. Chaudhury suggested that I inspect the Sylhet tax office; after all, Sylhet was considered the Texas of Bangladesh, he said half-jokingly. On learning that Sylhet was the birthplace of my paternal grandfather he said that his mother, too, was from there, following which a grand tour of my ancestral home was organised. The visit to the Sylhet tax office was routine, as was a visit to a tea garden on the hillside. The visit to Maulabi Bazar was, however, a surreal experience for me. The country is filigreed by rivers, and we crossed a huge river on a barge to reach the town. I asked the train of officers accompanying me to take me to the Shome *para* or neighbourhood. By the time we reached, a huge full moon had risen. A local person was asked to show us around. The Sonali Bank building, the main high school and sundry other landmarks were pointed out as "Shome property". I knew that all of these were taken away by the former East Pakistan government, one at a time, without compensation to a great uncle who had stayed on behind. With the local ranting on about Shome properties, it was now the turn of the accompanying officers to become concerned, if not belligerent, until one of them came forward to ask me if I was visiting to reclaim ancestral properties. I reassured them that I had relinquished ancestral properties even in India, so they had no cause for worry. Instead, I was keen to find out if any Shomes still lived in the area.

As we drove on in the bright moonlight, I saw a man in a silk *dhuti* and *chador* walking by our side. I had been told politely by the Sonargaon Hotel staff in Dhaka not to walk around in a dhoti, which was identified as Hindu attire. My curiosity aroused, I had the jeep stopped and asked the man who he was. He said he was the local school headmaster, and was going to a gathering to sing the *kirtan*s of Shri Chaitanya Mahaprabhu. This information came as a shock for I could never have imagined open Hindu worship in a Bangladesh village despite the fact that Chaitanya, a saint deeply revered by the Vaishnavites, hailed from there. We reached the centre of town and I was taken to the house of my great grandfather's brother. He had died and his octogenarian son, my grandfather's cousin, was now the head of the Shome Chaudhury family. I recalled that my own great grandfather had been called Pyarilal Shome Chaudhury, and that my grandfather had dropped the last surname as it depicted a title.

At my grandfather's cousin's home, there gathered many a Shome, for the word had gone out that a Shome was visiting from across the border. A simple, almost rural, Bengali meal was served; I ate heartily following which it was time to talk. The inspectors sensed their unwanted presence and politely left. What followed was a heart-to-heart chat between Shomes from two sides of the border. The substance of the talk, the tears, the laments, the joys from the knowledge of good news will all remain within me, and within the family. It was and remains a Shome matter. When I left, something had changed in me, touched me deeply, and would forever hail me back as if from a fantastic land. And yet, by the time I was back on the boat, the ever practical side of me concluded that had my grandfather not left for Calcutta in his late teens, I would right now be living in interior Bangladesh!

China

Another Asian destination that I visited several times was China, for providing technical assistance in Beijing, teaching corporate tax planning to officials in Qingdao (see Plate 9), participating in a conference at Shanghai Law University, and for inspecting the tax office in the Shenzhen SEZ near Shanghai. I found the Chinese to be highly disciplined at work, yet jolly at dinner. While there were gala dinners, especially away from Beijing, and officers were outgoing, in Beijing there tended to be a veil of formality. I often wondered if the reticence I encountered among the Chinese reflected the treatment they had received when ten powers—nine European and Japan—invaded China around 1900 to open it up for international trade. The Germans occupied the area around Qingdao, and unable to do without beer, established a factory there. The globally famed Qingdao, or Tsingtao, beer was thus created, continuing into the modern era.

In seriousness, there were several lessons from China. The first was that, contrary to expectations, I found that intensive and open discussions on a tax policy or administration matter would take place at all levels of bureaucracy but, once an issue was decided, it was strictly adhered to. In general, this has not been my experience in India, where controlling field implementation of the law or policy has remained a challenge for management.

Second, the local tax offices sparkled in China. In 1997 I was taken to one in Qingdao, and I found one-touch machines with on-screen icons that farmers and small entrepreneurs could touch and pay their tax instantly. Managers monitored the lines at the counters and shifted more staff to attend to longer queues. Third, the students in my class attended throughout with rapt attention—through an interpreter—and asked many a thought-provoking question. This again contrasted with my experience in India where, as Director of NIPFP, a research and teaching institution, I cancelled a class due to absconding attendees from the Indian Administration Service and, when I threatened to cancel the course, I received calls from the appropriate directorate to please resume the course. The following day the attendance was better, but their eyes darted fire.

Fourth, as I looked out of my hotel room in Qingdao, I found a complex being constructed that to me resembled a space station of sorts. When I enquired, I was informed it would be the new municipal centre. I was taken for shopping a little out of the modern city that I had seen being built and, upon entering an older, living city, was informed that this was the old Qingdao. I was amazed to see the clean, neatly organised and wide, expansive living spaces. As we went through miles of newly constructed housing blocks, the Chinese Deputy Minister joked that I was welcome to buy property there. I was taken to the top of a television tower from where I could view the entire complex. The minister boasted that five years back it was just farmland. When I spontaneously asked what had happened to the farmers, there was a perceptible pin-drop silence, following which the minister said that they had of course been resettled. I believed him since that kind of policy did work successfully in China.

In India, resettlement hardly ever occurs, and so many instances could be provided that it may no longer be interesting to cite them to the reader. It was serendipity that, on a trip to Delhi, I found that an NGO had taken the case of a group of eighty families of rag-pickers to the Supreme Court. They lived and worked on a hillock on the main Vasant Kunj Road that the municipality had plans to level in order to construct a connecter road between two thoroughfares going to the airport. They were scheduled to be removed from their meagre abode. When the Court asked where they would be moved and did not receive an acceptable response, it apparently granted the colony of destitutes long-term rights to live and work atop their vantage point. Today I remain ever amused when passing through that bottleneck very near one of Asia's largest shopping centres. Indian courts appear to remain the last solace for seeking justice in Indian society, for the other branches of government—legislatures and the bureaucracy—could politely be described as having fallen into disrepute. Reflecting more recent trends, however, it seems even the Indian judiciary has to be watched in the future.

From the first observations by Marco Polo when the Grand Canal had already been built and trade, economic success and a high quality of life had already been achieved, through Mao Tse Dong's Cultural Revolution, to the current formidable, if not unachievable, example of progress and prosperity that they have set for the rest of the world, the Chinese have remained invincible. An honest and bold analysis of whether and why India's experience through millennia of enslavement by foreign powers has emaciated any preparedness to excel at all costs and, instead, to survive through corruption, caste and class discrimination, and lacking basic nutrition, health and education, remains a matter of fundamental enquiry in socio-economic policy.

Yet, as the world well knows, the Chinese administration has been known to be severe. On two visits I found ordinary Chinese being led away quietly but in handcuffs from Tiananmen Square, and this was years prior to the Democracy Movement. The first time I asked my interpreter why, he calmly responded that they must have entered Beijing without an entry visa and would be put back on the train heading out from Beijing. Imagine an Indian citizen having to travel in and out of Delhi only with an internal visa! How are China's restricted political freedoms in combination with its economic strength to be compared with India's extreme poverty and worsening income distribution? This remains a terrible dilemma.

China may be a huge success, but far from flawless. Over the last four decades, it has amassed huge international reserves through an extreme export policy, by which I mean using artificially low exchange rates, dumping goods in international markets, and producing goods under compulsion of transfer of foreign technology. The West and the East have been essentially unable to contest it in the past. It is only recently that the US has been raising trade barriers through high customs duties that China has had to revisit its head-on international trade behaviour. Certainly there will be clashes, but the correction was needed. Whether it will actually take place is yet to be seen. In the past, policies initiated by the West for correction did not survive. India, too, has been affected, having had to apply World Trade Organization (WTO) sanctioned, high anti-dumping customs duties against China for significant periods of time. But it is China's historical resilience that may nonetheless make it the winner.

FIVE

POLICY WORK AT THE IMF
Early Years

Other than financial programming and technical assistance missions, there was a considerable amount of policy work and background research that I undertook while at the IMF. It is not feasible to cover the gamut of issues I had to address over the decades; hence I have picked just a couple of issues that I was excited about. I have selected from and around a field for which the Fund has not been recognised for being overly concerned about. These were in the area of reinstating countries that had built up arrears in their payment schedule to the Fund, as well as attempting to incorporate poverty as a criterion in the Fund's financial programming model. I would conclude that the Fund made progress in the former but showed less ability in 'formalising a model' with respect to the latter.

INTENSIFIED COLLABORATIVE APPROACH REFLECTING THE GENESIS OF THE FUND'S LENDING POLICIES

In 1989–90, I went to the office of the Managing Director in the new position of Senior Economist that was created for his office. Mr. Camdessus's deep concern had been poor countries that struggled to repay Fund loans. Hence much of my focus was on articulating the Fund's experience with postponement and rescheduling of loans. This was by and large cast in a framework that was developed during this period termed the Intensified Collaborative Approach (ICA), an approach that remains of interest even to the modern reader.

Certain countries that had borrowed heavily externally in the 1970s found their economic and external payments positions worsening in the early 1980s in the form of unsustainable fiscal deficits, high rates of inflation and nonviable balance of payments as a result of both adverse exogenous developments as well as inadequate domestic economic policies. While most Fund members with difficult external circumstances stayed current on their financial obligations to the Fund—to no small extent reflecting that their first obligation was to the Fund in terms of external payments of all member countries prior to all other multilateral payments—some did not manage to do so and eventually accumulated sizeable arrears against the Fund during the later1980s. The Fund did not have the flexibility to disburse to a member that had overdue obligations against it; hence further lending to them by the Fund automatically stopped. In turn this implied that such members could not benefit from Fund stabilisation programmes that were effectively a prerequisite for rescheduling of commercial bank loans or 'official' credit from other sovereign powers. Thus the members with arrears faced a drying up of normal external inflows while other Fund members had to share the additional burden on the Fund caused by the arrears.

At that time arrears to the Fund had been increasing. At the end of 1988–89 (May–April), overdues were almost 7 percent (comprising SDR 2.9 billion out of SDR 42.9 billion) of the Fund's ordinary usable resources accounted for by eleven members, of which eight had become ineligible to draw on the Fund's resources. But they represented 63 percent of the flows of lending and repayment for that year, thus imparting considerable concern for the Fund's management. Thus, in September 1988, a committee of the Board of Governors comprising the members' finance ministers welcomed a proposal by the Fund's Executive Board to pursue a multifaceted approach to solving the arrears problem. And, at the Managing Director's Office (OMD), I had the opportunity to support the different committees that were designing and negotiating these aspects. One of my responsibilities was to track each country on a weekly basis for the Managing Director to see if it was worsening or improving, and also to identify potential arrears cases. Needless to say it required constant cooperation with and from the area departments that enabled me to establish strong professional contacts within the Fund. It was a unique experience since I could form a clear lateral view of activities across the board.

The ICA had four pillars. First, the ICA among member governments and multilateral and bilateral institutions would provide exceptional financial assistance—from sources external to the Fund—to eliminate existing arrears. Each arrear case would involve a support group for all activities chaired by a member closely associated with the arrear country. Second, in order to assist the country to get back into the mainstream of international economic relations, a strong economic programme would be required that would involve major adjustment encompassing budgetary, monetary and exchange rate policies, buttressed by structural reforms aimed at reducing economic distortions and allowing appropriate price signals to work. Third, early warning signals would be identified to obviate emerging difficulties. Fourth, where ICA did not work, other remedial measures would be identified and pursued. Once a track record of good performance was established, the Fund would resume making available its own resources.

The first test case that I was exposed to was Guyana. Canada chaired its support group, with Belgium, France, Germany, Italy, Japan, Sweden, Trinidad and Tobago, UK, US and Venezuela as members. It mobilised financing for a three-year adjustment programme that the Fund would monitor as well as clear the country's multilateral arrears by the end of 1989. That in turn would enable the Fund to resume lending. What I perceived was the immediacy of the need for negotiations with the support group members to garner sufficient resources, first, to coordinate the flow of funds from their finance ministries or treasuries rather than from the aid agencies, and second, to decide the forms—commodity versus cash support for the balance of payments—in which such extraordinary financing could be disbursed. But most importantly, a careful yet achievable set of economic measures was constructed and monitored by the Fund before Fund resources—loans—could resume.

Interestingly, with the success of the Guyana case, a support group for Somalia was formed, which had already begun to take strong macroeconomic measures in anticipation of a Fund-monitored programme. Very soon Zambia, Sierra Leone, Liberia and Vietnam came into the fray, though not all overdue countries expressed equal interest in undertaking reform, their financial policies slackening even further. The Fund had to use dexterity to encourage protracted overdue members that had tended to stay away from the international financial fold to be more willing to rejoin the international financial community.

Indeed, as a number of support groups for other countries were formed, not least was the concern that members often duplicated their roles across several support groups, and care had to be taken to maintain equity among them in terms of sharing the work burden and to treat the availability of funds as a finite pool. I participated in what seemed like a continuum of meetings with potential donors, including Canadian, French, German, Italian and Nordic delegations and authorities together with multilaterals like the Paris Club made up of advanced economy creditors. The latter were given a menu of a few options from which they could select their preference for rescheduling the loans that an overdue Fund member independently owed them. There remain some interesting stories regarding the variations in their views on financial and commodity aid. Some other members like Japan preferred to simply maintain an account with the Fund, delegating the responsibility of administering the account for all support group purposes to the Fund. The overdue obligations situation did not disappear altogether, and its solution demanded continuous attention and efforts toward its resolution. The ICA and its component support operations contributed significantly to that process.

This was so in particular because, moving half a century backwards, I found the evolution of *purchase* (members borrowing from the Fund) and *repurchase* (members returning the loan) to be fascinating. Today's conservative members of the Executive Board were, at the inception of the Fund, themselves borrowers rising from the ashes of the Second World War. The resulting tensions were clearly perceptible. I scoped the information from the history of the Fund by Joseph Gold, for I had to write several memos as background information on ICA, and it is worth laying out the paradox. In 1947–48, 27 drawings totalling $430 million were approved. Belgium, Chile, Czechoslovakia, Denmark, Ethiopia, France, India, the Netherlands,

Norway, Turkey and the UK made drawings. In the early Board deliberations, the UK Executive Director (ED) typically favoured automaticity in borrowing while the US preferred conditionality. In January 1948, the US ED was arguing that the existence of the European Recovery Programme (ERP) financing should enable a tightening of the Fund's evaluation of requests for borrowings, and should indeed limit ERP members' use of US dollars. On 5 April 1948, the Board clarified that ERP members should request dollars from the Fund "only in exceptional and unforeseen cases". Termed the ERP Decision, it limited subsequent drawings from Western European countries.

Some examples would be illustrative. When the Netherlands requested a purchase after the ERP Decision, the US ED expressed serious doubts as to whether the purchase would be "temporary", pointing to the member's lack of effective policies, large budget deficit and high investment rate leading to inflationary pressures. However, other EDs argued that the Netherlands had not been put on notice that the Fund would raise objections; in the event, the Netherlands did make a drawing. Subsequently, when in July, Mexico requested a purchase to meet a serious loss of exchange resources resulting from capital flight, the EDs felt that the argument was sound and that capital controls were ineffective. Nevertheless, rules prohibited a Fund purchase to arrest capital flight. Consequently, Mexico's request was not approved. A Fund mission was sent to Mexico that reported to the Board in September that Mexico should put in effect strong fiscal and credit measures so that its international reserves might be built up and a new par value—fixed exchange rate—established. Thus in 1948–49, total drawings remained small at $89 million, of which $84 million were drawn by India, Brazil and South Africa. Indeed, the US questioned these drawings, giving rise to divisions within the Board between the US and members who still believed that members had automatic rights to draw. In the calendar year 1950, there were no drawings. The first actual repurchase was made by Costa Rica in May 1949 equivalent to $8,74,000 through a mix of gold and US$, reflecting an increase in its monetary reserves.

In October 1948, the Netherlands wanted to undertake another purchase, thereby abrogating an informal understanding that it would not make Fund drawings. The US ED questioned whether, given the

Netherlands' economic outlook, the purchase would be temporary and asked for details regarding how it would be repaid in a relatively short time. Other members again came to the rescue by pointing out that it was the first time that a member had been asked to reveal arrangements for repurchase. The UK ED remonstrated that there was an "increasing number of interpretations reading into the Fund Agreement. ... Because of such limitations the Fund was now of no use to its European members; it carried obligations but no benefits". The US ED objected and pointed out that the Fund had to play the role of policymaker and administrator of rules of fair conduct in foreign exchange policies and purchases. But he did not oppose the Netherlands' setting aside of the informal understanding.

Of course, strong repurchase policies were developed steadily with clearly specified conditions and formulae for calculations. The first input was a review by the US authorities on the Use of Fund Resources (UFR) policy. Accordingly the US ED reported to the Board that Fund drawings had to be temporary and thus be subject to close scrutiny. Any doubt regarding a proposed drawing should be resolved in favour of the Fund. Importantly, proposed drawings should be considered against four criteria: the member should have an appropriate par value; the disequilibrium should be temporary and the member should not be rationing its dollars which would be symptomatic of fundamental disequilibrium; drawing could not be for rehabilitation or economic development; and the member would take steps to maintain convertibility, avoid restrictions on current payments, multiple currency practices or discriminatory practices. This was immediately tested against a new request by Mexico—seeking to establish a new par value—to draw from the Fund. The above criteria were applied to Mexico and it was allowed to draw $22.5 million over the next twelve months. Mexico established a new par value in June, and the Board formally confirmed in January 1950 that Mexico's access to Fund resources was unimpaired.

Over the following decades, the Fund's purchase and repurchase policies rose to the occasion of ever changing and evolving global economic developments with varying conditions, charges, rollovers, remedies and sanctions for non-participating members. A proper review and analysis of the evolution would comprise the subject of a voluminous treatise. To end, Gold's view on sanctions is noteworthy in that he raises a basic question as to whether sanctions at all encourage the observance of a member's obligations towards the Fund. He cites Louis Henkin's *How Nations Behave* (1968):

> Much is made...of the...lack of effective sanctions against the violator... In fact, we know...that nations do generally observe laws and obligations. The preoccupation with sanctions seems largely misplaced. The threat of such sanctions is not the principal inducement to observe international obligations.[1]

The contribution of remedies will be less when the system of obligations appears defective. Failure to fulfil obligations under these circumstances is evidence of a need for reform of the system rather than of a need for retribution.

During that phase, another example of extreme adverse economic experience that drew the Fund's attention comprised Bolivia and Peru. I looked into Bolivia's successful experience with controlling hyperinflation, and lessons for Peru. Bolivia had taken once-off strong orthodox measures coupled with step-wise measures in exchange rate, fiscal, monetary and price policy. The rate of hyperinflation in the last quarter of 1988 (4,000 percent annualised) was down from the third quarter (13,000 percent). I concluded that, combined with the manner of implementation, there were alternative strategies to successfully address adverse ramifications, such as hyperinflation, of the heterodox policies of ephemerally populist governments.

POVERTY ALLEVIATION IN COLLABORATION WITH THE WORLD BANK

Another area that I had the opportunity to work in while at OMD was poverty alleviation. In the mid-1980s, poverty began to be placed at the forefront of the Fund's concerns with a growing recognition that raising growth rates—with its concomitant beneficial impact on the poor—was a longer-run objective than previously understood. Over the 1980s, poverty indices including life expectancy, daily per-capita caloric intake, primary education enrolment and per capita incomes in several developing countries worsened as their ability to cope with world recession and mounting debt service weakened. Worse, prospects for the 1990s seemed no better. The World Bank, in association with the African Development Bank and the United

Nations, was addressing structural issues associated with this global problem through a Social Dimensions of Adjustment (SDA) targeted at 26 African nations as of January 1989. It was making long-term credit available to help develop food security and enable imports for the poorest of the poor. In light of this, the Fund could allocate resources for vulnerable groups within the macroeconomic framework of Fund-supported programmes. Some ways needed to be found so that the Fund could actually participate in measures to ameliorate the temporarily adverse effects of an adjustment programme.

The stated objectives of the Fund's SAF and ESAF—loan programmes designed to enable structural policies over periods longer than the Fund's usual three-year cycle—could incorporate specific poverty-related measures. But for this, additional financing was needed. Thus, recognising that there exists a social cost of adjustment, in a 1988–91 ESAF for Ghana, the Fund was instrumental in allowing for budgetary allocations comprising current and capital expenditure for the redeployment, retraining and relocation of displaced public employees. For this, a donor's conference was organised to garner additional resources of $85 million.

Similarly, a SAF in Mozambique used identifiable instruments to lessen the adverse social consequences of adjustment with a detailed component list of measures to be implemented by the government. These were enabled by the Fund's recognition that a safety net might be required as a temporary means to redress distributional challenges such as by allowing food subsidies to continue rather than removing them. Soon more and more SAF and ESAF programmes were incorporating a budgetary line item on the allocation for vulnerable groups. Reflecting the MD's intentions and pronouncements in that direction, I sat in many country meetings pertaining to poverty alleviation in Fund programmes with a responsibility to report back on the emerging directions being charted.

Eventually, as always, this experience helped me to advance theoretical work jointly with my colleague Sheetal Chand on how to incorporate poverty alleviation as an explicit element in the Fund's financial programming framework. Essentially that would imply that poverty would become a binding constraint in the model so that governments would have to necessarily allocate funds for poverty alleviation. In turn, that would require further revenue effort than they were already making under Fund-assisted financial programmes. Obviously, poorer countries in particular would find this difficult to swallow, and the paper did not find official sanction. Instead, our research became a Fund Working Paper and was included later in a festschrift for Vito Tanzi. I have always felt that in Mr. Camdessus's absence, such an approach had little chance of being officially recognised by the Fund. And, sadly, it was not incorporated formally into the Fund's financial programming model.

CONFERENCES LINKED TO POLICY WORK

Vito never discouraged me from continuing my research efforts, sometimes into the late hours, as long as it came out of my own time. A clear benefit I reaped from such extensions of my official policy work, as well as the self-generated research that I undertook, was the opportunity to accept invitations to conferences across the world. Among them I may mention—though most will have to remain untouched—were those at the twenty-fifth annual conference of the Centre for Inter-American Tax Administrations (CIAT) in Montego Bay, Jamaica, where I presented taxation trends and comparable patterns observed across Latin America that became quite popular for future investigations. I presented newly emerging trends in Buenos Aires in the University of San Andres in 1999. I presented a treatise on Mexican taxation at both the Autonomous Technical University (ITAM) and the Autonomous National University (UNAM) in Mexico City in 1998. After those conferences, the newspaper *El Financiero* reported that I had suggested that, while simplifying its overall tax structure, the rate of VAT be increased to 20 percent. I had found that there was always work that remained to be accomplished in completing tax reform in Mexico from the time of that early 1985 mission when I had used Mexico's detailed input-output tables—being compiled in a United Nations project—to estimate VAT evasion.

That was not the end of this story. A comment came from very near home as reported by *Reuters* on 25 June 1998. Referring to the former Republican vice-presidential nominee who now headed Empower America, a conservative foundation, the report said, "Jack Kemp had some tough words for the IMF ... calling [it] a 'menace to mankind'". It added that Kemp criticised a suggestion by IMF official

Parthasarathi Shome for suggesting that Mexico raise its VAT rate to 20 percent from 15 percent. The report further said that Kemp said the Congress should not approve President Clinton's request for an $18 billion funding package for the multilateral institution until it recommended tax cutting measures.

Vito sent me a one line note that I shall keep to myself. Suffice it to say that he was more than supportive as always. No one in the Fund raised an eyebrow, an expression of resilience and quiet confidence in its staff that I had invariably experienced.

After this, let me recall a congenial experience for I cannot forget a conference on fiscal federalism in La Paz, Bolivia, in January 1999, where I gave a talk on the international experiences in fiscal federal arrangements jointly organised by the Ministry of Finance and the Senate (usually a rare occurrence). The Minister of Finance arrived well before most of the guests and welcomed them with a smile as they arrived, chatting pleasantly with them, and with me in particular. Just before the conference, I had completed a mission analysing the Bolivian tax system whose recommendations I had discussed in detail with him and his colleagues. On return to headquarters I found a letter sitting on my desk from the Minister to Vito in which he had extolled "Dr. Partho Shome's brilliant work in the analysis and recommendations for the Bolivian taxation system". I wondered if his early arrival at the conference had anything to do with his assessment of the technical assistance report I had presented to him.

Thus quite often I found myself in Brasilia, Mexico City, Buenos Aires or Bogota at their central banks, ministries of finance and at academic conferences to speak on a panoply of topics on fiscal policy. In 1994 I also gave a well-liked lecture on how tax policy needs to be reinvented in an increasingly open international environment at the Institute of Fiscal Studies, Santander, Spain, where, apart from three days of hard conferencing, I got an immersion course in Spanish merry-making comprising endless dinners with the invariable accompaniment of sangria.

I found myself at Hitotsubashi University, Tokyo, in 1997 to talk on India's economic reforms and macroeconomic dimensions. In Seoul I presented a joint paper with Vito on the suboptimal role of tax incentives explaining why, other than investment oriented incentives, they are by and large unproductive and a source of revenue depletion.

The paper was included in an edited volume from University of Chicago Press by Takashito Ito and Anne Krueger in 1992. These were most enjoyable experiences, though the prior preparation, presentation and completion of research papers always posed a challenge through all the office work that took obvious priority. And there were numerous opportunities to present my views in India on fiscal and tax policy matters. Suffice it to say that my interest and familiarity with the Indian economic scenario had grown and was a supportive element when I landed at NIPFP in June 1995.

ENDNOTES

1. Louis Henkin, *How Nations Behave: Law and Foreign Policy* (Published for the Council on Foreign Relations [by] F. A. Praeger, 1968).

SIX

EARLY INVOLVEMENT WITH INDIA

Back and Forth with the Fund

My early involvement with India had three phases: first, at the Fund in 1988 as India desk economist examining various aspects of the Indian economy; second, as Director of the National Institute of Public Finance and Policy (NIPFP) during 1995–97 which gave me the opportunity to carry out intensive research and policy work on India; and, third, as Chairman of the Working Group on Tax Policy and Administration of the Ninth Five-Year Plan during my stay at NIPFP, which required me to travel the length and breadth of India in understanding and making recommendations for tax reform.

EXAMINING INDIA AT IMF'S ASIAN DEPARTMENT

Reform of the Tax Structure

During the first phase at the Fund I was assigned to the India desk in the Asian Department in 1988 as part of a so-called 'mobility programme' that encouraged Fund economists to spend some years away from their presumed home departments. One of the first documents on my desk was a position paper, 'Long Term Fiscal Policy' (LFP), issued by India's Ministry of Finance in December 1985, which laid out what should comprise its dimensions. The goal of the LFP was to identify means of financing burgeoning current expenditures. The emerging strategy was expected to lead to greater revenue mobilisation through increased tax revenue as well as larger surpluses of public sector undertakings. The means deployed would comprise expansion of the revenue base through healthy economic growth, moderate tax rates and strict enforcement. It suggested introduction of input tax credit in domestic excises on a selective basis to decrease 'cascading' of the indirect tax structure by minimising embedded taxation on a tax already paid. This so-called modified VAT (MODVAT) was meant to be revenue neutral, but collection suffered. Thus, though raising the share of direct taxes in total tax revenue was an objective, the share of indirect taxes rose as revenue was made up through discretionary trade tax rises.

Thus, I observed that there had been a spurt in the tax revenue to GDP ratio in 1985–86, after which it maintained—rather than significantly improving—that trend. It could be explained by an examination of the nature of the measures actually introduced. While the LFP incorporated some of the canons of fundamental tax reform, it also made significant departures. For example, it justified the continuing role of quantitative controls on the imports of 'universal' intermediate goods—those used in a large number of industries—if indigenous industry was felt not to be able to compete.

The LFP led to a reduction in individual income tax rates and increased standard deductions to unleash supply-side effects, but expressed no intention to expand the tax base directly. Instead, it mentioned the use of differentiated incentives to encourage financial savings as well as differentiated incentives for preferential investment, despite the possibility of both leading to serious economic distortions in the medium term. It stayed away from mentioning presumptive taxation even where it could have reduced inequities and the efficiency costs of the income tax structure. Thus the LFP departed significantly from the correct framework for an efficient and equitable structure of taxation. Finally, improvement in the internal resource generation of public sector units (PSUs) seemed to receive little remedial action.

In mid-1988 when I studied the LFP, it became clear to me that of the five avenues through which the goals of the LFP were to be attained, the tax revenue base did not expand and significant revenue expansion did not occur; there had been some though not major progress in reducing the distortionary effects of the tax structure; equity in the tax structure had not improved substantially if the direct to indirect tax ratio were to be taken as a guide; tax administration had not moved from a discretionary to a rule-based approach; and internal resource generation by PSUs had improved only slowly. I realised how challenging it must be to carry out fundamental tax reform in India, a challenge I would have to grapple with for three subsequent decades in my professional life.

India's Poverty Challenge

I have remained deeply concerned about India's poverty as I write this memoire, and increasingly surprise myself by recommending radical tax measures to contain it. But it is not a fundamental transformation for, as far back as 1988, I studied the issue and brought it to the attention of my superiors at the Asian Department based on data and information from India's National Sample Survey (NSS), the World Bank's 'Social Indicators' series and country poverty profiles, International Labour Organisation publications, and a wide range of research papers and government studies including those from the Planning Commission and the Overseas Development Institute, among others.

At the time, India's population was about 750 million with a per-capita GDP of $260. It was one of the poorest countries in the world. One-third of its population lived below the 'officially' established poverty line—the cost of daily purchase of 2,400 calories in rural and 2,100 calories in urban areas. This has varied with more stringent international definitions that place India's poverty at much higher levels. It is interesting that, even three decades later, the extent of India's poverty and its pattern and distribution remain about the same, and about which I have been writing elsewhere incessantly. For example, there was a persistent geographical concentration of poverty in four eastern states—Bihar, Orissa, Uttar Pradesh, West Bengal—and four arid zone states—Karnataka, Madhya Pradesh, Maharashtra, Rajasthan—where three-quarters of the poor lived. The proportion of rural poor was higher than the proportion of urban poor.

The poor typically belonged to occupational groups such as landless agricultural labourers, marginal farmers, urban construction workers, domestic servants, hawkers and peddlers. Mostly they were without assets—illiterate (no human capital), unemployed or underemployed (no or little wage earning capacity), and without any tangible wealth (no financial or non-financial capital). Any progress in poverty reduction was slower in the agriculturally lagging eastern and central states so that their share of the total poor population increased with time. It also led to rural-urban migration, which had accelerated in the 1980s.

The central government's poverty alleviation efforts could be divided into direct intervention policies and its overall policy stance. Among the former were the Integrated Rural Development Programme (IRDP), the National Rural Employment Programme (NREP), and the Rural Labour Employment Guarantee Programme (RLEGP), accounting for about 2 percent of overall government expenditure. The IRDP provided income-generating non-land assets to the poor. The other two provided employment through the building of physical infrastructure. Among the latter—governmental policy—were the government's general incentive and subsidy policies that could have different impact on absolute vis-à-vis relative poverty. For example, on the one hand, agricultural growth through fertiliser subsidies was said to have had a negative impact on poverty. On the other, agriculture's share in GDP had fallen at a faster rate than rural-to-total population. This was pointing to an increase in rural poverty relative to urban poverty. In any event, the success of these programmes was a subject of much debate. The fact remains that over three decades and despite more and complex government programmes, India remains one of the poorest countries in the world.

In the late 1980s, the Fund was seriously considering what its stance should be in using policy instruments to address poverty. The methodology would comprise several steps. A detailed analysis of the socio-economic characteristics of the poor would be undertaken. Components of the country authorities' macroeconomic programme and associated policy measures would be identified. The short-term impact as well as the medium-term ramifications of the measures would be studied; thus, for example, not only the immediate impact on prices, employment and income, but also the medium-term effects on the earning capacity of the poor through structural changes in relative prices would be studied.

If the before-measures status of the poor could be compared with the after-measures status, conclusions could be made on changes in poverty. Policy measures that affected poverty would include money and credit, pricing including exchange rates, price and import controls, revenue and expenditure measures and, last but not the least, labour market policies. In 1987, India weathered one of its worst droughts. The previous two years had also suffered poor harvests. In this context, the Fund took deep interest in discussing their effects on the poor employing, where possible, the methodology and associated policy measures.

I found poverty to be the catch phrase not only for Indian politicians but also for most government documents espousing its eradication as a primary objective as well as for domestic researchers who scribed volumes on the issue. There was little agreement over the outcomes of the government's poverty alleviation efforts. Needless to say, this was a sensitive area for discussion with the authorities. To give them their due, such academic interest or activity might have been expected of any Fund member. The difference today is that poverty seems to have degenerated into a total lack of concern to the extent that an increasing number of politicians openly express their lack of responsibility in tackling the matter while related bureaucratic branches issue meaningless statistics and, on that basis, unreliable reports.

Yet, even in 2015, India's poverty situation was drastic. To put it in perspective, India has signed on to the UN's Human Development goals for 2030. Just twelve years remain for not just reducing inequality, but also leaving no one behind, eradicating extreme poverty, ending hunger, and making all of them sustainable. Indeed, a listing of comparisons for 2015 is an eye-opener. First, India's overall rank is low as are its component values. India's Human Development Index (HDI) is ranked at 131 out of 188 countries.

Second, during 2010–15, India's improvement in HDI rank (4) still lagged behind Brazil (7) and China (11). Brazil's poor income distribution was well known. And now India has surpassed even Brazil. This is revealed through a Coefficient of Human Inequality (CHI)—derived using the familiar Atkinson's Inequality Index—which is 5.4 for Norway, 7.8 for UK, 12.9 for US, 25 for Brazil, and 26.5 for India (China's is not available). Third, once CHI is incorporated into HDI to obtain an Inequality-Adjusted HDI (IHDI), India's percentage loss in HDI (27.2) is the highest, even higher than Brazil's loss (25.6). Fourth, while India's HDI value is one-third of Norway's, India's more meaningful IHDI value reduces to half of Norway's. However much one may critique Pickety's recent conclusions on India's worsening income distribution, the comparisons emerging from UN statistics are telling enough of India's unsuccessful performance in poverty alleviation or HDI improvement.

The United Nations Human Development Report (UNHDR) also reveals the extent and intensity of poverty. It uses a 'multidimensional' concept incorporating education, health and income components. Multidimensional poverty headcount is defined as 33 percent of the population in deprivation of the components, and severe multidimensional poverty as 50 percent or more. While Brazil, China and South Africa results are based on 2012–14 information, India's is almost a decade older, and hence not fully comparable. But a decade could not have bridged the kind of gap the UN reports, for the percent of population in multidimensional poverty in Brazil, China, South Africa and India are 2.4, 5.2, 10.3 and 55.3 percent respectively; the percentages for severe multidimensional poverty are 0.3, 1.0, 1.3 and 27.8 respectively. India may spat internally over its domestically generated, much lower poverty statistics, but these UN numbers lay bare what India's reality is if, that is, humility allows India to view it as such rather than nonchalantly talking out of it.[1]

Radical innovation—including streamlined population policy, rapid expansion in taxpayer registration rather than spending public resources on pursuing existing registrants, steeply progressive income taxation for newly created top brackets, reintroduction of wealth tax on real and financial wealth for above Rs 600 million (£6 million), massive redistribution of income, wealth and land if required through Constitutional amendments, and stipulated private sector commitment to corporate social responsibility (CSR) that needs to be enhanced multiple times—should be wrought by the new policy makers, for there are just twelve years left to achieve India's international commitment to sustainable development and eradication of poverty. Under these circumstances, leaked information—as has emerged through Panama and Paradise Papers or others—may well be used by the authorities to garner much needed public resources.

Otherwise, if India remains toothless in its ability to surmount its entrenched poverty problem, no number of claims, however much shrieked from rooftops, about its economic achievements, will be taken seriously by the international community; rather they are increasingly embarrassed about India's insistence to be counted in, for example, as a permanent member in the United Nations' Security Council. The argument against economic success is simple: it is not impossible, in fact it is quite achievable, for a country of India's geographical proportions to effectively shift disproportionate resources for selected economic activities and thus enter comparably high global numbers in certain sectors like mining, manufacturing and services production (beware—not productivity, however). And this has to be necessarily achieved only through diversion of resources from sectors that could, and should, have generated more acceptable benchmarks of equity and equality.

There were several other lines of investigation that I undertook at the India desk including its public debt burden and whether it was entering into a debt trap, reflecting excessive credit not only for production but also for consumption, its agricultural output patterns based primarily on rain-fed irrigation leading to regular seasonal drought conditions, its misdirected fertiliser subsidy policy, and its heavy subsidy burden from artificially fixed prices of petroleum products benefitting mainly the urban population and rich farmers.

On the political front, despite vocal opposition in Parliament, the Constitution was amended in March 1988 by majority vote to (1) widen the circumstances under which a state of emergency may be declared; (2) lengthen the period of direct central rule (President's Rule) of a state from one to three years; and (3) tighten restrictions on freedoms of speech, assembly and movement during an emergency. These changes were introduced to counter Sikh terrorism in the Punjab more effectively. Important by-elections were held in May, with a populist Finance Minister V. P. Singh posed as an opponent of the popular Prime Minister Rajiv Gandhi. In the event, the latter was assassinated while campaigning by Tamil guerrillas who had slipped into the state of Tamil Nadu from Sri Lanka. I wrote a series entitled, 'India: Current Issues' that went every month to the Director of the Asian Department, and helped me keep abreast of a broad array of economic, political and social developments on a daily basis in India. And I kept up my deep interest in Indian developments even in the years that followed when I left the Asian Department and the Office of the Managing Director and returned to the Fiscal Affairs Department (FAD).

Thus I felt quite prepared when I left for India in June 1995 to take up the position of Director, NIPFP in New Delhi. I had been approached by Amaresh Bagchi, the outgoing Director, who had come on a visit to Washington DC. I was Chief of Tax Policy at the time, having completed three years in the post, a position that my predecessors had typically occupied for longer tenures. However, India herself, my father's expectation about my serving India, and my own inner compulsions together pushed me to accept the offer. To divert myself from thinking about the immensity of the impending upheaval in my professional and personal life, I amused myself by observing how uncomfortable Dr. Bagchi was with the luxurious continental lunch at the Fund's formal dining room where I had invited him. He just fiddled with his food leading me to wonder if the gentleman would not have been more comfortable at the Fund cafeteria that offered a wider menu. As we conversed, I realised he was quite familiar with my published work and must have heard reports of my field experience through the Fund grapevine. As time passed after I went to NIPFP, I was myself amazed at this man's scholarship on India's public finances. It was a sad day some years later when he passed away well before his time.

MY WORK AND RESPONSIBILITIES AT NIPFP

I worked at the Fund until the very end of May. My belongings—furniture, art and artefacts from all over the world—filled my three-storey townhouse in Adams Morgan, an area of urban renewal, where I had moved a few years earlier from Georgetown, the slickest Washington neighbourhood. Family and friends supervised the packing process; otherwise I would probably have had to abandon the venture altogether. I had convinced myself that I should not be backward looking, hence had resolved to move lock, stock and barrel. I sold my townhouse at a 20 percent actual loss in a recessionary real estate market, subject as I was to my father's caution never to be an absentee landlord, a practice I have maintained despite many a national and international move across globally dispersed locations. I sold—almost gave away rather than bargain—my dream car, a Chevy Monte Carlo, even smarter than the Chevy Impala that the parents of a classmate of mine owned when we were in school and in which I had many an occasion to ride. I was ready for India.

Research and Administration

The NIPFP had a memorandum of understanding with the Revenue Department of the Ministry of Finance. In lieu of carrying out research on its behalf, NIPFP received a certain proportion of its finances from the Ministry. Much of its resources also came from research projects funded by other ministries, state governments and from teaching courses to returning government officers. It was a thriving crucible of research and intellectual discourse on government tax-expenditure policies. I undertook many a research project on any number of taxation matters pertaining to India, and learnt the Indian case along the way. One person who accompanied me on several field trips was Sukumar Mukhopadhyay, who had recently retired as a member of the Central Board of Excise and Customs (CBEC) and possessed a range of information on India's customs and excise tariffs and operations in the indirect tax field. We travelled together to inspect many customs and excise offices and factories across India, on the basis of which we wrote a report on indirect tax administration in India.

My earlier experiences in Latin America and Asia served very well as a backdrop to our comprehensive report, and I also edited a book on the VAT reflecting part of the work. Paul Bernd Spahn, a colleague and friend at the Fund, also contributed a paper in it. Years later, this work reflected in my *Tax Compendium* in 2014, for its relevance had not waned. Another project was on tax deduction at source (TDS) in the income tax, and Kanwarjit Singh, a retired income tax official who had ideas for reform in this area, worked with me, and I included this work, with Pawan Agarwal, another colleague, in a commemorative NIPFP volume mentioned below. The government subsequently expanded the use of TDS in a number of areas. There were several other research projects that I led or supervised or undertook on my own, rendering my stay fruitful and full of anticipation and surprises.

An area of research of which I could still say I was quite satisfied was a lecture I prepared on Indian taxation and expenditure policy experience for the Purushottamdas Thakurdas Memorial annual lecture organised by RBI on behalf of the Bankers' Association of India. Dr. Rangarajan, the Governor of RBI, called to invite me, and I took the invitation seriously. To this day I feel that the accompanying tabular analysis remains valid for the years covered in the study.

Commenting on the study after its delivery, one observer said that the "details are to be found in Shome's footnotes; so do not miss them". I still recall that statement fondly.

I did some interesting work with Dr. Carlos J. Moreno Leguizamon, an expert in qualitative research methods, and Dr. Kavita Rao, a quantitative economist. I used the joint work for my speech at the thirty-second annual conference of the Indian Econometric Society in March 1996, which was subsequently published in *Economic & Political Weekly* in July that year. The possibility of combining the two approaches in social science enquiry had always intrigued me, and the joint work of the two experts provided me an excellent opportunity to discuss with them the possibility of a via-media. In the question-answer session after my speech, I encountered several critical comments from econometricians who asserted that they already carried out qualitative studies. In reality, only later, with the advent of behavioural economics could it be claimed that advances were being made. Further, my contention was not *what matters* economists tended to address, but *in what manner* they addressed them. After the economic collapse of the global economy in 2008, there was alarm in advanced economies as to the exclusive quantitative approach of economics that had failed to predict the collapse—even the British monarch asking about it—and promises were made that economics education would be corrected. But, as of now, it appears that by and large we are back to square one.

One surprise for me as I became familiar with the condition of NIPFP staff was the state of its administration. Part of the staff seemed to spend much of their time on union representations and there were any number of litigations brought on by them against the institution. I found pervasive dissatisfaction among administrative staff of whom there were just too many. I could not do anything about the excessive number but I undertook to promote the good and efficient staff, thus setting them apart from the rest. Remarkably I was informed that, in two years, I had been instrumental in promoting more staff than in the past twenty years under previous NIPFP administrations. The outcome was that there was more competition to work well and for the smooth functioning of the entire NIPFP community. I had been advised by many that I should not 'touch' administrative staff dissatisfaction for that could only attract more woe. On the contrary,

I found that facing issues directly and genuinely attempting to resolve them remarkably improved the overall environment.

The members of the administration proved their worth at NIPFP's twentieth anniversary celebrations that stretched over two days in December 1996. Mr. Chidambaram was the chief guest while Dr. Vito Tanzi was the keynote speaker. Both delivered scintillating speeches, followed by a conference of speakers on scholarly subjects. I edited the conference papers and produced a volume entitled *Fiscal Policy, Public Policy and Governance* from Centax Publishers during the last few days prior to my return to the IMF in mid-1997. The reason I mention this somewhat lost volume is the collection of brilliant papers included in it. I shall only mention Vito Tanzi on corruption and governmental activities; P. Chidambaram on economic policy goals, ideology and governance; Bhaskar Dutta on coalition governments and policy distortions; Sumon Bhaumik and B. V. Kumar on economic crime, corruption and destabilisation; A. K. Ghosh on budgetary control for expenditure management; and Amaresh Bagchi on the federal dimension of fiscal management. For the celebrations, I also organised 'variety entertainment' comprising classical dance and giant Scandinavian puppets, the likes of which the community there had not witnessed earlier. Of course it all ended with a grand meal, Indian style, all this delivered in impeccable style with the unwavering support of the administration.

Another challenge was to hire and productively employ young professionals in the taxation area, and then to shape and sharpen them so they could shine as internationally competitive economists. I recall Hiranya Mukhopadhyay and Soumen Chakravarty with some satisfaction as, over the years, after serving terms at the NIPFP, they assumed important positions at the Asian Development Bank and Jawaharlal Nehru University respectively. In some cases the hiring was a bit of a hit and miss, mainly reflecting a less than best fit into a particular specialisation though, in all cases, as I recall, I did not give up on finding a suitable job for them if asked for assistance in that endeavour. Through my entire professional career I have felt energised in working with young professionals as, by and large, I have found them to bring with them new knowledge and, of course, enthusiasm. This was also the case when I was Chief of Tax Policy at the IMF when I had some freedom to hire economists into my division.

Various Committees

And there was government committee work while at NIPFP, eventually comprising a heavy portion of my overall responsibilities. Most committees were formed in the Ministry of Finance and others at the Planning Commission, Ministry of Environment and Forests, and so on. Thus, my chairmanship of the first centre-state committee to suggest reform of the Central State Tax (CST) that thwarted India from becoming a common market by distorting trade among states was an extremely challenging one. The CST was considerably revenue productive for the states, and abolishing it was not a straightforward solution despite its obviously distortionary ramifications. CST was a 4 percent tax on all trade among states that was collected and retained by an exporting state without the importing state government giving input tax credit to the importer in their own state. This led to wide-ranging cascading caused by the CST across states.

The members of the centre-state committee were mainly finance secretaries of important states and a selection of academics. I pushed for a lowering of the CST from 4 percent to 2 percent and eventually for its removal, and for the revenue sources to be made up from other non-distortionary sources. It was sheer camaraderie that resulted in all finance secretaries signing the document since, initially, they had all been concerned about immediate revenue loss. Their signatures on the final page of that report paved the way for a steady rate reduction and eventual abolition of the CST. From that early participation with experienced government officials who were knowledgeable in state level finances, I learnt how to deal with the diverse personalities hailing from different corners of India—an experience I found to be more beguiling than dealing with the twenty-odd nationalities that were under my care in Washington.

I must point out that initially, Dr. Amaresh Bagchi, a committee member, desisted from signing, indicating that lowering the CST was a sign of the central government's attempts at scaling back the revenue intake of states. He was a strong federalist. I explained to him in two meetings that the reduction in economic distortions in business decision-making by lowering and then removing the CST would impact the GDP positively and, in turn, impulse tax revenue. I also told him that, of course, he had the option of writing a dissent note. Finally Amareshda came around and signed on the report.

With his subsequent early death, India lost a deep and erudite public finance scholar. Few professionals have the advantage of government experience combined with that of academia and research. Amaresh Bagchi, who had also been an income tax official, possessed that advantage.

A major event was a meeting of state level finance ministers convened by Union Finance Minister Manmohan Singh in December 1995 that I had the privilege to participate in as Director of NIPFP, reflecting the background work, nay history, of India's fiscal federal relations. I also had the opportunity to brief him through Dr. Raja Chelliah, Chairman of NIPFP, about the manner in which CONFAZ, the committee of Brazil's state level finance ministers, operated. That meeting was a precursor to a similar meeting that came much later in November 1999 in which it was decided to simplify the prevailing sales tax system and introduce a VAT. Subsequently, following the recommendation of the chief ministers, in July 2000 an Empowered Committee of state finance ministers was set up to chalk out appropriate methods to switch over to a VAT.

Another committee that I chaired was one on market-based instruments for environment protection, the report of which was resurrected by the Environment Ministry after a decade by an interested and concerned minister. Another committee was on examining instruments—including tax instruments—for the enhancement of household savings in view of international practice, even though Indian households already comprised the main source of private sector savings. There were several competent members including Amaresh Bagchi and Amit Mitra, then Secretary General of the Federation of Indian Chambers of Commerce and Industry (FICCI), currently Finance Minister of West Bengal, among others. We had to be innovative in our recommendations, in particular keeping in mind my general dislike for tax incentives and reflecting the already high household savings rate in India. In retrospect, there were many such committees and studies that I chaired that, together, sharpened my understanding of Indian public finance issues and my ability to successfully handle diverse personalities.

I was at NIPFP for two years. Dr. Manmohan Singh was Finance Minister during the first year, and Mr. Chidambaram in the second. I recall having several chats, if not conversations, with Dr. Singh who had also been an officer at the Fund for a short while in his early years. He also discussed India's centre-state relations in depth, revealing his deep desire for composite reform of indirect taxation comprising both levels. I informed him of comparable systems of Argentina, Australia, Brazil and Canada which also had fiscal federal arrangements. He was quite fascinated and, while implicating the lack of time for his inability to spend adequate time on intellectual matters, always mentioned that I should return to him soon. This was a practice he maintained even while he was Prime Minister, sometimes complaining that I did not come to meet him at least every month. I tried to, provided his office allotted me the time; and indeed, as I see it in retrospect, his office indulged me quite a bit that way. But I always mentioned my visits to Dr. Singh to Mr. Chidambaram when, years later in 2004, the latter became my direct superior.

However, we are now at my years at NIPFP. During my second year there, Mr. Chidambaram was Finance Minister. I recall that when I went to make a protocol visit, he said to me after a couple of minutes that two minutes had been allocated for the meeting since it was only for purposes of protocol. Having met some thirty finance ministers across the world, I was taken aback, but it was a good lesson to realise that one should not take anything for granted in India's official circles. Yet, by the time I left NIPFP, he was first in wanting me to stay back, and I felt his genuine desire that I do so. He pursued the matter even at the Fund-Bank Annual Meetings held in Hong Kong in September 1997 when he sent word to meet me there. I had gone there with Vito Tanzi, who had selected me as a member of a small delegation from the Fiscal Affairs Department. But I thought returning to the Fund was the best decision I could make at that point. It was serendipity then that, almost a decade later, I worked with Mr. Chidambaram during his second term as Finance Minister. It was an excellent experience. More on that in the next chapter.

CHAIRMANSHIP OF THE NINTH PLAN WORKING GROUP ON TAX POLICY

In December 1995, I was asked by Dr. Arjun Sengupta, Member Secretary of the Planning Commission, to chair the tax policy working group that was being set up. I realised that it would enable me to travel widely to attempt to understand the tax preferences from the point of view of the states, and why they always expressed that their interests were ignored by the centre. I also knew that, while fully recognising the states' perspective, finally I would need to make recommendations for the fiscal federal nation state of India of which the central government was the anchor. I welcomed the thought of attempting to take on this mammoth task and accepted the invitation. It turned out to be an experience indeed.

The working group was asked to suggest a suitable tax policy regime to generate new resources for Plan expenditure needs. Its scope was the impact of tax reforms on revenue from major taxes, an analysis of central excises including its Modified VAT (MODVAT) and the possibility of a state-level VAT, reform of tariff policy for customs duties, Octroi and entry tax at the municipal level, CST on inter-state trade, prohibition and its impact on resources of the states, and the gamut of direct taxes—including income tax—with special reference to an assets-based minimum income tax. The report was submitted in June 1996 to Dr. Bimal Jalan who, by then, was Member Secretary. After its submission, it was requested that a chapter on tax administration be added. This was done subsequently.[2] I felt somewhat dissatisfied with it until, almost two decades later, I had the opportunity to chair the first nationally named Tax Administration Reform Commission, whose report was submitted in 2015. More on that experience in a later chapter.

India's tax to GDP ratio in 1995–96 was 16.5 percent of which the central government yielded 10.2 percent, states 5.7 percent and local governments 0.6 percent. Additional resources of 1.8 to 2 percent of GDP would have to be generated for the Plan. Accordingly, after much investigation and discussion, we drew up a menu of recommendations comprising immediate and medium-term measures for the tenure of the Plan. Shorn of the detailed analysis and calculations, among immediate measures at the central level were included a minimum alternate tax (MAT) on companies, scaling back concessions and incentives from the corporate income tax, extending the MODVAT base to include services, reinstatement of traditional excises—no input tax credit—on selected demerit goods (cigarettes, motor cars, petroleum products and alcoholic drinks) without removing them from the MODVAT base, eliminating inappropriate exemptions from both the MODVAT and customs duties. And, in the medium term, introduce presumptive income norms for the taxation of non-corporate businesses.

At the level of states, immediate measures recommended comprised the urgent need for state-level finance ministers to implement their agreement to minimise tax competition through sales tax incentives including exemptions, tax deferment and tax loans, rationalisation and reduction of the incidence of sales tax exemptions for sales by, or to, particular types of institutions, inclusion of services in the sales tax base including transport, private nursing homes, computer maintenance and consultancies, automobile repair services, leasing, works contract and advertising, rationalisation of stamp duty and registration fees, motor vehicles tax, passenger and goods tax, and increasing other tax rates and bases commensurately to counter revenue loss from prohibition policies. We also recommended that, in the medium term, the sales tax should be replaced with a harmonised state-level VAT with a floor rate and a broad base.

At the local government level, we indicated that the resolution of the rental value interpretation of the property tax base must be modified and modernised. Also, rationalisation of entry tax structures in various states and the reform of smaller local taxes were much needed and suggestions for change were made.

Finally, an innovation in taxation was suggested through the introduction of a presumptive environment tax on energy-consuming industries at the rate of 1 percent of fuel consumed. In many respects, therefore, I took the tax policy framework forward reflecting my international experience and throughout received an enthusiastic response from academic professionals. Government action also followed albeit at a slower pace, for example, reformulation of the MAT, introducing selected aspects of presumptive taxation, expanding the base of a service tax, however, only at the central level—services could not be taxed by the states without a constitutional amendment—firmly putting floor rates to the sales tax to reduce tax competition among them, beginning preparations for a state-level VAT, and initiating rationalisation of the customs tariffs structure even though it would take a decade to steady customs tariffs reform.

However, one matter which was never adequately addressed was that of scaling back tax incentives. As a result, years later in 2004 when

I entered the North Block of the Union Finance Ministry, with the finance minister's consent, and using the practice of the US Congress, I initiated an exercise of calculating 'tax expenditures'—revenue loss from tax incentives—assisted by Arbind Modi and Gautam Ray, the two joint secretaries in the Revenue Department in charge of tax analysis of direct tax and indirect tax respectively. The calculation became an annual feature of the published Budget documents and continues to this day, though the method needs urgent repairs at this point.

I departed from NIPFP exactly to the day upon completion of my two years there. I had edited and written volumes, held conferences celebrating a grand twenty-year anniversary of the institution with pomp and glory, participated at the highest levels of India's central and state governments, and given recognition in newer forms by the day, delivering lectures on tax policy to various chambers of commerce and industry across the nation and attempting to convince them about the benefits of a level playing field for all. Nevertheless I came away with a bittersweet experience for, while my professional experiences were singular and brilliant, some of the human encounters were complex and challenging. Yet they opened new corners and corridors of experience hitherto unfamiliar to me in my own background and culture, surprising me time and again. Peculiarly though, by and large, I believe my overall cultural, philosophical and ethical stance has not changed. It is just that one has to skirt in and around such challenges, persevere with one's convictions and surge forward.

BACK AT THE FUND, 1997–99

After NIPFP I returned to the Fund, though I found that the technical work at the Fiscal Affairs Department had altered in its approach and substance. While I continued to lead technical assistance missions to Latin America and elsewhere, I was also involved in garnering financial aid for post-crisis countries such as Rwanda. Such experiences were interesting in that they left me confounded as to how a country full of such sharp-headed government executives could have gone through internal genocide just a couple of years earlier. I had read reports in *The New York Times* detailing how the brunt of local hatred had been generated and sponsored by European colonists over the last century, using one ethnicity against another to suit their ulterior purposes. It thus came to pass that local populations that had lived in harmony for millennia across creed, class and caste came to hate one another within a span of just half century or so. Amazing ability there!

Apart from Rwanda, I found this in Ireland and Ulster, Malaysia and Singapore, Palestine and Israel, and most of all, in India and Pakistan, and West Bengal and East Pakistan, the latter being essentially of identical ethnic extraction. In such cases, historical observers have commented on the prosperity and peacefulness of such contiguous communities that were subsequently lost in one breath. Yet, it is also true that, once the cord was cut off from the temporary European masters, the people were left in the vacuum of plunder, exploitation and abominable selfishness resulting in abject poverty, dragging education, health and nutrition to the drain, precipitating maldistribution of income and increasing concentration of wealth in few hands and, worst, living in and encouraging extreme corruption at every rung of society. Perhaps the exception that stands out is Singapore, which nevertheless has had a non-pecuniary cost that I shall comment on later.

I also found myself at odds with some of IMF's approaches. I shall mention one here. Professor Jerry Eichengreen, a reputed American professor, wrote a paper for the Fund Executive Board on theoretical and practical aspects of capital account liberalisation. The responsibility of reviewing the paper in my department fell squarely on me. While I respected his work, I found its scope to be narrow. Yet the issue concerned me deeply in an environment of urgency in which the Fund was recommending that the capital account of the balance of payments be liberalised in many countries—almost irrespective of their international reserves position—as if liberalising the capital account would solve the reserves problem. It was like putting the cart before the horse, and I had discussed the matter informally among selected colleagues.

I shall not go into the details of my short review of 6 July 1998; suffice it to say that I brought out my reservations, and that the review was circulated to all the area and functional departments concerned. It was happenstance that the Asian Crisis of 1997–98 floated in, and that Malaysia and a few other countries were vehemently opposed to the Fund's recommendations, refused to follow them, eschewed

Fund loans, and emerged with good prospects at the end of it. I had accompanied Vito to the Fund-Bank Annual Meetings in Hong Kong and I had already shared with him my deep reservations on capital account liberalisation at that point in time.

My technical assistance missions of course continued apace during this period to Argentina, Bolivia, Brazil, China, Colombia, Mexico, Nepal, and Paraguay—eleven missions during those two years I was at the Fund, and two additional missions immediately after I returned to India—while I attempted to control the spate of international invitations from the far corners of the world to speak on a plethora of subjects on the challenges and reforms in tax structures, and my international amity was thus further bonded. At the same time, I could not but observe once again that some of my immediate cohorts were sitting comfortably at headquarters, and that their careers had progressed quite well.

Focussing instead on the positive side, it may be worth recalling in passing my lectures to Brazilian civil servants at ESAF, Brazil (see Plate 5), a training institute comparable with those of the Indian tax departments in Nagpur and Delhi. I consider all of them to be of exceptional quality, though it is worth pointing out that the syllabi in the Indian counterparts have to be updated more regularly than what they actually undergo since this training early in the careers of budding officials is the backbone of both technical and character formation for the rest of their professional lives.

BACK IN INDIA AS RBI CHAIR PROFESSOR AT ICRIER, 1999–2001

Coming back to the theme in focus here, I was in Paraguay, heading a mission I mentioned in Chapter Three, with my friends Bernd, Erik and Osvaldo. That evening Osvaldo had ordered a giant fish from the Paraguay River to be baked by the hotel chef, and it had been a fantastic success. After dinner, Bernd had sat down at the grand piano in the hotel lobby with a rendition of several of his classical repertoire. I had gone to my room contented, looking forward to reading a few pages before sleeping. At 1:30 am, I got a call from India. It was Isher Ahluwalia. She said she had just taken over as Director of Indian Council for Research on International Economic Relations (ICRIER), her first full-time executive job after years of working from home and being a domestic engineer so to speak, and asked if I would join to support her and take up a professorship there that would be funded by the RBI. I was moved by her plea, impractical though it was. I had barely settled back in DC, and yet the attraction of returning to India played its wiles on me. I agreed.

Vito appeared a little doubtful, though not terribly surprised perhaps, and half-jokingly commented that I seemed to be happiest on top of the Atlantic! However, correctly assessing my resolve, he went along with my decision. I recall a few hallmarks of the two years I spent at ICRIER as RBI Chair Professor.

India's Fiscal Matters

While at ICRIER, I delved deep, investigating all aspects of India's fiscal challenges and in 2002 came out with a book, *India's Fiscal Matters*, from Oxford University Press, burning the midnight oil when I had already left for Singapore. The book covered fiscal policy in a macroeconomic framework, financing of fiscal deficit, sustainability of public debt, the impact of subnational governments, and overall fiscal strategy. I anticipated introduction of the VAT at the state level and examined and recommended its potential structure as well as that of taxation of services.

I also carried out an exhaustive analysis of Indian fiscal federalism and the fiscal effects of decentralisation in light of my experience with Argentina and Brazil as well as, by then, my continuing experience as adviser to selected Indian states. A particular area I examined was the impact of decentralisation on overall expenditure, a hot topic at the time, in particular in the Planning Commission which monitored states' efforts to control their fiscal deficits and maintained a magnifying lens, so to speak, on state-level expenditure. Sunil Ashra assisted me in the data work for estimating the associated equations.

I found most interesting a conclusion that development expenditure could not be linked to the fiscal deficit, possibly reflecting the former's positive underlying link to economic growth:

> First, decentralisation that is based on a state's own total expenditure, or its development expenditure only, has a dampening effect on the fiscal deficit, but decentralisation based on non-development expenditure has uncertain and insignificant effects. Second, only when

> decentralisation is expressed as a ratio of a state's own expenditure only, rather than a sum of the state's plus the centre's expenditure, does decentralisation tend to raise the fiscal deficit.[3]

Thus it was also true that the central government's supplementary support to a state's own resources tended to dampen the latter's fiscal deficit:

> As it were, the absence of central expenditure from the denominator puts the focus entirely on a state's own resources, highlighting the limited capacity of any state to fund its own expenditure.[4]

The lengthy volume, needless to say, had many conclusions and recommendations. As the work proceeded, I often presented my ongoing research with a palatable policy perspective and found my suggestions to be well received in business chambers such as Assocham, CII and FICCI and their branches, as well as in several academic discourses. The work was published when I was already in Singapore. Many reviews appeared in newspapers and magazines, and I was also called for television interviews during short visits from Singapore to India. These included ones by Manas Chakravarty in *Business Standard*, S. R. Kasbekar in *The Financial Express*, Debasish Roy Chowdhury in *Hindustan Times*, Jayant Kher in *Business India*, Dharmakirti Joshi of *BusinessWorld*, apart from articles in *The Economic Times*, *Outlook Money*, *The Hindu BusinessLine*, and several local papers, with interesting titles such as: 'The Shome diet for fiscal excess', 'Chalking out a fiscal roadmap', 'Addressing fiscal concerns', 'Overview of matters fiscal', 'India and her economy', 'What are we reading now, That fella behind the tree—A smart fiscal policy generates revenue, but it must also stoke growth', and so on.

There were also scholarly and comprehensive reviews including one by Deena Khatkhate in the *Economic & Political Weekly*, August 2004, and one by Shri Rajmal in the RBI journal *Occasional Papers*, Volume 22, 2001.

I concluded that readers found the book to be practically oriented and useful. Possibly the most detailed analysis of the book titled, 'Rake's progress—writing on the wall,' was by the well known economist Ashok Desai. Apart from a crystal clear analysis of the book, he made several conjectures on the personal side, one of the milder ones being, "he is bitten by the bug of patriotism", the satire typical of this avuncular man. Someone sent me a Xerox copy dated 20 March 2001 with interesting handwritten notations such as, "We must consider getting Dr. Shome! Advice", and, "Isn't he working with us?" The upshot of all this fun and frolic was that I was truly delighted, and even more so when I found that the book had been included in the syllabus for Delhi University economics major students.

An interesting aspect of my stay at ICRIER was my involvement with states. Some of them invited me as adviser or committee member, and I usually responded positively out of curiosity and for the possibility to learn and assist. I recall some of these below.

Madhya Pradesh

In terms of policy work, I worked as adviser to the Madhya Pradesh government when Chief Minister Digvijay Singh had found that the state was being weighed down by the heavy burden of public debt. He asked me to meet him during a visit to Delhi, which of course I did. Subsequently he wrote to me on 24 May 2000:

> I was happy to....learn that you have agreed to assist the Government of M.P. in its efforts at increasing buoyancy of tax and non tax revenues .... and in developing a medium term budgetary framework....I will be particularly interested in your views on our proposed VAT scheme (which) we have decided to introduce from 1-4-2001. I will also look forward to your recommendations regarding the management of public debt of M.P. in the context of the medium term budgetary framework.[5]

Accordingly, apart from examining their VAT, whose proposed structure I found to be simplistic and conveyed as much to the Chief Minister, I built a model revealing the eventuality of incurring public debt to repay interest. Sunil Ashra assisted me to put in the numbers. The model was convincing and, in my final meeting with the CM, it was obvious that he was seriously concerned with the precarious economic condition of his state. The meeting was cordial and I wondered if he recalled the first time we had met. It was during my tenure at NIPFP some years earlier. P. Chidambaram was Finance Minister then, and Digvijay Singh was Chief Minister. Presumably, I was considered a young Turk for me to have been invited with them on the same public podium by an important chamber of commerce in Mumbai for, by then, I was known to possess a measure of fearlessness in speaking my mind on the state of the Indian economy. Each of us had been given twenty-five minutes to speak to be followed by Q&A. Digvijay Singh started by saying that he cherished being on the stage with P. C. for they had been together some years earlier as first term Parliamentarians. Then he went on to sing praises of the Madhya Pradesh economy. By the time he finished, forty minutes had elapsed.

Mr. Chidambaram spoke next but only for fifteen minutes, saying that the following speaker should not lose any time. I did not know him at the time, my only encounter with him having been that protocol visit I already mentioned. I had no idea why he would be concerned with the time I would lose; rather, was he once again pointing out the value of time? There was pin-drop silence in the otherwise rambunctious audience. I made an especially critical speech of the faults in government fiscal policy that held the audience spellbound. It was not easy since Mr. Chidambaram had presented the contents of a brilliant Union Budget package. At the end of the Q&A, I went to Mr. Singh and said a particularly friendly hello, to which he gratefully responded. Thus it was that, sitting half a decade later before him trying hard to convince him of his state's debt problems, my mind could not but float to that event in Mumbai, and the public consternation I felt he had then endured.

At the same time I also learnt from Mr. Chidambaram that one has to express disagreement in certain situations, in particular in India where speakers routinely exceed their allotted time without consideration for subsequent speakers. I was myself at the receiving end of this several years later when Kaushik Basu invited me to speak at a huge conference he had organised. The chairman of the panel—I shall not name him except to say he has acquired a reputation of being an efficient private and public sector professional—let an elderly professor speak on and on in quite unrelated a fashion to his topic. Then the chairman bent over backwards from his chair, looked at me, and indicated, "So you could shorten your talk". I was aghast for as always I had prepared detailed statistical analysis to speak on poverty and development, my topic. I did not say a word, recalled that early experience, and spoke for my assigned length of time, ignoring the chairman. I recall, later, Professor Pranab Bardhan and a couple of others asked for my slides, which I gladly provided.

Karnataka

A surprise call I received while at ICRIER was from Shri Veerappa Moily, who had been finance minister of the Karnataka government. He informed me in a friendly way that he had been named chairman of the just-formed Karnataka Tax Reforms Commission by Chief Minister S. M. Krishna, that he knew of my work in the taxation area and wanted me to be a member of the commission. I told him that I was humbled by his invitation but that it would be impossible to participate since I was based in Delhi. He indicated that I could fly out once every month and that he would not hold a single meeting without me. I had no choice but to agree. It turned out to be a nice experience, in particular, working with Renuka Viswanathan, an IAS officer of the Karnataka cadre who had been named secretary to the commission. Renuka's knowledge of the nooks and corners of Karnataka's tax system was impressive, and we developed a good professional acquaintance that continued into the years when she was posted as additional secretary in the Union Agriculture Ministry.

And the work at the commission took me to every corner of Karnataka in Moily's company to hold a continuum of consultations with stakeholders and state tax administrators alike. I came to know S. Madhu, Commercial Tax Commissioner, another brilliant IAS officer who continually provided alternative laptop generated models of the optimal VAT rate for the state. I ended up writing much of the chapter on the VAT for the commission and overseeing several chapters at Renuka's request. Not because I was a member, but I feel to this day that it remains the most comprehensive report on a state's tax reform in India, and I continue to recommend it strongly in countries with a fiscal federalist tax structure. It is lamentable that so much high quality technical work is lost with the vagaries of time in the archives, if those, of bureaucracy. And that association with Veerappa Moily continued through the subsequent years when he came to Delhi as chairman of the Administration Reforms Commission when he insisted that I read drafts of the chapters and even later when he became Union Minister of several portfolios. Despite excessive demands on my time, I never said no to him while keeping Mr. Chidambaram informed whenever I went to see Mr. Moily.

West Bengal

The decision to introduce a VAT at the state level had already been taken. It was a matter of achieving uniformity among states in terms of rates and the base. Since the states had no taxing rights over services, the complexity of taxing services could be avoided. Many states were in full preparation over the VAT. Ashok Gupta, Chief Finance Secretary of West Bengal, and a sterling IAS officer who had been member of the CST Committee that I had chaired some years earlier while at NIPFP, was instrumental in inviting me to be adviser to the West Bengal government to prepare it for the introduction of the VAT. Dr. Asim Dasgupta, the Finance Minister, appeared cordial and welcoming. I negotiated for Sukumar Mukhopadhyay to also join me in my work on the same terms and conditions as mine and the government agreed; thus I came to accept the invitation with full satisfaction.

My role as adviser to the Government of West Bengal allowed me to visit the field many times, perhaps the most interesting being to Jhargram at the confluence of Bihar, Orissa and West Bengal. I found the young officers there in decent living conditions for they had to be located there in residential posts. But despite their best attempts, I found the serpentine lines of trucks going in and out of the state very like the ones I had encountered not that long back in Paraguay going in and out of Argentina. Reflecting Paraguay's administrative development, I impressed upon the Finance Minister, in no uncertain terms, the urgent need to computerise the administration of way bills—documents that truckers were expected to have in their possession during travel—at state borders. The preparations for the VAT proceeded apace with the rest of the advanced states and, for me, it was a fulfilling experience participating, sleeves rolled up, with the state tax administration while remaining mindful of erratic, untoward practices that I might encounter. I continued in this role until my departure from India as the Fund's Ambassador to Singapore in 2001.

CHAIRMANSHIP OF THE TENTH FIVE-YEAR PLAN WORKING GROUP ON TAX POLICY AND ADMINISTRATION

It was mid-2000. I was waiting at the airport VIP lounge for a flight, immersed in as many newspapers as I could lay my hands on, though they all provided the same news, much like the same product of different brands, when I heard someone say "Hi" and looked up. It was Montek Singh Ahluwalia, Member Secretary of the Planning Commission. I said "Hi Montek" and stood up to greet him. He gestured to a pair of sofa chairs in the corner, and we occupied them. He started asking me about the Indian tax structure, and, essentially, I began telling him that the reforms needed were known to every expert by now. It just depended on the political will to take the measures. He listened carefully and finally indicated that, even if the measures were known, they needed to be updated and reemphasised for such measures had short shelf lives. I began to feel uncomfortable as I did not want to blow my own trumpet by informing him that my report for the Ninth Plan had the necessary contents, and that all he needed to do was to take it off his own office shelf.

We chatted on. Then his flight was announced. As he got up, he said that the Tenth Plan financial resources committee would need a good report on Indian tax reform, and that I was the man to do it. I began to protest and informed him about the existing Ninth Plan report. He ignored my protestations, simply informing me that he had dictated the official announcement for the Tenth Plan tax policy and administration working group, with me as chairman, and it might have already been issued at that point. I felt frustrated that I would be reinventing the wheel, but knew I had no recourse. I noted one interesting factor—I would be working with the NDA government being led by the Bharatiya Janata Party. I had heard that Yashwant Sinha, Finance Minister, was able and K. C. Pant, Deputy Chairman of the Planning Commission, was scholarly (see Plate 10). I took these pieces of information as pluses. In the event I also realised that, by then, several concerns in the national taxation area had altered, and it was time to look at them with a fresh approach. The experience turned out to be a good one.

I had little say about the list of committee members since most of it was government determined, but I could select Arbind Modi as adviser and D. K. Srivastava as member, for both of whom I had a high professional esteem. D. K. wrote an excellent introduction on fiscal policy from a macroeconomic stance, while Arbind assisted me in drawing up an exhaustive list of tax incentives that should go from the income tax code. Of course the ultimate responsibility for the recommendations was mine, and occasionally Montek would organise large meetings with K. C. Pant chairing them. I got his rapt attention and clear directions. Addressing me as 'Professor' in one meeting, he said that I should recommend the best menu of measures despite the eventuality that others might pare them down. Thus, a strong recommendation was made that,

> ideally, tax incentives under Sections 80CCC, 88, 80L and 10(15) of the Income Tax Act be abolished, at least in phases. Further, 'tax concessions under Sections 80D, 80DD, 80DDB and 80E be given as a tax credit rather than an income deduction to reduce their inequity.'[6]

Finally, any

> rollover provisions relating to capital gains under Sections 54, 54B, 54D, 54EA and 54EB be removed. This reform should eventually enable further reduction in the overall tax rate structure that should enable improved savings behaviour by all tax payers.[7]

Indeed in the 2002 Union Budget speech, Finance Minister Yashwant Sinha declared that he had read the committee's report and agreed with most of its recommendations, and that he would steadily remove the tax incentives that had been listed for removal.

There was a long menu of other recommendations also submitted to the Planning Commission,[8] for all of which there is no space here. However, it is important to mention a few aspects that have relevance even today. One such aspect was in the individual income tax in light of what has transpired over almost two subsequent decades. The committee emphasised that the maximum personal income tax rate should be retained at 30 percent while a surcharge whose revenue was not shared with the states, should be removed. (The surcharge was removed in 2001–02 but eventually crept back in various incarnations). Also, a correction should be made to remove 'bracket creep' from the structure by broad-basing the different income brackets even though it might lead to some revenue loss at existing levels of compliance. Hence the change had to occur *pari passu* with containing the erosion of the tax base due to incentives.

Paradoxically, two decades later, India's poverty, income distribution and wealth concentration have fallen to such a low state that my view on the matter, I am not reticent in admitting, has also strengthened with time. Thomas Piketty, an economist based in France, has recently co-authored a research paper[9] from which it may be derived that the rate of growth of income of the 0.001 percent of the population has been higher in India than even China. And the poor comparison persists as one climbs down the lower decile groupings. I have thus felt obliged to recommend in a recent writing, first published in *The Economic Times* on 26 September 2017, that:

> What can be done about the failed ramifications of the trickle down of liberalisation? Recall that, first, marginal income tax rates were slashed in the 1997–98 Union Budget for incentivising work effort. It appears that it, and subsequent sundry policies, by and large incentivised non-job-generating growth.[10]

Further, in the same recent writing, I have said on the capital gains tax,

> Second, capital gains taxation has been fully flawed. Capital gains from the stock market are free of tax just after one year since that is deemed 'long term'. Yet an elderly couple selling a home after whatever number of years of possession has to pay capital gains tax. Relatedly, third, an elderly person acquiring a second flat at retirement even in his same cooperative from incremental small savings is taxed on the second property, while blanket exemption is given to ownership of a single house irrespective of value or height. Clearly, this should be limited to a consolidated value of Rupees 5–10 crore for all owned properties.[11]

Returning to the Tenth Plan working group, another area of great discomfort to me from early years was the exemptions for foreign exchange earnings from exports of goods and services. Thus the committee found

> no justification in the continuation of the incentives under Section 10A and 10B since the international competitiveness of exports covered under Section 10A is greater than exports from outside the special economic zones (SEZs). Similarly, the incentive under Section 10B is a premium on licensing. It is, therefore, recommended that the provisions of Section 10A and 10B be phased out.[12]

In the corporate income tax area, the committee recommended that the "rate should not exceed the maximum marginal personal income tax rate" and thus be reduced to 30 percent. We also recommended

> the abolition of the distribution tax on dividends and consequent reduction of the tax rate for foreign companies to the rate recommended for domestic companies. Further, 'The 20 percent dividend tax should

> be abolished. Instead, the Minimum Alternate Tax (MAT) should be reconstituted as a tax equal to the aggregate of 0.75 percent of adjusted net worth plus 10 percent of the dividend distributed. The MAT should be carried forward for setoff against future tax liability in excess of the MAT as provided in Section 115JAA. The adjusted net worth for tax purposes would be the average of capital employed as on the first day and last day of the previous year. The definition of capital employed should be the same as was in the case of Section 80J of the Income Tax Act, 1961.'[13]

While there is no doubt that the MAT structure over the years proceeded to approach that recommended, again, my views of the dividend distribution tax have changed in light of the lamentable prevalent income distribution situation, and in the same recent column I have argued that,

> Fourth, the tax on dividends at 10 percent over Rupees 10 lakh calls for drastic reform. Why is the rate not 30 percent or, simply, the marginal rate applicable to the assessee? The argument that the company has already paid dividend distribution tax can be answered in several ways. Its rate is only 20 percent, hence there is room for higher taxation at marginal income tax rates. It could actually be abolished and fully merged with the income tax. Or, a tax deducted at source at 30–40 percent could be applied and small owners could adjust it against their probable, smaller TDS on interest.[14]

In the indirect tax area, the working group recommended reducing the number of rates of the excise tax and also the scaling back of the customs duty structure. These recommendations were accepted and followed significantly. However, a couple of issues would be useful to air. I had found to my dismay while at the NIPFP that capital goods were not given input tax credit (ITC) under the central VAT (CENVAT) system in the first year of purchase but over two years.[15] This vitiated the system and caused cascading since capital goods could represent a big chunk of purchases by a manufacturer in a particular year. Thus it was recommended that,

> both capital goods and other inputs 'used in the factory of the manufacturer' should be allowed CENVAT credit. Thus, capital goods and other inputs should not be distinguished for purposes of ITC.[16]

Despite this recommendation in 2001, the non-immediate ITC on capital goods continues to exist to the present day even after the GST was introduced on 1 July 2017.

In addition, the report made extensive recommendations for the design and administration of a state-level VAT whose structure was reflected in the VAT that was subsequently introduced in 2005. Treatment of inter-state trade and interim reform of the then prevailing sales taxes of the states were also addressed. Thus this Tenth Plan report could well be considered a precursor and a detailed treatment of the VAT that took a few more years to be introduced and put in place.

Finally, the Tenth Plan report visualised a fiscal federal or 'Integrated VAT'. Thus it recommended

> a comprehensive VAT whereby the central and state VAT stand integrated. To achieve this end, our proposal of a state level VAT would be for one that could co-exist with the present arrangement of the central VAT (or CENVAT). The central jurisdiction would give setoff only for central duties and state jurisdictions for state duties. Such a national integrated centre-state VAT arrangement can easily exist in parallel or dual format. However, respective tax jurisdictions (and administrations) would have to be careful about excluding the taxes paid to the other jurisdictions from the assessment of value bases.
>
> ...the Centre may levy the service tax and authorise the states to administer/collect.... (a list of) services whose consumption is of an intra-state nature.
>
> After the initial introduction, services could be incorporated into the VAT.
>
> The rate structure for the VAT on services should be identical to those for goods to obviate distortions in producer and consumer decisions.
>
> State taxes such as luxury and entertainment tax on restaurants, hotels and other lodgings, professions tax, motor vehicles tax, goods and passengers tax and electricity duty should be integrated with the state level VAT.
>
> The assignment of the power to tax services to states must be viewed as adequate compensation for revenue loss on account of abolition of the central sales tax (CST).
>
> The VAT on services should be fully integrated with the VAT on goods, both in its design and administration, with an appropriate mechanism to set off service input tax against goods output tax and vice versa. Therefore, a destination based, invoice credit method, dual VAT—one at the central level and another at the level of states—comprising both goods and services could be envisaged at the end of the Tenth Plan.[17]

Thus the committee had proposed a full-fledged, fiscal federal GST in India that came to be introduced one and a half decades later. Though the former was during the National Democratic Alliance (NDA) regime and the latter during a BJP government, intensive work continued in between, and they will always remain the imagination of technical professionals and experts in reflection of their global experiences albeit being thrust into reality by the political class. Needless to say, much remains to be sharpened in the GST that the taxpayer faces today.

DEPARTURE FROM INDIA

As my two-year visit to India was coming to an end, I was once again beset by the dilemma of leaving or staying. Then an unanticipated offer made me relent. It was a post as IMF ambassador to Singapore to take up the directorship of one of the three training institutes of the Fund, the other two being in Washington and Vienna. I accepted it, thinking I could fly back and forth to India more often, as indeed I did with continuing discussions in the media of the Tenth Plan taxation report and also post-publication media coverage of *India's Fiscal Matters*. In summary, my stay was congenial and luxurious. I was presented as Ambassador of the Fund to Sellapan Ramanathan, the President of Singapore popularly known as Nathan, in a grand ceremony for new diplomats (see Plate 11). He found out that my father had been a nephew of Netaji Subhash Chandra Bose, and I received a call from his office to have coffee with him and his wife. The meeting was most interesting for he indicated how much he admired Netaji.

During my stay in Singapore, there were probably three more tea invitations from him during which he related his affinity to India, and also his views on how India could speed up and step up. Indeed, he contrasted Singapore with India relating how, in its early epoch, the former had to reinvent its existence and then progress rapidly. Eventually, Nathan had a long presidential term between 1999 and 2011, reflecting the commonly known fact of his loyal services to Singapore. At my presentation, I also met Lee Hsien Loong, then Finance Minister, who assumed the position of Prime Minister since 2004. We had a long conversation at the diplomatic presentation during which he informed me of the need for the Fund's role in Asia (see Plate 12). Being the son of Lee Kwan Yew, he had been groomed for becoming Prime Minister, but had also developed a stature befitting the post, one he currently occupies. He has been observed to conduct governance successfully, albeit with a soft touch.

I found Singapore to be a bit unbelievable in that it revealed day in and day out that bureaucracy could actually work. It was under the leadership of Lee Kwan Yew that the city-state had gained prominence and phenomenal economic growth, leaving behind several Western economies in the process. The place was spotlessly clean except for—as a government official lamented to me once—Little India that would just not buckle under. Even public housing projects, of which there were plenty, had sparkling swimming pools, shopping areas but government allocated living quarters that avoided concentration of minority ethnic groups—Malaysians and Indians—in any area. I found little evidence of Malaysians at high positions in the army. Another point the officials made was that Singapore did not believe in providing foreign aid to a bottomless pit but was interested in providing technical assistance only to countries that were seriously willing to learn. Taxis were clean and drivers were honest, though they would also caution you that many drivers are government spies, so it was better not to talk too much though it was fine to talk with him. Officials in receptions only spoke of the weather, and I found that among university professors as well.

Another amusing yet significant characteristic I observed in first and second generation Bengali gatherings was that they spoke in English, though in local Singapore and East Bengal accents, something I had not found even in the heart of Texas. Bengalis are correctly infamous for invariably speaking in Bengali even in the presence of non-Bengalis, a phrase which by itself is unique though commonly used. And the conversation often focused on meaningless critique of India. I soon lost interest in attending those dinners. Instead, I preferred the grand receptions of the diplomatic circle, to which I had many an invitation now that I was ambassador; though, here again, I realised that they had their own groups and history of who had been, or was, or headed to, where.

I did make a few friends, among whom I recall the Korean ambassador at the top. We met now and then at one of Singapore's many clubs and exchanged notes on our respective civilisations. The extent of his dislike for the Japanese surprised me. When I confessed what I had thought of until then as a minor point, that I preferred the earth colours of Japanese pottery over the red and gold of the Chinese or Korean, he bristled to respond that even as the latter had taught the Japanese—who had been a mix of warring clans and warlords—the rudiments of civilisation including pottery, painting and other forms of art, the Japanese had started attacking. Thus they had stopped short at earth colours before they could proceed to red or gold! And subjugating was an innate character of the Japanese that had remained intact to the present day.

Singapore also gave me the opportunity to travel all over Asia, for the Institute taught a variety of courses to a mix of officials from thirty-five countries in its premises at the Monetary Authority of Singapore (MAS). But I also went on consultation visits to discuss and assess the reactions of the officials to the courses the Institute was offering, which took me to Bangladesh, Cambodia, China, India, Indonesia, Malaysia, Japan, Sri Lanka and Thailand during the two and a half years I was there. But the component of work that was most challenging was renegotiating the memorandum of understanding (MoU) that the Fund had with the Government of Singapore on cost-sharing. This took me the entire period and the Fund received much enlarged premises in MAS itself. On the day the Fund Managing Director and Singapore's senior Finance Minister were signing the new MoU, I was flying back from Singapore to Washington. Fund headquarters had desired that I return and resume putting out Latin America's fiscal fires once again. The Director that followed me in Singapore would continue in the post for many years to come.

ENDNOTES

1. See my article, 'Mind the (Widening) Gap—Worsening income distribution can be redressed by tax policy and targeted expenditure policies', *The Economic Times*, 26 September 2017, New Delhi.
2. National Institute of Public Finance and Policy, *India: Tax Policy for the Ninth Five-Year Plan (1997–98 to 2001–02)*, Planning Commission (New Delhi, 1997).
3. Parthasarathi Shome, *India's Fiscal Matters* (Oxford University Press, 2002), 140.
4. Ibid.

5. Letter from Digvijay Singh to Parthasarathi Shome, 24 May 2000 (author's personal correspondence).

6. Government of India, *Tax Policy and Tax Administration for the Tenth Plan*, Report of the Advisory Group Constituted by the Planning Commission (New Delhi, May 2001).

7. Ibid.

8. Ibid.

9. 'Indian Income Inequality, 1922–2014: From British Raj to Billionaire Raj?', World Wealth and Income Database, WIDER, Helsinki, 2017.

10. Parthasarathi Shome, 'Mind the (Widening) Gap'.

11. Ibid.

12. Government of India, *Tax Policy and Tax Administration for the Tenth Plan*.

13. Ibid.

14. Shome, 'Mind the (Widening) Gap'.

15. When CENVAT was introduced, full ITC was given in the first year itself. From the second year, ITC was stretched out over two years, reflecting a fear of revenue loss by the government. Thus it was recommended that ITC should be immediately restored by giving the credit in the year of the purchase.

16. Government of India, *Tax Policy and Tax Administration for the Tenth Plan*.

17. Ibid., 4–26, selective pages.

PLATES

1. Reverend Father P. Gatti SDB, Rector and Principal, Don Bosco, Madras (1965–68).

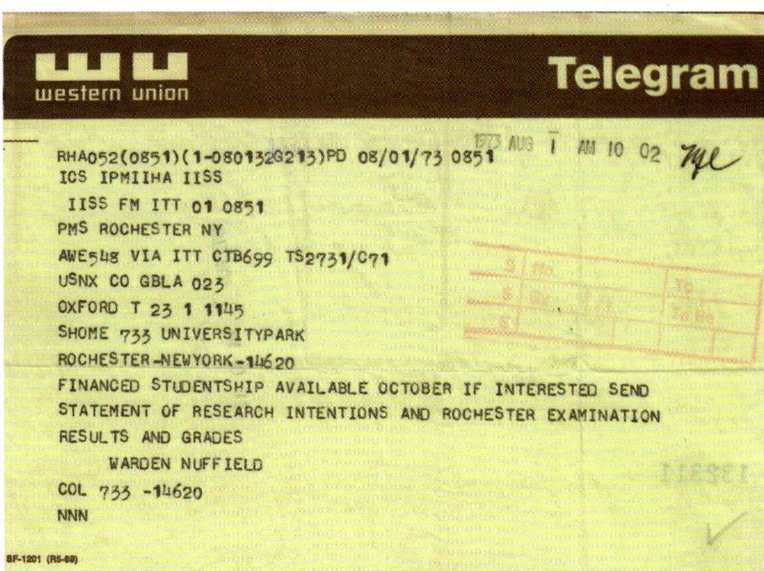

western union Telegram

RHA052(0851)(1-080132G213)PD 08/01/73 0851 1973 AUG 1 AM 10 02

ICS IPMIIHA IISS

IISS FM ITT 01 0851

PMS ROCHESTER NY

AWE548 VIA ITT CTB699 TS2731/C71

USNX CO GBLA 023

OXFORD T 23 1 1145

SHOME 733 UNIVERSITYPARK

ROCHESTER-NEWYORK-14620

FINANCED STUDENTSHIP AVAILABLE OCTOBER IF INTERESTED SEND STATEMENT OF RESEARCH INTENTIONS AND ROCHESTER EXAMINATION RESULTS AND GRADES

WARDEN NUFFIELD

COL 733 -14620

NNN

SF-1201 (R5-69)

2. A Western Union telegram, 1 August 1973, informing me that Nuffield College was ready to offer me a full studentship.

O Presidente da República Federativa do Brasil, Grão-Mestre da Ordem Nacional do Cruzeiro do Sul, houve por bem outorgar ao Senhor Parthasarathi Shome, Economista, de nacionalidade indiana, o grau de Comendador da mesma Ordem, por Decreto de 2 de fevereiro de 2000.

E para constar, mandou expedir-lhe o presente diploma, que vai por mim assinado, e selado com o selo da Ordem.

Brasília, 3 de fevereiro de 2000. 179° da Independência e 112° da República.

[signature]

Secretário da Ordem

3. Letter from the Secretary of the Order, Government of Brazil, 3 February 2000, conferring upon me the 'Commander of the Order of the Southern Cross'.

4a and b. Being presented the award for 'Commander of the Order of the Southern Cross, 2000' by Vera Machado, Ambassador of Brazil to India, at her residence.

5. Giving a speech at a seminar on fiscal policy, Brasilia, Brazil, 25–28 January 1999.

6. Explaining that a minimum alternate tax does not harm investment. *Ambito Financiero*, Buenos Aires, 4 March 1998.

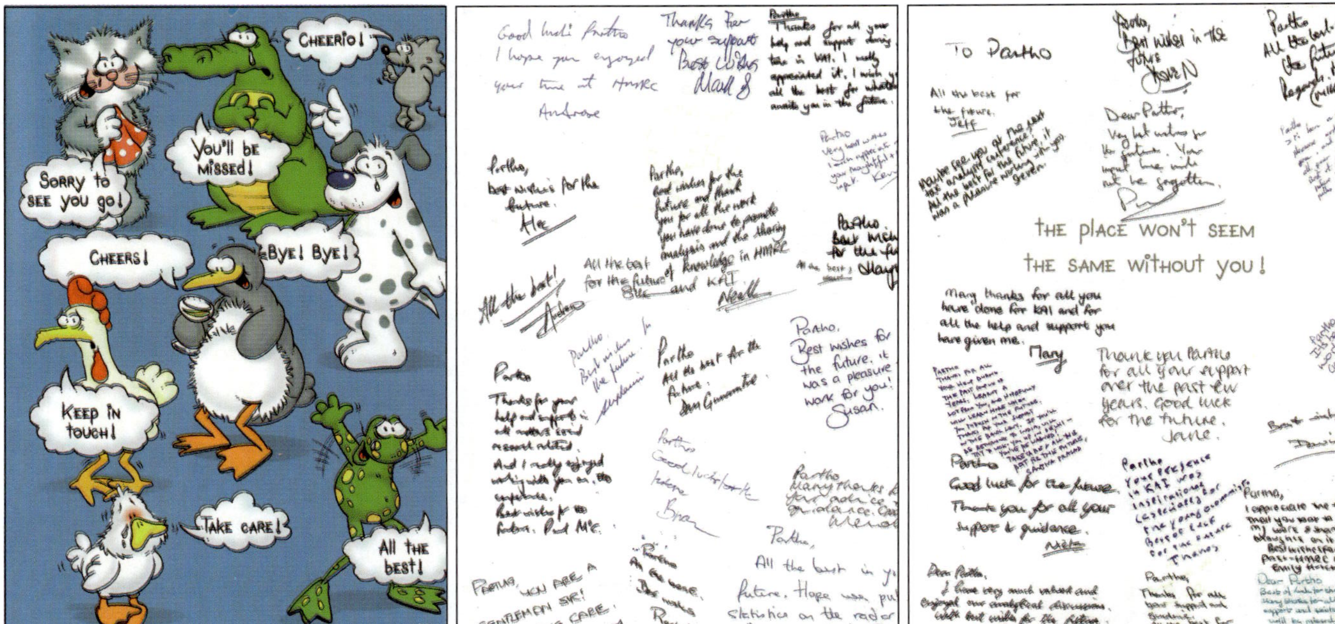

7a, b and c. Goodbyes from the IMF for NIPFP, New Delhi, May 1995.

8. At a seminar on tax policy at Trinity College, Dublin, November 1993.

9. At an international seminar on enterprise income tax, Qingdao, China, 1997.

10. Presenting the final report of the advisory group on tax policy and administration: Tenth Five-Year Plan, to K. C. Pant, Planning Commission Deputy Chairman. First published in *Business Standard*, 22 May 2001.

11. At the investiture ceremony with S. R. Nathan, President of Singapore, 13 June 2002.

12. With Lee Hsien Loong, Deputy Prime Minister of Singapore, 13 June 2002.

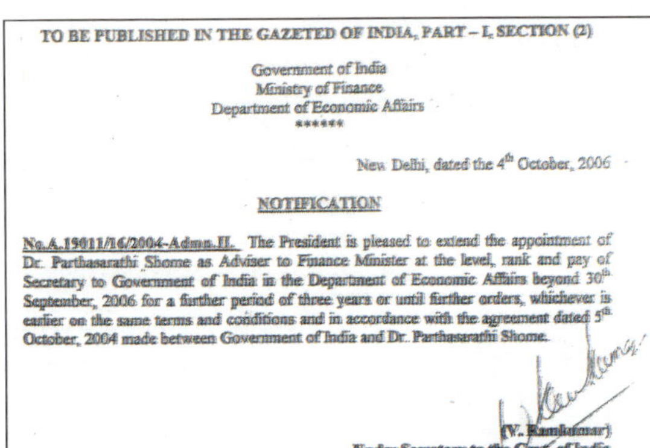

TO BE PUBLISHED IN THE GAZETED OF INDIA, PART – I, SECTION (2)

Government of India
Ministry of Finance
Department of Economic Affairs
******

New Delhi, dated the 4th October, 2006

NOTIFICATION

No.A.19011/16/2004-Admn.II. The President is pleased to extend the appointment of Dr. Parthasarathi Shome as Adviser to Finance Minister at the level, rank and pay of Secretary to Government of India in the Department of Economic Affairs beyond 30th September, 2006 for a further period of three years or until further orders, whichever is earlier on the same terms and conditions and in accordance with the agreement dated 5th October, 2004 made between Government of India and Dr. Parthasarathi Shome.

(V. Ramkumar)
Under Secretary to the Govt. of India

13. Letter from the Ministry of Finance, Government of India, 4 October 2006, confirming my reappointment.

14. 'Commander of the Order of the Southern Cross : In his new role, Shome is expected to give tax reforms a big push'. First published in *BusinessWorld*, 22 November 2004.

15. 'VAT: The rollout and the fallout'. First published in *BusinessWorld*, 18 April 2005.

16. 'VAT no fear'. First published in *The Economic Times*, 2 February 2005.

17. Emerging with Finance Minister P. Chidambaram after pre-Budget discussions with Prime Minister Manmohan Singh. First published in *Business Standard*, 10 February 2005.

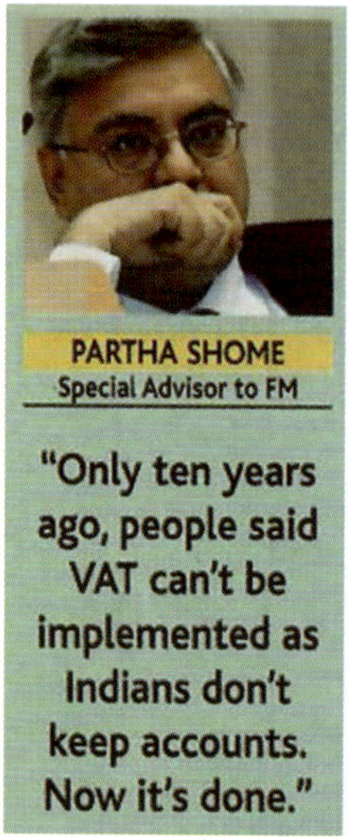

18. 'Walk on the fringe side'. First published in *Outlook*, 14 March 2005.

19. Non-VAT states hindering CST phase out, ASSOCHAM, 11 June 2005.

20. 'TN, UP may introduce VAT soon'. First published in *The Hindu*, 21 May 2006.

21. With Secretary General, ASSOCHAM, D. S. Rawat. 'Single GST: Centre will share revenue with states'. First published in *The Hindu BusinessLine*, 5 April 2007.

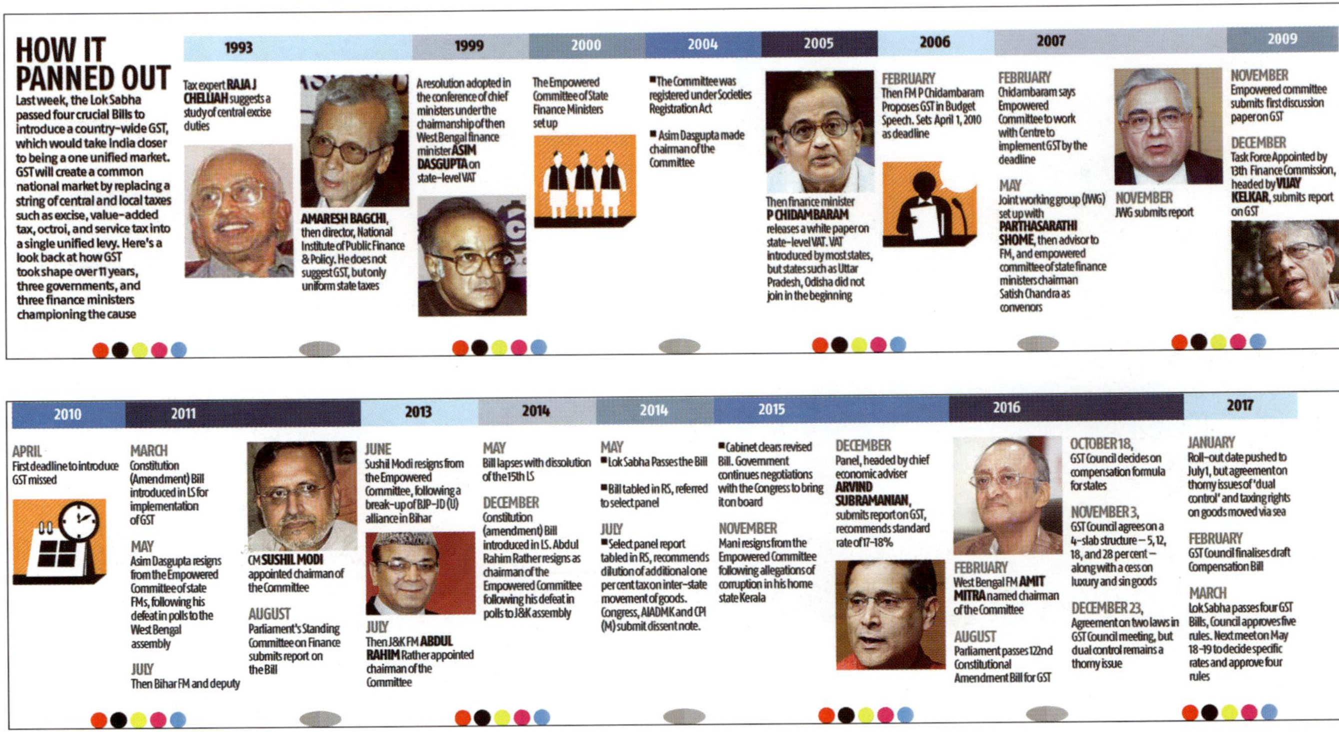

22a and b. GST: 'How it panned out' (1993–2017). First published in *Business Standard*, 5 April 2017.

23. Interview on Budget analysis by Anjuli Bhargava, 'People have not perceived what we've done'. First published in *BusinessWorld*, 14 March 2005.

24. Interview on Union Budget 2006 by Anjuli Bhargava, 'Budget Speak'. First published in *BusinessWorld*, 13 March 2006.

25. Speaking on 'Bank loss due to sub-prime crisis' at a CII conclave. First published in *The Hindu BusinessLine*, 6 October 2007.

26. As head of the first mission on taxation to Myanmar, May 2012.

27. Release of *Tax Shastra: Administrative Reform in India, United Kingdom and Brazil*, February 2012.

Cabinet Office

The Rt Hon Oliver Letwin MP
Minister for Government Policy

9 Downing Street
London
SW1A 2AG

Email psoliverletwin@cabinet-office.gsi.gov.uk

Telephone +44 (0)20 7276 3846
Web www.cabinetoffice.gov.uk

Dr Parthasarathi Shome
Adviser (Minister of State) to Finance Minister Government of India New Delhi
Room No 137B
North Block
New Delhi 110001

2 July 2013

Dear Dr Shome,

Very many thanks for sending over your extremely interesting paper on the differing fiscal paths chosen by different governments.

India is lucky to have you!

With best wishes,

OLIVER LETWIN

28. Letter from Oliver Letwin, UK Cabinet Minister, 2 July 2013, on my paper 'Fiscal Stimuli and Consolidation', in *In the Wake of the Crisis* (2012).

29. With Dr. Manmohan Singh with the GAAR report, New Delhi, 2012.

No. A.12011/11/2012-Admn.II
Government of India
Ministry of Finance
Department of Economic Affairs
****

North Block, New Delhi
Date: 13 Decemeber, 2012

ORDER

The President is pleased to appoint Dr. Parthasarathi Shome as Adviser to the Finance Minister in the rank of Minister of State.

2. Dr. Shome's appointment will be with effect from the date he assumes charge and shall be co-terminus with the period of office of the Finance Minister.

3. The detailed terms and conditions of appointment of Dr. Shome will be issued separately.

(Ashok Kumar)
Under Secretary to the Government of India

30. Letter from the Ministry of Finance, Government of India, 13 December 2012, announcing my appointment.

31. At North Block as Adviser to the Finance Minister, Minister of State level, 2013.

32. Release of *Taxation Principles and Applications: A Compendium*, with Daniel Witt, President, International Tax and Investment Center (ITIC), Washington DC, Sudipto Mundle, Emeritus Professor, NIPFP, and K. L. Krishna, Emeritus Professor, DSE, New Delhi, 2014.

33. Release of *Development and Taxation: Sixty Critical Commentaries*, Academic Foundation, New Delhi, with S. Mahalingam, Member, Tax Administration Reform Commission, and Ram Tyagarajan, industrialist, Chennai, 2017.

SEVEN

GOVERNMENT OF INDIA
North Block

I was chairing a particularly difficult meeting with a visiting delegation from Venezuela, some two decades after my first visits to that country. Based on the Western Hemisphere Department's (WHD) prior briefing, I was explaining to them that, reflecting the economy's fiscal challenges, tax reform would be a pre-condition for entering into a Fund arrangement for macroeconomic financing—a thankless task. So when my Blackberry began to ring incessantly, I was frankly relieved at the welcome break. I excused myself and slipped out of the meeting to take the call.

"Is this Dr. Parthasarathi Shome?"

"Yes, I am. Who am I speaking to?"

"This is P. Chidambaram."

I checked my watch. It was 4:35 pm Eastern Standard Time or 3:05 am Indian Standard Time. P. C. was calling smack in the middle of the night. This must be important, I told myself, glad to be out of that stuffy office filled with polite yet stern colleagues and surrounded by newly elected representatives of the proletariat led by Hugo Chavez, the newest heterodox Latin American President. Chavez had demonstrated that he possessed the verve to once again change the look, approach and solutions to Venezuela's economic problems, but without much, nay any, recognition of the necessary tightening of the belt to ensure the future sustainability of his declared policies. I was increasingly reminded of the last chapter of Harold Robins's *The Carpetbaggers*, a novel I had devoured during the heady days of college when I read voraciously. In that part of the world, revolutions come, leaders change, but the way of life and the challenges of the common people appear to continue unperturbed.

"Yes, Mr. Chidambaram," I tried to sound calm despite a racing heart contemplating the exact nature of this unanticipated call.

"Dr. Shome, my party has formed a government at the Centre a couple of months back. I have been appointed Finance Minister."

"Congratulations. I have been following the news," I said somewhat noncommittally.

He continued without pausing, "I have heavy responsibilities. I need your support for a variety of technical issues. I would like you to join me as my Adviser to take charge in these matters."

My thoughts were aflutter. After two and a half years as IMF's Ambassador to Singapore and having successfully negotiated a new memorandum of understanding with Singapore's financially cautious authorities on cost-sharing for running the IMF's training institute for Asian officials located there, at the same time gaining a significant area of extra space in the Monetary Authority of Singapore building, I had felt victorious returning to IMF headquarters. I had come lock, stock and barrel just six months ago, and been reassigned to once again "put out the fires", as a senior colleague had put it, explaining the determined call back to IMF headquarters.

I hesitated. Quick came the response to my momentary silence.

"The Prime Minister is also keen that you should come. When can you join?"

I at once knew that my role with respect to P. C. would soon assume new tones. I used the manner of address embracing Indian practice.

"Sir, when would you like me to join?"

"In fifteen days."

I fell from the sky. Perhaps he meant for me to visit Delhi for initial discussions. I had just returned from Singapore and was in the middle of negotiations with the Venezuelans on a tax reform programme, and preparing for a forthcoming technical assistance mission to Italy to lead a team of experts to analyse and recommend changes in its complex revenue and expenditure sharing system under its framework of fiscal federalism. Few Indians, if any, in those days led missions to Western Europe at least for technical assistance.

However, having dealt with P. C. earlier, I knew there would be little point in enumerating contradictory details. Nevertheless, I asserted, "Sir, I am in the midst of some ongoing tasks. I would need to complete them."

His answer astounded me further. "Of course complete them. That's why I said fifteen days."

"I also have to pack my belongings and so on."

"You are single. You should be able to do so quickly." At this point, touching a rare personal note, he did sound a bit softer, though this common view or presumption about single individuals had driven me up the wall for decades. I had never been able to convince the world that I did not have the advantage of "economies of scale" that couples enjoyed where a spouse could share in bearing the fixed costs of any endeavour jointly undertaken. I had to do everything myself, from start to finish, with some support from sibling or friend.

Being single had other manifestations as well. At the IMF, I had to take on travel assignments several times that of some of my married colleagues under the assumption that I could just pick up and go, go, go. After initial consternation, I had resolved to turn the disadvantage into enjoyment by immersing myself in the heritage of every culture that I was exposed to. Now P. C. was making the same assumption, the same error, but it did not dislodge my equilibrium too much, inured as I had become to this quintessentially inalienable societal law.

"Sir, there are several steps that I must comply with at the IMF prior to departure."

"Okay. Follow up on them and get back to me in a couple of days."

Click.

P. C. wrote me a letter confirming the appointment and informing me that he was communicating the same to Anne Krueger, First Deputy Managing Director of the Fund, writing to her on 1 August 2004:

> ....It is the Government of India's desire that Dr. Shome should join.... as Adviser to Finance Minister. This post is a senior post at the level of Secretary to Government of India. He will be specially tasked to advise the Government on fiscal reform, including tax reforms.
>
> I shall be grateful if you could kindly facilitate Dr. Shome joining us by October 4.[1]

A senior FAD official suggested that I take leave without pay for two years, in particular because it was FAD's desire to put me up for the important post of Senior Adviser in November. Dr. Krueger called me up urgently, expressing her view that I had already gone to India twice for considerable periods on leave without pay from the Fund and, if this time India were to take up tax reform in all seriousness, it could certainly be carried out in two years. The same mutual friend—for everyone knew everyone well—placed highly in the Indian bureaucracy who had been instrumental in pushing for my assignment, wrote to me,

> Dear Partho,
>
> How nice to have many choices....My view is that an appointment at Secretary level is usually not associated with taking leave and given the views of the Left one cannot rule out someone making this an issue.
> [Then referring to my Fund colleagues,]
> You obviously draw out the [good] instinct but [name omitted] doesn't realise how much damage [an internationally reputed economist] has caused to the IMF.
>
> The main thing is pack up quickly and get here soon. There is a lot of work to be done and the new team in Finance will all be coming in around early October. Best to be there at the same time so they don't view you as the Johnny come lately.[2]

In an immediate phone conversation with my friend, I mentioned my being put up as Senior Adviser at the Fund in a month's time, and should I not wait until that happens, but he asked me, in no uncertain terms, to turn round and not fret over it. I wrote back,

> Attached is the Government Order. It is final now.
>
> I had a chat with [my FAD senior colleague] this morning. The matter is resolved. I shall leave the Fund. She was genuinely concerned and unhappy but I explained that I would not be effective if I maintained a lien with the Fund and must, therefore, take this step on professional grounds. I hope she understood.

In the event, I took up my appointment from 1 October 2004. When I reflect on what made me take such a drastic decision at a time when I had not known any of my colleagues to have resigned and returned to India while enjoying a fast-track career at the Fund, I can only say that the same heavy burden of soul-searching and its outcome propelled me, coupled with adhering to the word I had given someone. On the one hand, this comprised the final break with the Fund in practical terms, and with the distant countries and cultures I had been deeply involved with. On the other hand, I was fulfilling my father's desire, receiving my mother's approval, and enjoying a tremendous sense of fulfilment in anticipation of direct participation in policy-making for my beloved country.

The adulation from print and visual media, friends, ex-colleagues and staff was immense and, for some time, seemed endless, but I knew that my work in India was cut out. In the print media, I recall several articles by Anjuli Bhargava and Ashok Desai in *Business World*, Nivedita Mukherjee in *The Week*, to name a few and, of course numerous newspapers.

Certainly this was an altered scenario from the one in 1991 when, at the time of economic liberalisation, I had been informally approached by Nitish Sengupta, then Revenue Secretary, to join the Ministry, following two meetings I had with him in Washington at his suggestion. I would never say no if the job were offered, not just because of my parents' views but because of my own inner compulsions. Soon, I heard that there had been alarm within the Ministry if I were to join, though the newspapers were already reporting on it. For example, *The Indian Express* reported on 19 November 1991 under the heading, 'IMF man to join Finance Ministry', that with my appointment as adviser to the Revenue Department, the "ideological hold of the IMF and the World Bank over the Government" now seemed complete. It said that experts (who were not named) believed that with an office of the multilateral institution in the capital, and a former employee placed in a key post, Finance Minister Dr. Manmohan Singh could expect a "good working relationship" with the IMF. It further stated that Dr. Singh had brought me in "to advise him on the revenue raising implications of the IMF loan" as I was familiar with the workings of the Fund.

As it transpired, I was never offered the position, and Mr. Sengupta subsequently apologised to me. A year later in 1992, I became the Chief of Tax Policy at the Fund, and came to India as Director NIPFP in 1995. It seemed that all of this had happened a long time back. Nevertheless, now in 2004, I braced myself for the new responsibilities even as I found myself looking at photographs, cartoons and congenial reports every morning as I read the news (see Plate 14).

ENTERING NORTH BLOCK

Following that mid-July call in 2004, I entered North Block on 1 October. The office I was located in had been previously occupied by a Joint Secretary, though I was appointed at the level of Secretary. While I was happy to be there, the Finance Minister (FM) explained, almost apologetically, that he had situated me near his office along the same corridor as his immediate officers, as opposed to the other secretaries—revenue, expenditure, finance—from the Indian Administrative Service (IAS) who were away around the corner. Later I noted that the Expenditure Secretary was from the Indian Accounts and Audit Service, which seemed unusual, and revealed the rare selection of an officer to fit a job perfectly. The contiguous physical location of the top Ministry officials from an exclusive public service cadre seemed a metaphor preserving its autonomy, if not monopoly, over job fitment. Ignoring the lack of professional specialisation that comes with it, I settled down in my smaller designated office a few doors down from FM's—as he explained to me, it was on the corridor he had reserved for his own officers—even as I broached him to explain exactly what responsibilities he had in mind for me.

On that first visit to his office, FM was matter of fact. "What do you prefer to be addressed as?"

"Sir, I am used to being called Partho. Please feel free to call me by my name."

The slightest ever smile escaping his lips, he headed straight to his agenda. "Partho, I want you to address all matters of tax policy for me." He first described to me the units of Tax Policy and Legislation (TPL) and Tax Research Unit (TRU), the singular arms of research in the direct tax and indirect tax areas respectively, comprising all of a dozen officers, overseeing the sum total of the government's policy research and writing legislation on taxation in a country as large as India. I was incredulous at the meagre number of officers; he must have read me for he immediately asked me to pluck any officer I deemed capable from the vast Indian Revenue Service (IRS) to staff TPL and TRU. I asked if he would write a memo to that effect, already aware of the obstacles posed from the corridors around me. He asked me to draft the memo, which I did that evening. I took it to FM, for he was still at his desk at 9 pm. He asked me to leave it with him. The next morning the signed memo was out.

Second, the FM emphasised that all files on tax policy matters would come to him directly from me. I did not fully comprehend the need for his emphasis at that point since I thought this to be the natural, normal procedure. Within a fortnight the new Revenue Secretary (RS) arrived upon termination of a foreign assignment. Soon thereafter I was called in by FM. With an apologetic smile he explained that all files, including on tax policy, would pass through the RS prior to the FM's desk even though, he elaborated, I would effectively be the final point as far as the FM was concerned. I came out dumbfounded. That evening I spent an hour re-reading portions of Paul Brunton's *A Search in Secret India*, with Nikhil Banerji's eloquent sitar playing in the background, until I fell into a fitful sleep.

In the long haul I have realised that meritorious pursuits and commensurate professional successes carry with them stringent tests that may be better assuaged by accepting and digesting, to a not insignificant extent, the inexplicable penalties that accompany those tests. Amelioration is feasible through alternative pursuits that stand apart from the source of those injustices. Incessant reading and writing, music and art appreciation, for instance, come in handy while also simultaneously aiding the accumulation of cultural wealth. Unfortunately these are generally lacking in the overall cultural milieu in the vast Indian population base other than in an embarrassingly narrow, rarefied layer of society. Instead, the post-independence focus has inexorably shifted from material and financial sacrifice that achieved independence to, by and large, a deep-seated self-centredness, the outcome of which appears to be the singular goal of achieving career success at all costs if not financial wealth for oneself and family, irrespective of the incompetence or waywardness of the family unit. This has left India in the forever-developing mode where family comes first with country a distant third. Worse, it is among the most corrupt countries in a global line-up, against which I have fulminated increasingly in recent years.

THE VALUE ADDED TAX

I immediately found myself deeply immersed in the push towards a Value Added Tax (VAT) at the level of the states as well as in background calculations at FM's initiation of the 2005–06 Union

Budget process. FM explained to me that the introduction of the VAT was a foremost tax matter on his mind. He also indicated that he had particular ideas on taxes for the forthcoming Budget that he would soon discuss with me and that the discussions should be considered one on one (see Plate 17). It was an exhilarating period.

After several countries where I had assisted in carrying out VAT reform, I found the design of the VAT structure in India comparatively smooth sailing. Whenever I had visited India from Singapore I took the opportunity of analysing the prevailing thought process on the VAT and emphasised its importance in several media interviews and lectures at industry chambers across the country. But from North Block I found the VAT's political milieu and challenges to be complex. This reflected the heterogeneity of the states that had to jointly arrive at a common and comprehensive VAT base and rate structure. In my experience, the only two other comparable experiences were Argentina where provinces could never agree to introduce a coordinated VAT, and Brazil, where the state-level VAT was four decades old and attempts at reduction in its complexity had taken enormous effort on my part in convincing the concerned authorities, especially at the level of state finance ministers, towards reforming its structure.

The Empowered Committee of State Finance Ministers

The Empowered Committee invited me to join it as Permanent Invitee, and so I did to a warm welcome. I began to represent FM in EC meetings, bringing back to him my views on the progress towards introduction of the tax. The main challenge was, first, to bring in all the states to accept the VAT; second, to find a formula to compensate them in case of revenue loss after the change; and third, to arrive at a meaningful structure that would comprise a significant improvement from their prevailing sales taxes.

On the first matter, some opposition states were clearly not playing ball, Tamil Nadu, Madhya Pradesh and Uttar Pradesh being foremost. So FM, with me accompanying him, went to Lucknow to meet and convince Chief Minister Mulayam Singh. There was a grand reception in the form of a sit-down lunch, prior to which we had to drive through hecklers against the VAT. The CM started by saying that he had completed all fiscal reform there was to be made in Uttar Pradesh, and enumerated a spate of micro socio-economic expenditures such as bicycles for school-going girls and sewing machines for married women. I turned and softly asked FM if he would allow me to speak. FM gave me permission, indeed subsequently to speak in Hindi on his behalf when he wanted to make a point. Having just arrived after resigning from the Fund, I had the temerity to inform the big man that all his reforms comprised expenditure items that would need revenue to sustain them; hence would he consider the VAT? I added that this was what the FM was also emphasising. I recall Mulayam Singh laughed loudly and said he would have no difficulty in introducing the VAT provided we also convinced the crowd that we had driven through on the way to his home. Later, I asked FM how had the CM known that there had been a large crowd. He looked at me with raised eyebrows. I do not know if that meant that the crowd had been organised. I soon began to realise the intricate game that was Indian politics. Interesting indeed.

Rajasthan was another case in point. It had insisted that the Central State Tax (CST) should be abolished prior to the introduction of the VAT, and Chief Minister Vasundhara Raje wrote to the FM in September, October, December and January, reiterating that as a pre-condition. The newspapers had full information on all this and had a heyday reporting from every which corner. Here the push and pull between states reared its ugly head. States that imported more from other states than they exported wanted the CST to go since it was collected and retained by exporting states, while exporting states protested loudly against its immediate abolition and were determined to extract substantial compensation from the Centre. Having chaired the first government committee on the CST while at NIPFP, I was well aware of the issues but had to politely carry the argument at EC meetings. The state finance ministers always listened politely but the cacophony resumed as soon as I stopped speaking. Soon I learnt to listen more, realising that the states would have to come to their own equilibrium. Of course I kept FM fully informed, through memos and discussions, about the status of VAT implementation and the pace at which the different states were progressing, on the possible impact of the VAT on prices and on state finances, or the EC's reluctance to immediately abolish the CST, and meetings on the matter right up to the VAT's introduction on 1 April 2005. Meetings regarding alternative schedules to phase out the CST continued right through my departure for the United Kingdom at the beginning of 2008, and even after.

The issue of compensation followed. I took the liberty of explaining in the Empowered Committee for VAT (EC-VAT) that, after all, introduction of the VAT, its subsuming small and distortionary state taxes, and abolition of CST would all converge in improving resource allocation in productive sectors and thus have a positive supply effect, in turn improving revenue. In North Block, FM told me that while my argument was correct, the states would not admit it, and I should make compensation calculations on that basis. Lalit K. Gupta, an IAS officer, and I sat together for hours, discussing and arriving at agreed numbers. I found out later that he had been a chartered accountant; no wonder he was sharp at his work. FM would have to allocate Rs. 5,000 crores in the Union Budget for compensation on account of any revenue loss from VAT and CST. The basis of calculation was as follows. Of the previous five years prior to VAT moving backwards from 2004–05, the three best years were taken in terms of revenue from which a past average revenue growth was calculated. It was agreed that, after the VAT's introduction, that is, beginning 2005–06, any lower rate of revenue growth than the three-year average would be compensated. Compensation would be on a declining formula of 100, 75 and 50 percent for three years. Compensation was based on meticulous reporting by states in a template provided by the Centre.

In the event, after the completion of one year, seventeen states had enjoyed in excess of 20 percent revenue growth or thereabouts, and did not claim compensation. But Maharashtra claimed most of the allocated amount as the VAT moved to a destination basis, robbing the state government of the revenue collected from the earlier origin based sales tax. It was also rumoured that it had given built-up sales tax refunds in the form of the VAT's input tax credit. There was a special audit that set aside such fears. Seven other states also made small claims. Thus ultimately, much of the allocation for compensation was spent even though most states could not claim any. However, some states that did not enjoy high revenue growth attempted to raise tax rates in their own state, which called for immediate complaint and correction from within the EC itself.

On the third aspect, after much wrangling among themselves, to which I was a silent observer, the states worked out for themselves a good VAT structure, nevertheless with a few idiosyncrasies. For example, while there were two tax rates of 4 and 12.5 percent, capital goods were at 4 percent even though tax on inputs would anyway be credited out. On exemptions, the ministers agreed on a basket of forty commodities from which each state could exempt eleven that were of local importance to them. This was a unique way of keeping in check the size of the basket of exemptions. This was remarkable reflecting that, even a few months prior to the VAT's introduction, states were outcompeting one another on tax exemptions, with the aggrieved states writing to complain to the Centre. As FM directed me, I would then caution Dr. Asim Dasgupta, EC Chairman, who would bring back his colleagues to the narrow path of preparation for VAT implementation.

On 21 August 2006, under FM's instructions the Press Information Bureau of the Government of India issued, under my name and authorship, a statement entitled, *Implementation of State VAT* (FINANCE, 37, AB/RTS/VN, SS-147/SF-147/21.08.2006) that described the genesis of the VAT, the role of the central government, providing a measure of flexibility to the states to enable them to meet their local requirements, the revenue enhancement experienced under the VAT, the compensation that the central government had agreed to provide the states—at that point eight states had asked for a compensation of Rs 2,500 crores—and the need for the remaining states to implement VAT. Indeed, slowly but surely, as states experienced a surge in revenue growth with the VAT, the remaining three—Uttar Pradesh, Tamil Nadu, and Pondicherry—joined in. Of course they wanted 100 percent compensation in their first year of the VAT. My view was they should be compensated only for the remaining months of the three-year period of compensation. However, FM argued that since compensation was being calculated on a yearly basis, any state joining during any month of a particular year should receive full compensation for that entire year. Thus Tamil Nadu got full compensation for the second year though it joined just before the end of the second year. I appreciated his perfect legal argument but felt there would be no effective cost to the state for coming on board so late. At the same time, as a possible measure to alleviate future compensation costs, at the Centre we calculated the revenue impact of moving towards a rate structure of 4-8-12.5 or 6-12.5, and concluded the latter to be better for the Centre. However, such an eventuality never occurred.

North-Eastern States

During intensive preparations by states for introduction of the VAT, the north-eastern states expressed a desire for the Centre's assistance in VAT implementation—in particular the computerisation aspect—in the region. FM asked me to visit Kolkata for the purpose and a meeting was held on 9 January 2005. We already had knowledge of existing problems in the region. More cement, for example, was destined for the north-east than was feasible given its construction index. Thus much of the supply remained behind in West Bengal, escaping its sales tax. Robust systems would need to be installed under the VAT that would address leakages in real and financial terms.

It was interesting for me to view how, even in a region that was, and is, usually just addressed as the 'North East', as if the ancient dimensions of Assam had remained the same, actual experience reveals the vast differences and conflicts of interest that exist in the region. It was as if I had returned to Andorra. The turnkey project was with Tata Consultancy Services (TCS) as the vendor for hardware and software while the government information technology department—National Informatics Centre (NIC)—was undertaking the task in Meghalaya and Sikkim. Though the states using the NIC expressed doubts, eventually TCS and NIC would have to be coordinated for seamless flow of information through a central server across all the states. However, the location of the central server had not yet been decided.

Assam proclaimed that it would have no objection if it were located in Guwahati, while other states had a variety of reactions to this ranging from agreement, cautious optimism and strong objection. Indeed, several said that the administrative rules being currently applied were being taken directly from Assam, but that handholding was needed to set up state-specific rules. Some insisted that for data entry and systems administration support, only local youth should be employed while others felt that such functions should be outsourced. Some looked into the medium term pointing to the need for developing a cadre for audit. Needless to say, officials from the states put forward their special financing needs.

The central government's Director General of Excise and Customs for Computerisation and a senior officer were present at the meeting. I sent him a hand-written note asking,

> Can you announce that you are willing to put (said officer) full time on the job, including visiting some of the states including training? That would be very helpful.

He immediately wrote back, "Agreed". That was the genesis of the Centre's involvement.

As we moved forward, I perceived tensions between the TCS engineers and the central government officer in the role of commercial tax commissioner. Thus I had to keep in mind FM's keen interest in the matter apart from my own and pushed forward by focussing on monitoring TCS on the establishment of the essential technical components for setting up appropriate inter-state IT systems, the need for state-specific software, the establishment of a disaster recovery site in case of a systemic breakdown, provision of hardware in remote areas where wiring could not reach, and getting agreement on a viable system of inter-state exchange of information. It was a rich experience also to visit states such as Arunachal Pradesh, Sikkim, Tripura as well as the usually traversed ones in order to clinch agreements, rather, the cooperation of respective regimes and bureaucracies on project details.

As if the technical and financial assistance provided by the Centre were not enough, however, the EC Chairman insisted that the Centre should compensate states that had already spent some of their own monies on computerisation. There was also the matter of running costs after the establishment of the system and the need for continuing handholding and training. While I could understand how well he played the role of addressing the interests—in his interpretation—of his fellow states, all this would escalate the Centre's budget by a third or more, and I did not see the basis to agree but bore it with a smile since FM, after I reported the matter to him, agreed to bear it, such was, and remains, the pull of the North East on the political economy of India. Thus, while there was considerable brouhaha in the media over my external role in the VAT, in reality I was spending many an hour in the background, visiting the far reaches, burning the midnight oil, and bringing it all back to FM. There could be no richer experience.

VISIT TO BRAZIL

Right from the time of my entry into North Block and getting involved with the introduction of the VAT, I had pushed the idea of the EC visiting Brazil to analyse and study its VAT and learn what pitfalls should be avoided. This was to obviate conclusions that state finance ministers were making based on the Canadian and Australian structures that were appropriate for small populations with little tax evasion and a high degree of computerisation—in other words, quite irrelevant for India. Finally the approval to go to Brazil came in August 2007, and I literally bundled them together and all of us went off to different Brazilian cities to check on their rather dated fiscal federal VAT. It was an interesting mission to see the gradation of objectives with which Indian politicians approached the foreign trip, from mastering the VAT and its implementation to those farther afoot.

Media Coverage

I was myself surprised, not so much on the media coverage of the VAT, but on the accolades I received through articles and interviews. Though they continued to appear over perhaps two years, my favourite remained a two-page cartoon of selected individuals intrinsically involved with the VAT that appeared in *BusinessWorld* on 18 April 2005 soon after the VAT's introduction (see Plate 15). Of course, from what I came across, *Business Standard*, *The Financial Express*, *The Economic Times*, and *BusinessLine* had rapid, regular and intensive coverage, but *The Times of India*, *The Hindu*, *Deccan Herald*, *The Telegraph*, and *The Statesman* had extensive coverage with attractive titles and pictures of events through the following couple of years (see Plates 16, 18, 19, 20).

Of course, on FM's instructions, as I circled the chambers, I was trying to prepare them on what was to come not just before but also after the VAT. I always tried to keep the story simple but, in the Q&A sessions after my talks, had to answer the countless intricate questions put up by traders and suppliers reflecting the extremely complex systems of clearance, inter-state transport, filing and so on under the prevailing state sales taxes and the CST. In other words, they were more interested in the administrative hurdles that made compliance onerous and difficult, if not impossible, than on the VAT structure itself. Often they talked about corruption in particular at the level of state tax administrations, to which I usually had to respond rather limply that to clap, one needs two palms. I realised that India had to face the issue societally, through a Truth Commission such as in South Africa, rather than through a discussion in an industry chamber. Government after government comes and goes, only the colour of corruption changes. Here I have to make a confession. Despite my experience in governments, I have never encountered corruption among policy makers, and I have wondered if and how they did it. I have at times felt like a schoolboy brushing his teeth in front of a mirror, but so sleepy that he just wants to jump into bed after saying goodnight.

HARBINGER TO GST

As the VAT took hold, in his 2006 Union Budget speech, FM announced his intention to introduce a fiscal federal GST covering goods and services under one umbrella. Though there was much in the VAT that still needed to be sharpened, leave alone the central excises, as could have been predicted, the states saw the announcement as an opportunity to immediately push their agenda on the share of the revenue pie from the taxation of services which, at that point, was taxed only by the centre. At FM's suggestion, I began to contemplate an acceptable GST structure in the context of fiscal federalism, or, comprising both the Centre and states. By January 2007, I found myself giving lectures at chambers which had been pressing the matter. On 16 January 2007, an indication by me at Assocham, New Delhi, was reported widely the next day by *The Economic Times*, *The Hindu BusinessLine*, *The Indian Express*, *The Telegraph*, and *The Statesman* (see Plate 21). As the spate of work continued, the press continued its coverage, revealing the intensity of interest in the GST in India. In September, November and December, as I had to deliver more lectures, the same papers and others continued to report on a probable GST structure as our work became more widely known.

In January 2007, FM had expressed his plans for the Centre and the states to work on a GST structure. As a precursor to the GST, he asked me to draw up a list of local services that could be assigned to the states, and he went through the list meticulously. By mid-2007 he had agreed on thirty-three services to be transferred from 2008–09 with some additional services at the request of the states that were not being taxed at all, thus bringing the number up to seventy-seven services altogether. The states asked for more, but any extension would have to await the GST. My suggestion to FM was not to transfer any exclusive list to the states, and that the Centre should also tax those services, keeping in mind the eventual dual structure of a future GST. I also suggested that the EC liaise with the central service tax administration in different states and organise training in service tax administration, which he put down in writing.

A Working Group on GST was set up that held its first meeting on 13 June 2007 where discussions over the GST were born. I was one of the two convenors, the other being the Secretary of the EC, but it also included all finance secretaries and VAT commissioners—the most senior tax official—of states, four joint secretaries and an observer from the central Finance Ministry. Keeping in mind that both the central and state governments should be benefitted, we discussed a host of topics including which taxes other than central excises, service tax, VAT, central sales tax (CST), and remaining state-level sales taxes might be brought under the GST without arriving at too high a GST rate; how to design a better administration system of set off or input tax credit at both central and state levels; how to comprehensively address the interests of industry and trade including exporters and consumers; and whether the GST should or should not remain in the prevailing formula of 30.5 percent devolution from the Centre to the states as stipulated by the quinquennial Finance Commission. Of course there was keen interest from state-level officers for training in service tax administration, which I conveyed to FM, and which he encouraged as strongly as possible. The first report on GST was completed in December 2007 by the two convenors and submitted to FM and the EC just prior to my departure for the United Kingdom (see Plates 22a and b). Just before I left, FM expressed his doubts that the GST work remained unfinished. I reassured him that the report had recommended the right structure, that the EC had in principle agreed on the framework and that, in any event, I had promised the Prime Minister that I would return in three years. When I returned to India in 2011, interim events revealed an essential breakdown in centre-state equations. Once FM returned to North Block, the work began in earnest once again in 2012.

ON THE JOB AT NORTH BLOCK

While the work on VAT and GST took up time, all through 2004 to 2007 at North Block, I was busy putting out fires in different directions.

Tax Incentives

My dislike for tax incentives including area-based incentives is well known. My research and experience have time and again proved that they are useless other than enabling the extraction of economic rent by the entirely undeserving. At the cost of losing friends, I would say that many industries and services have received incentives over the years that have resulted in fat pockets. India has been no better, perhaps worse; yet as a researcher and adviser I have seen governments support private sector self-interest. As an example, take incentives for capacity expansion. This was inexplicably defined differently under the income tax and excises. When I raised the issue, I was politely informed that they were defined at different points in time with no reference to one another, although no officer suggested redefinition to coincide the two. Definitions also differed for the north-east, the western hill states, and Jammu and Kashmir, with similar explanations when queried.

An interesting case of differential excise incentives given to special category states that had an adverse impact on the prices of Gujarat's manufactured goods, was rightly submitted by then Chief Minister Narendra Modi. But reflecting the status quo in the excise structure, internal arguments were against making any change. I realised that the only way to bring the matter of tax incentives upfront was to initiate an exercise on 'revenue expenditure', that is, the annual loss in revenue due to tax incentives. However, I found flaw in the methodology; while on the income tax side it was fine, on the indirect tax side the revenue loss was calculated on the basis of initial law that had been irrelevant for several years for the rates were changed in every annual budget. Gautam Ray, a clear-minded head of Tax Research Unit and always respectful and cooperative, took the legal interpretation and FM, not surprisingly, agreed with him. I lost, though defeat by two erudite minds was not too hard to bear. The exercise became an annual feature for the Budget's presentation. To this day that flaw in calculation appears to remain, and should be corrected.

Special Economic Zones

A terrible measure in the area of tax incentives in the name of economic growth was the Special Economic Zones (SEZ) Act in 2006. FM asked me to join the Finance Ministry officials after quite some time had elapsed in the wrangling between Commerce and Finance, with the latter taking a more cautious approach in terms of revenue depletion from SEZs. The law made no sense to me; any supply to an SEZ would be considered an export item, thus attracting all prevailing export incentives. However, only selected recipients of such supplies located within the boundary of the SEZ would be considered to be located abroad, but other SEZ activities would be considered domestic. Thus selected activities in an SEZ would receive tax incentives, but not others though both were located within the boundary of the same SEZ. How could this be monitored? It was clear to me that it would be impossible.

The answer I received to the puzzle was that upwards of 3,000 new excise inspectors would do the monitoring. Given that 160 SEZs had been approved—against less than 20 in China—it would be a Herculean task and fraught with corruption. In the meanwhile, vast tracts of land were being sanctioned, yet single buildings were also being designated as SEZs. As I participated in meetings with the secretaries and officers of concerned ministries, I understood the extent and depth of fallacious policies that bureaucrats might undersign as routine work that would be verboten for a specialist. As I accompanied FM to the empowered group of ministers on SEZs, my fears were further confirmed. After one such meeting when we returned to North Block late at night, I felt so uncomfortable that I went to FM's office to explain my extreme discomfiture. FM heard me out and said, Partho, we have to lose a few battles to win a war. Then he elaborated on the remaining work on the VAT, preparation for a

GST and other major reforms we had to push ahead with. I left him in resignation, yet noting his resilience.

During the decade 2004 to 2013, I gave some twenty-five substantive newspaper interviews not counting magazines and visual media. Among them, in the tax sphere, one that has stood out in my mind was by Sunil Jain, then with *Business Standard*, now editor at *The Financial Express*. His relentless pursuit of the erroneous policy on tax incentives impressed me, while I too felt I had not done too bad a job in justifying government policy from a sticky corner. I probably felt a bit amused during the tête-à-tête. I provide a few excerpts from Sunil Jain's interview of 21 March 2006, first published in *Business Standard*.

> One of world's top tax experts explains the natural ceiling to the pace of India's tax reforms. He's won the Brazilian equivalent of a knighthood for his work on reforming that country's tax system...As part of the IMF, he's worked on reforming taxes in most Latin American countries and his work on calculating tax evasion under VAT a decade ago became popular enough to be called Shome index....So has the finance minister's adviser on tax policy met his match in the India taxman:
>
> Shome resumes, 'Latin American countries were always more market-oriented, they didn't seek to fine-tune every tax policy in the manner we do. The government here wants to....ensure no one gets hurt by changes in policy—you tend to recognise every distress you cause—so changing tax policy is inherently different.' In no other country, not even in Bangladesh, where he helped restructure tax policy, has Shome seen the tax authorities pay so much attention to petitions made by various associations/lobby groups. 'Democrazy' is the term he has for it.
>
> That said, Shome says the government has made major reductions (81) in exemptions this year including changes in depreciation and investment allowances, and the one removing tax exemptions on non-religious charities was a difficult bullet to bite. But isn't that too slow and, in any case, what's the point of reducing exemptions, I ask, if new ones such as the hilly areas—ones in Uttaranchal—and the ones for SEZs are going to be added on?
>
> Shome gets diplomatic here, and argues structural difficulties. Once these incentives were announced, he says, a lot of people have begun shifting/organising their production facilities to take advantage of them, and so it becomes difficult to end the exemptions quickly.
>
> ...
>
> On Latin America's slashing and flat-rating customs duties,

> How did they do it in Latin America, I ask, and has he become a 'realist' now, succumbing to all the usual explanations given by people who want to preserve the status quo? Apart from the fact that Latin America didn't have this huge baggage of exemptions to clear, an additional issue is that the industrial bases there were a lot less diverse in comparison—so there was a lot less industry that got hit in Latin America.
>
> So, exemption raj cannot be unravelled, I ask dejectedly. No, Shome is reassuring, about a third of the quantum of exemptions the Budget talks of (Rs 158,000 crore) can be removed provided the government comes out with focused policies to deal with such industries. That involves retraining and this has been done in Latin America. It doesn't help that setting up and exiting businesses in India is also a lengthy and tortuous process—another reason for going a bit slow.[3]

The interview flowed, in Jain's inimitable hard-hitting yet friendly style, into many other taxes such as the service tax, securities transaction tax (STT), the banking cash transaction tax (BCTT), the fringe benefits tax (FBT), inverted import duties, for all of which he somewhat erroneously claimed that the strong perception was that I had been the man responsible for the 'slew of bad taxes'. Jain concluded his report,

> He mentions a paper of his a decade ago where he concluded a financial transaction tax was not a great idea, but seeing the success of it in raising revenue in Brazil, he was persuaded to change his mind provided it was low enough (as the STT is) to not distort (business decisions). On the FBT, he points out without absolving himself, others have recommended the same.[4]

But there was also Anjuli Bhargava, another economist journalist also trained at DSE, who visited my office soon after I came into North Block and kept a steady check on my activities and interviewed me many times and penned several articles on me (see Plates 23 and 24). She was hard-hitting in approach yet with a soft touch, the kind of woman who can have a profession, manage a home and come out on top. I cannot set aside Anjuli's critical contribution in my initial and ongoing assessments of hot economic issues emerging and ebbing all around me. She would say, "Dr. Shome, what do you think of...", and I would think, "Not another fire to fight! Leave it to her to push me relentlessly." But, of course, being a reporter she would also probe me on impending policies and their pros and cons; I would protect private information but have a hearty discussion on overall tax policy strategies for India. At the end of it both of us would be quite satisfied with the exchange. Just before I left for the UK, Anjuli did an interview of me. I have appended most of it to this chapter because it reveals my frame of mind prior to my departure that is critical in placing to the reader, and it is best to show it through someone else's assessment perhaps rather than my own.

Inequity in Corporate Income Tax

I surmised that large firms were possibly not paying an equitable share of revenue, as I had found during my investigations in so many countries. Whenever I spoke at Indian chambers of commerce and industry, and the frequency seemed to be on a continuous scale rather than discrete, I encountered small firms that perennially complained about their unbearable tax burden while large firms pointed to anomalies in the tax structure rather than about tax burden. I decided to ask Tax Policy and Legislation (TPL), the income tax research unit, to carry out an exercise on the incidence of the corporate income tax. We found it to be regressive in terms of the size of firms. The effective tax rate diminished with the size of firms, becoming slightly higher at the end of the series where the corporate financial sector came in. Thus the incidence curve was downward sloping though it rose slightly upward at the very end, making it marginally U-shaped in economic parlance. In the subsequent budget, FM abolished the surcharge on small firms that corrected the regressivity mildly, and the exercise was presented in an appendix. There were quite a few such terrific, small victories that were satisfying at the end of the day.

Experimenting with a Banking Cash Transaction Tax

Many professionals I encountered pointed to FM's inclination to introduce a new concept, a new tax, in every budget right from his first term as finance minister in 1996–97 when he slashed the income tax rate structure and introduced a so-called 2×5 scheme for filing income tax returns in which every individual who satisfied two out of five stipulated criteria would have to file a return even if he did not have to pay tax. While the first was needed at the time and stayed on in the income tax structure, the latter too was useful in bringing in new filers though, as the numbers increased, it was eventually removed.

Soon after I joined, FM came into my office and asked me about Brazil's financial transaction tax (FTT). At a time when Brazil's fiscal deficit was soaring, and the Fund was extremely unhappy about it, Brazil introduced the FTT though I had felt it would distort the financial sector by increasing the cost of financial transactions. The FTT was imposed on literally every financial transaction in the economy other than a transfer from one own-account to another own-account within the same bank. Though there was evidence of some capital flight after its introduction, the temporary need for revenue was satisfied since this tax made a considerable contribution to revenue. Later, Brazil brought down the rate of FTT to zero but did not abolish it in case there was need to raise the rate in the future. I explained the Brazilian experience to FM, weighing it against likely market reaction.

FM introduced the BCTT in his 2005 Union Budget speech. To quote,

> I am concerned about large cash transactions, especially withdrawals of cash, when there is no ostensible purpose to withdraw such large amounts of cash. These cash withdrawals leave no trail, and presumably become part of the black economy. Therefore, I propose to introduce two anti tax-evasion measures: Firstly, I propose to levy a tax on withdrawal of cash on a single day of over Rs. 10,000 or more from banks at the rate of 0.1 per cent. Thus, a person withdrawing Rs. 10,000 in cash would have to pay a small sum of Rs. 10. Secondly, I propose to require banks to report to the Government all deposits which are exempt from TDS on interest. I intend to observe the results of these steps before I propose any further measures.

The objective was to control, if not eradicate, hawala transactions that operated presumably through multiple bank transactions by agents who assisted tax evaders to launder money. The tax was levied on all cash withdrawals from scheduled banks exceeding Rs. 10,000 on a single day, as well as on purchase of bank draft by cash, and encashment of term deposits, of the same amount. The mechanism had been agreed to with the banks after FM held an extensive meeting with their chairmen who confirmed that an algorithm could be designed with successful built-in controls on withdrawals.

The Parliament's reaction to BCTT was adverse and immediate, the arguments being various. Firstly, Rs. 10,000 was too small even for small operators to pay wages, leave alone other costs. Second, hawala did not operate through savings accounts; hence there was no need to put any withdrawal limit on them. Third, black money was generated in many ways that the BCTT had not addressed. Media reaction was also strong and wide. I recall an article in *The Economic Times* dated 16 March 2005, with the title, 'BCTT: 0.1% Tax, 100% Hassle', which aptly reflected the pervasive feeling against the tax. I proposed to FM to remove the withdrawal limit from savings accounts and increase the limit from other accounts to Rs 25,000 per day. Further, administratively, to ease and improve compliance, banks should report their daily total cash transactions—rather than submit withdrawals per account—since that would suffice to indicate where cash was being stashed. Eventually BCTT brought in some Rs 600 crores.

The next year, in his 2006 Union Budget speech, FM declared,

> The BCTT has turned out to be a boon, not for the modest revenues it brought which was never its purpose, but for the remarkable trails that it has helped establish. To cite just one example, huge cash withdrawals in a bank branch in Chandni Chowk, noticed through the BCTT, led the Department of Income Tax to three entities which were carrying on the business of purchasing demand drafts from traders at a discount and helping the traders to avoid both sales tax and income tax. These entities would deposit the demand drafts in their own accounts and withdraw the cash. In a period of 18 months, they had laundered Rs. 1,500 crore. BCTT has also helped the Department to detect bogus bills, accommodation entries, artificial loss claims and dummy firms. I propose to continue the BCTT for some more time until the AIR system is able to capture all significant financial transactions.

In his 2007 Union Budget speech, FM justified BCTT further,

> The BCTT continues to be an extremely useful tool to track unaccounted monies and trace their source and destination. It has led the Income Tax Department to many money laundering and hawala transactions. Having regard to the experience gained, I propose to exclude cash withdrawals by the Central and State Governments from the scope of BCTT. Further, I propose to raise the exemption limit for individuals and HUFs from Rs. 25,000 to Rs. 50,000. As other instruments become more effective, I think it would be possible to review BCTT next year.

Thus FM had provided an argument to back him up when he subsequently declared in Parliament that the tax had been successful, had served its purpose, and that he was removing it.

Annals of the Fringe Benefits Tax

The most misunderstood tax in the annals of Indian taxation has perhaps been the Fringe Benefits Tax (FBT). This was the second ill-fated tax in the 2005 Budget. The prevalent belief in the tax department was that while perquisites received by the salaried from their employers were taxable under the Income Tax Act (ITA), there was little reporting by the taxpayer of such perquisites. FM asked me about international experience, and I provided a note on Australia and New Zealand that had used the FBT to revenue benefit. Following that overall model, I worked closely with TPL officers to work out a structure for an FBT. The central idea was to determine a presumptive value of fringe benefits deemed to be provided by the employer. It would include expenses on entertainment; festivals; gifts; clubs; hospitality, food and beverages; guest houses; conferences; health clubs and sports; sales promotion and publicity; conveyance; tour and travel; hotel boarding and lodging; motor cars; fuel; telephones; and scholarships for children. The presumptive value would be 50 percent for the first ten items, 20 percent for the next five, 10 percent for the next item, and 100 percent for the final item. The tax rate to be applied on the truncated value would be the corporate tax rate.

In the 2005 Union Budget speech, FM introduced the tax with the words,

> I have looked into the present system of taxing perquisites and I have found that many perquisites are disguised as fringe benefits, and escape tax. Neither the employer nor the employee pays any tax on these benefits which are certainly of considerable material value. At present, where the benefits are fully attributable to the employee they are taxed in the hands of the employee; that position will continue. In addition, I now propose that where the benefits are usually enjoyed collectively by the employees and cannot be attributed to individual employees, they shall be taxed in the hands of the employer. However, transport services for workers and staff and canteen services in an office or factory will be outside the tax net. The tax is not a new tax, although I am obliged to call it by a new name, namely, Fringe Benefits Tax. The rate will be 30 per cent on an appropriately defined base.

The reaction from trade and industry and the media was immediate and sharp. Reflecting this, FM asked me to meet representatives of the major chambers. Accordingly I, together with the joint secretaries of TPL, met six senior-most technical representatives of the national chambers on 17, 18 and 24 March 2005 for two to three hours each. By and large they claimed that perquisites in the FBT list were legitimate business expenditure, that the proportions proposed were wrong, that there should have been an applicable threshold, and so on. The inclusion of charitable organisations was especially opposed. They asked, if FBT were nevertheless to continue, for a combined return for FBT and the corporate income tax. FM also asked me to visit Mumbai and other places to check the nerve on FBT, which of course I did. After further internal discussions at North Block, we proposed several amendments to make the FBT more acceptable to taxpayers.

There were some critical scholarly articles as well. One claimed that fringe benefits had positive multiplier effects on the economy, hence FBT should be removed. FM asked me to comment on it. On 2 June, I explained in a note the nature of multiplier effects based on Keynesian assumptions based on a demand orientation, as opposed to the neoclassical approach of economic growth based on savings and investments. I explained that the discussion on economic growth and its determinants had moved from the Keynesian basis. Experience had revealed that countries that had blindly followed 'heterodox' policies had found themselves in hyperinflation and collapse of growth. The late 1990's global economic crisis could also be perceived as the outcome of heterodox policies of unbacked loans. Directly on FBT, tax policies should certainly not be too short-term so that they killed economic growth, but the prevailing tax environment did not reflect that. FBT might have cautioned the taxpayer regarding legitimate tax liabilities (of the perquisites portion of the income tax), and the corporations were certain to oppose it. But if we believed in the market, they would either adjust salaries appropriately (of which there was already some evidence) or they would bear it themselves. The FBT's tax incidence was likely to be shared between employee and employer, hopefully, more by the employee. I was gratified when I found on 12 June that FM had marked the note at several places and had written back, "Thanks. Very useful."

I was impressed to occasionally find a positive reaction to FBT. One that politely skirted the matter was an article by Sutradhar in *The Economic Times* dated 20 December 2007. I mention it here because, among the many assessments over the years, it caught the essence of my convictions in taxation matters in the flow of the times; it was accompanied by not too unpleasant a cartoon. As introduction Sutradhar said, among other things, that the "soft-spoken" former IMF official received "liberal encomiums" in Latin America and rendered "much heeded advice" to East Europe. On India, Sutradhar acknowledged my "able tutelage" in introducing the VAT and my "motivational force" in drawing up a roadmap for the GST proposed by a two-member joint Centre-state committee of which I was one. He said that with "Shome in the saddle", tax exemptions were being scaled back and "India now has FBT". Sutradhar mentioned several other components of tax reform we were pursuing, adding that these would not be "put on the backburner if...Shome...continue[s] with the government".

It was happenstance that I left for the UK a fortnight after this article appeared though FM, with PM's full encouragement, had extended my term for another three years through September 2010 (see Plate 13).

The reason for the long sojourn into the FBT is that the tax taught me to realistically assess the unpopularity of a tax even while believing in its efficacy. One challenge might have been the tax administration's demand that the minutest receipt and invoice be maintained on file and produced on demand more often than essential, as reported informally by many in the industry. If that were true, though I have no proof of it, then it revealed the power of a tax administration to vitiate the objective of good tax policy. On the other hand, it was equally probable that commerce and industry would not accept responsibility to pay appropriate tax on perquisites. And the maximum reportage containing significant articles that came across my desk—and do even to this day—were on FBT, enumerating various reasons why the tax was being judged negatively.

FM continued to adhere to his position even after I had left for the UK. When the next Cabinet reshuffle took place with Pranab Mukherjee taking over as finance minister, he called me over to his hotel in London during two visits. He asked me about FBT and I informed him in some detail that, by all accounts it had stabilised and should remain in place. He expressed his doubts given its unpopularity, and we moved on to other polite topics. He also sent an emissary from the Ministry to strongly and insistently reiterate the need to remove

FBT. I politely explained why India needed FBT. He left in a huff from my HMRC suite of offices. FBT was removed in the 2009 Budget, and I heard that the gentleman visitor had moved to Washington as India's representative at a major multilateral. I did not give up. Five years later, as Chairman of the Tax Administration Reform Commission (TARC), I resurrected the idea on the suggestion of some TARC members who had been senior tax officials. I noted that *The Economic Times* appeared to trash the entire report in its editorial. Such are the annals of FBT in India. I remain convinced that FBT is a tax reflective of the maturity of the taxpayer and tax administration, and that when India reaches that juncture, it will naturally embrace an FBT.

Large Taxpayer Units

Soon after I entered North Block, a matter that stood out—not that I had been unaware of it—was the complete separation of direct tax from indirect tax administration, including exchange of information that was crucial for reducing tax evasion. In particular the top brass of the income tax administration was opposed citing confidentiality of data. When I raised the matter at the Board level I encountered polite non-cooperation, to put it mildly. I decided to bring the matter to FM's attention and organised a seminar on large taxpayer units (LTUs) in Kalpavriksh, the seminar room of the Revenue Department. FM was informed that fifty countries already had LTUs where large taxpayers reported both their direct and indirect taxes, and administrators from both sides operated jointly. FM was clearly enthusiastic and, after much give and take with the boards, agreed to introduce them. Thus, in another innovative move in his 2005 Budget speech, he announced his intention to establish LTUs to serve large taxpayers paying excise duty, income tax, corporate tax and service tax under a single window.

In May I proceeded to arrange for two deputy secretaries from the two departments to attend a course on LTUs at the Fund. This by itself was a feat given my earlier experience, when I had been director of the Fund's Singapore institute, of encountering participants from India whose responsibilities did not match the topic of the course. In this instance, the deputy secretaries attended the course in late June and came back fully convinced. They gave another seminar for the seniors. The LTU modus operandi was set out in a detailed Central Board of Direct Taxation (CBDT) memorandum dated 27 July.

However, in my view, there was a strategic error in structuring the LTUs. I recall business and regular papers such as *BusinessLine*, *The Indian Express* and others reporting on the LTUs with fanfare.

The error was in offering an option. In no country was induction into an LTU optional. The idea was simply to direct large taxpayers to a special office where they could discuss and pay all taxes. Whether the tax administration exchanged information should have been an internal matter. In India, large taxpayers—defined as those who paid Rs 10 crore in income tax or Rs 5 crore in service tax—were allowed to opt into the LTU.

As I had anticipated, there was wide variability among large taxpayers in their desire to join or not to join, their overall numbers revealing not even 10 percent of those who qualified as willing to join. Cajoling them became an activity in itself and I had to fly out several times to the five metros where LTUs were planned. On the other side, cooperation from the administration was also slow in coming and different city administrations demonstrated different degrees of interest. While the Bangalore Chief Commissioner was quick to move, another Chief Commissioner told me, after a year, that he had had no time to move on the matter. He retired and moved to a post-retirement post. While in some cities large taxpayers were happy with the LTU, in others some were not and preferred to leave. There had been no explicit provision for exiting the LTU and the administration was tardy about it. Thus it was voluntary to get in, but not to get out. Papers were not slow in reporting dissatisfaction. I was not surprised that after Pranab Mukherjee assumed the finance ministership, by several accounts, LTUs languished.

Travelling through time, a joint committee of CBDT and CBEC was constituted in 2012 to assess LTUs and whether it should be made compulsory. The finding was that while the current LTU assessees were less than 200, those eligible were 4,000, and hence difficult to escalate to the latter in light of the prevailing infrastructure. The argument was of course palpably erroneous since reallocation of resources to the LTU function would obviously have to be carried out and other functions such as routine assessment of all taxpayers slashed. A taxpayer had even approached me indicating his desire to opt into the LTU, but he had been informed that, due to lack of resources, the administration could not take him in. This was a clear negation of the voluntary approach to the LTU. While I attended to this case, it became obvious to me that I should explore the possibility of reviving the LTU when I returned to North Block in 2013. Accordingly I convened a meeting to discuss nagging issues. Realising that I was facing quite a different climate, to put it mildly, than the one I had faced in my earlier sojourn at North Block, I saw that I must now pick my battles carefully. FM had asked me to work on the Direct Tax Code and set up a Tax Forum to solve immediate taxpayer obstacles. I thus decided to return to LTUs at a future opportunity perhaps. That opportunity came a year later as I assumed the chairmanship of TARC.

Automation of the Tax Departments

Among the various activities that FM asked me to take up was the chairmanship of an empowered committee (EC Comp)—that would report directly to FM—for the computerisation of both the tax departments under one umbrella. They included approval of a detailed implementation strategy including choice of technology for proper and speedy implementation; appointment of technical project consultancy for expeditious and effective implementation; approval to request for proposal and tender documents of technical proposals relating to procurement of hardware, software and systems integration, of evaluations of technical bids and short-listing of bidders, of evaluation of commercial bids, and several others to promulgating the readiness of the departments and of trade and industry. Obviously it was a sensitive activity reflecting its size and underlying decisions involved. The committee members included intra- and inter-ministerial officials as well external ones such as Mohandas Pai of Infosys and Kiran Karnik of Nasscom and several others. I felt strongly supported, yet the final responsibilities were mine.

It was clear that computerisation of the tax departments was not a straightforward matter. Huge contracts, tenders and expenditures were involved. In my thinking it was not feasible or rational for government officers to do it. Professional involvement was needed. I was aware of possible accusations of inappropriate leakages from formulation to delivery of large projects. I had witnessed it in my foreign missions too, and putting a stop to large inexplicable project expenditure could be done with a wave of the Fund's wand, which I had used when I had a hunch. India was considerably more complex, and I had to be careful. Accordingly I brought in two types of experts, engineering professors who could give opinions on the technical content of the proposals, and accountants who were to assess the practicality of the proposed finances. This was a good strategy since this reduced the number of project submittals. Even after selection, however, competitors—domestic and highly reputed international IT firms—did not easily accept the decision or shy away. Lobbying did not stop until they were categorically informed that I was not in the habit of meeting clients individually.

Reputation was to be protected at all costs. Throughout my career, in every facet of my life at North Block, I made sure that no client or high industrialist should visit my office or home or meet me in private, despite requests. It was not difficult since a wooden reputation takes hold quickly, and can well be complemented by a smiling face. Given the culture and the environment, I sometimes did wonder if Delhi thought me a fool of sorts, as the whiff that occasionally reached me seemed to imply, but my family example and innate self made it all simple and straightforward. For example, I recall my father's rule not to accept any gifts other than New Year calendars and diaries—that were mainly for distribution to eager recipients—sending away even Diwali sweets from the office room itself. I also recall an uncle visiting me in my office at the Fund and gifting me a bar of Maharani sandalwood soap. He had come to Washington to negotiate an agricultural credit from the World Bank. As he gave me the gift, he elaborated that it was from an uncle, and not from an official of the Indian government. This could be expected in the behaviour pattern of the extended Shome family, and I told him so. Both of us had a good laugh, even as I swallowed my sense of slight irritation. Over the years, I have realised that I too am imprisoned by the same set of unbendable values. While always keeping a smiling face—to the extent that the media would comment that it was a relief to see a smiling face emerging from North Block—I could be characteristically distant if I needed to deflect bothersome flies from around me. I did not shed blood or sweat tears over it. Thankfully, that reputation took hold soon enough.

Since computerisation was already proceeding in the income tax department, understandably there was some reluctance to change course. The indirect tax department was a bit behind, though it turned out to be a blessing in disguise since its Director General Yashodhan Parande was enthusiastic and quick to learn and implement. A. K. Raha, a predecessor, was also innovative, always full of new ideas. This chairmanship obliged me to travel to regional offices of the locations where work was afoot. Endless meetings took place at the Empowered Committee for Computerisation, and I was helped by the subcommittees of engineering professors for technological matters such as earthquake-proofing of buildings and laying of cables, as well as of chartered accountants for financial issues of tendering. At FM's behest, I got involved in a major computer processing centre (CPC) in Bangalore that successfully slashed the time needed for processing returns, and explored possibilities that eventually turned out to be a second major computer centre in Vaishali in the suburbs of Delhi. The CPC was a major success, reflecting public-private partnership (PPP) and, to this day, appears to run efficiently in serving the median taxpayer.

Just before my time, FM had directed CBDT to introduce the Annual Information Return (AIR) on individual taxpayers but to be filed by a list of 'third parties' including banks, credit card companies, mutual funds, companies issuing bonds and debentures, registrar of properties, and the Reserve Bank of India. Accordingly, reportable transactions included, above certain thresholds, cash deposits, credit card payments, purchase of mutual funds, receipt of bonds and debentures of companies, purchase of immovable property, and investment in Reserve Bank of India bonds. However, I found that even towards the end of 2005, less than one thousand AIRs had been filed, and pushed to see what could be done to improve performance from entities required to file AIR. Of course reporting improved, but there were anomalies in the interpretation and application of the AIR. One example was investment in mutual funds which came under AIR for purchase of units above Rs 2 lakh. This was being interpreted by the department in gross terms. Thus if a financial adviser was investing for a retired person by taking funds in and out of a total of Rs I crore, the system was nevertheless picking up only what was put in without accounting for what was taken out. Tax officers were reluctant to alter this interpretation until directed from above. This unnecessarily led to erroneous scrutiny selection and to considerable consternation among honest taxpayers. Speedy correction of mistakes within any tax department is thus terribly important and vital for tax compliance, and for the reputation and confidence that a taxpayer has in it.

Other Matters

There were many other interesting committees and responsibilities that were assigned to me. It is impossible to recall them all, nor is it necessary just for the sake of being comprehensive. But I am tempted to mention a few.

The first one included me as a permanent invitee in the Trade and Economic Relations Committee (TERC) as per an Order from the Prime Minister's Office dated 7 June 2006. TERC members were cabinet ministers, and their secretaries also participated. In our conversations, the PM had emphasised that India's structure of customs tariffs should ideally reflect that of the Association of Southeast Asian Nations (ASEAN) so that India could envisage having free trade with it one day. His inducting me into TERC was perhaps a reflection of that desire for he continued to press the point when we met occasionally. FM also participated in TERC; at the same time I had to write down for the Prime Minister's Office (PMO) the Finance Ministry's views on decisions taken at TERC. Though I had attended many empowered group of ministers meetings that took policy decisions at the sub-cabinet level, participating in TERC was an additional interesting venue for participation at the highest policy level.

The second was FM's asking me to coordinate the work on the Right to Information (RTI) Act for the Finance Ministry. It was possibly a result of my participation in a national colloquium on RTI on 11 December 2005 where other participants included the current and previous Chief Justices, Justices of the Supreme Court, and Nikhil Dey, member of an influential NGO in Rajasthan, who made a presentation on implementation problems arising from difficulties in dismissing corrupt officials and implementers. My presentation covered practical measures to make the RTI Act user-friendly while expressing reservations regarding confidential information from third parties. While work at the Ministry demanded an enormous amount of time both in terms of meetings and carefully reading the views of several branches and interpreting and retaining or culling them, I learnt immensely about the practical constraints on providing information while recognising its need in a maturing democracy.

On a regular basis, there were many ideas and concepts that FM would direct to me upon seeing an article or having conversed with someone. I looked forward to responding to them. I recall an interesting double-pronged matter on the 'sub-prime crisis' and investing fiscal surpluses—possibly he was contemplating that adhering to a strict Fiscal Responsibility and Budget Management (FRBM Act, 2003) path could lead to a fiscal surplus in India, and also that the international sub-prime crisis could lead to reserves and fiscal benefits to India. I informed him of practices in Chile, Saudi Arabia, Singapore and the United States, and specifically Alaska and Norway for oil revenue surpluses. I also emphasised transparency through regular reporting and publication of such funds' earnings, and accountability through audits of accounts, assets and budgetary transfers. Summarising, he wrote back, "Thanks; objectives may be 1) pre-paying public debt; 2) investment in financial assets (to earn returns?); 3) stabilisation fund(s) for primary products; 4) smoothing expenditure. Please hold." There were many such discussions, some of which were of a confidential nature and hence cannot be recounted. Once he said to me, "Partho, you are talking like an economist." I replied, "Sir, I am not an advocate and cannot compete in that sphere. I suppose you brought me here because I *am* an economist." I of course refrained from emphasising that I was reading and interpreting reams of tax law at his behest. FM was always sparse of words. His faint, almost embarrassed smile, reassured me.

Relatedly, I was thrown into the debate on the sub-prime crisis and found myself delivering public lectures in Bangalore, Mumbai and elsewhere essentially along similar lines. On 5 October 2007, I made my point at a Confederation of Indian Industry (CII) Conclave (see Plate 25). I explained that the Indian banks' losses included both first order losses—direct or indirect exposures to the sub-prime mortgage market—and second order losses—arising out of the impact of the banks' exposure to equity investments, but that the losses up to that point had been limited in view of the limited direct exposure of

Indian banks in US mortgage markets. Interestingly, in my address at CII I also anticipated that,

> there would be a surge of liquidity since funds were escaping the combat zones elsewhere for the Indian safe haven.... Managing this hot capital flow was of concern....one policy direction was to allow more funds to be taken out of the country.... (then) there could be a tempering effect on capital flows into the country....the ebb and flow phenomenon of global liquidity would increase the rupee volatility.[5]

The *Hindu BusinessLine* reported on it in detail the following day. One conclusion that was clear to me as 2007 turned into 2008, and 2009, was that India would not need to loosen its fiscal policy to the extent that other economies with more globally integrated financial sectors would need to. Unfortunately, India, too, loosened its fiscal belt, as the fiscal statistics from 2008 would reveal, and the gains made on revenue and fiscal deficit during 2004–07 were on the way to being compromised.

DEPARTURE FROM NORTH BLOCK

In 2006, Her Majesty's Revenue and Customs (HMRC) of the United Kingdom had proceeded to amalgamate its two tax departments—direct and indirect—into one. Dave Hartnett, Permanent Secretary of Revenue, a professional who had held possibly every line function from scratch in the Revenue Department, visited India with a team to see how India had organised its training of tax officials, and if there were any lessons they could learn. No doubt India's training centres at Nagpur for direct tax and Delhi for indirect tax stand out as among the best in an international comparison. I had a long meeting with him and his team in my office during which I recounted all the reform measures India was undertaking in tax structure and administration. Soon after his return, Hartnett called me to ask if I would join HMRC as Chief Economist. I was truly astonished, and asked him why. What he said could be summarised as that he had found me to be effective in inculcating change, and that the UK needed just that during that challenging moment of amalgamation. He indicated that I should go for three years, and that it should suffice.

I was torn between two directions. I dilly dallied, and calls from Hartnett's office became more frequent. On the one hand, I did not perceive how I could possibly leave North Block so soon after I had been given an extension, and while I was in the midst of so much activity including the beginning of preparing for a GST. On the other hand, I knew that being embedded in the British bureaucracy—in particular in the Revenue Department—was too unique an opportunity to be missed. I was told that Alistair Darling, UK Chancellor of the Exchequer, proposed and received approval for my appointment from the Cabinet, but that UK had to justify at the European Union as to why a European had not been identified for the post, though I never came to know the veracity of these nuggets of information. My experience would be enormous, I told myself, and I felt great satisfaction that the HMRC, known as a high-nosed institution, was inviting a complete foreigner to be one of them. It was also an acid test of sorts, for India had never embedded me in its bureaucracy.

I finally decided to join HMRC, and informed FM on 30 November 2007. He was not expecting it, and asked me to meet the PM about the matter. I did. Dr. Manmohan Singh expressed his unhappiness and asked me to join him for lunch on 13 December 2007. When I came out of his office and informed Subrahmaniam, his Joint Secretary, about the lunch, he was surprised and told me that the PM liked to have lunch with his family. I requested him to check, for I might have misheard. He ran in and returned to confirm that the PM would indeed have lunch with me. A formal invitation followed for 13 December. We had a longish lunch, perhaps spending an hour one on one. The menu was perfect. Dr. Singh expressed in soft terms what he thought about my contributions, and that I should stay. I already knew and had always felt a strong support from him regarding my work, and I need not, and should not, go into detail here. I perceived that he became a little agitated when he said he would call UK Prime Minister Gordon Brown to say that his tax adviser should remain in India. I requested him not to do so, and that my action did not behove one PM calling another. I reassured him that I would return. Gauging my determination, he became cordial and friendly, switching to questions about my intended work at HMRC and congratulating me that I would work in Whitehall, indicating he was pleased that an Indian would be placed at such a high position there, and added that I must return to India. I promised that I would. I left a bit sheepishly, impressed as always by his cordial personality. The notification of my departure was issued on 24 December 2007 and I completed my term on 10 January 2008. I joined HMRC on 13 January 2008, immediately after the weekend in between.

ANNEXE

Interview with Anjuli Bhargava, *Business Standard*, 20 November 2007[6]

His extensive travels have sharpened the FM's advisor's views on not just India's bureaucracy, but on even its new breed of writers and art collectors. This may sound incredible but when advisor to the finance minister, Parthasarathi Shome, first heard the word as a 17-year-old, he asked, "What is economics?" The answer he got from his brother-in-law was, "Oh, it's somewhere between physics and anthropology." Shome was then enrolled at the Presidency College in Calcutta to study physics, a subject he found 'dry' after his father gently persuaded him that anthropology, his personal choice, may not make the best of careers. Four decades later, Shome concedes that things probably worked out for the best. He went on to top his university and proceeded on scholarship to the US and the rest, as they say, is history, writes Anjuli Bhargava.

...Brought up by a father who firmly believed that travel is the best education, he has stayed at innumerable 'dak bungalows' and 'circuit houses' in India. Partho...has visited (many) countries, around 40 of them on work...His personal favourites are Norway and New Zealand, the former for its snow—as opposed to water—falls, and the latter for its ability to encapsulate and deliver every possible natural formation in a drive from the north to the south.

On an emotional plane, Latin America tops his list. Work for the IMF took him there time and again for long periods. He has some close friends there and speaks Spanish like a native. Although he's spent most of his professional life overseas (he's been in India 30 years and overseas for 27), he can't seem to shed his father's only request to him: that he serve the country. This is his third assignment at the request of the Indian government. One of his former bosses at the IMF hit the nail on the head and said at his farewell, "I think Partho is happiest when he's on top of the Atlantic."

Travel has also embedded in him a love for art...walking through a museum or viewing an exhibition...his weakness is naïve art, of which he has a small collection gathered from places as far flung as Haiti, Brazil, Ecuador, Peru or interior parts of Africa.[7]

...our conversation moves...to not so happy issues like India's poverty and problems. Growing up in Calcutta during those days, he couldn't help but be infected by some Marxist ideas and even today thinks the Marxists have their heart in the right place; it's only their solutions he doesn't buy. "You can't keep redistributing an ungrowing pie," he says. He likes the Scandinavian country models where a largely socialist system is followed after growth has occurred. Yet, he's conscious that in India's case, it's far more complex: India, unlike those countries, is not small or homogeneous. Here it's about redistributing both from the rich to the poor and from one region to the other. That redistribution, he argues, is critical.

"The inclusiveness of growth is more important than growth itself," he believes. Poverty is a shame, the widening gap in incomes is "frightening" and "300 million of us have overwhelmed the consideration of 750 million others".[8]...It's never too late. If we are "ruthless about accountability" and the judiciary takes on the role of monitoring, there is hope, he says.

...I quickly ask him whether he's as baffled by his colleagues in the ministry as they are by him.

I have clearly hit a tender spot. He sits up straighter, slams his hand on the table and proceeds to dig his teeth into the Indian bureaucrat. Nothing personal here but he's convinced that the "bureaucracy simply must change!" Its approach is too rudimentary, it needs to specialise ("you can't do housing one day, animal husbandry the next, and move on to whatever's the third, and be good at it all, it's not done anywhere in the world"), it has too many perceived systemic interests and no firm beliefs! Even in tiny Uruguay and Costa Rica, specialist lawyers negotiate for the country....In several countries, he's offered suggestions to the bureaucracy, and many of them, "despite the apparent impracticality," have been carried out to the country's greater benefit. The premier service of the Indian bureaucracy seems opposed to change, and change we must.

What, I ask, does he see as his main achievements during his stint in the ministry and what constitutes his unfinished agenda (his three-year (sic) term was smilingly yet determinedly extended by the finance minister to six (sic)). He visibly relaxes as he moves to a topic close to his heart: taxes. The reforms of the last three years, he says, have helped fundamentally change the basis for participation in tax payment. The taxpayer base (as opposed to the tax base) has expanded significantly and some sense has been brought into scrutiny procedures. The reforms are less visible to the public eye but will eventually lead to a simpler system for paying taxes. "We have given the tax administrator new and proper instruments to carry out (his) task, rather than just harass," he explains. State-level VAT and the Centre's large taxpayer units are other areas where he's been able to give his inputs.

On his agenda remain the committee report on the goods and services tax (GST) and its introduction (I point out that two years may be too little to introduce the GST; he lets it pass), the new income tax code, where he is partly involved, and computerisation of the tax departments. I exclaim that ever since I have been meeting him, he's been talking about this...it must be harder than it sounds. He explains that in the government, nothing is particularly easy, especially where tenders are involved. I guess we all know what that means.

...I ask him about some of his other interests, apart from travel and art. Well, he is into photography, and swims at the Delhi Gymkhana. A voracious reader, who grew up on Sarat Chandra and Rabindranath Tagore, he has a strange aversion to the Bengali writers of today ("Jhumpa Lahiri is insipid, Amitav Ghosh...anyone can write *Calcutta Chromosome*"). Vikram Seth is contrived. He dislikes Rushdie with a passion ("atrocious and grotesque"), but loves Arundhuti Roy's single creation with an equal passion (and Rohinton Mistry, sic.).

As we part, I ask him if his desk is any neater, my mind picturing the numerous times I've thought his room was unoccupied, so well hidden was he behind the mountain of files on his desk. "A bit, a bit. I'm a bit more in control now," he offers. The computerisation of the income tax department may or may not happen but, by the end of his stay, I think he'll crack this.

ENDNOTES

1. Letter from P. Chidambaram to Anne Krueger, First Deputy Managing Director, IMF, 1 August 2004, as shared with Parthasarathi Shome (author's personal correspondence).

2. Author's personal correspondence.

3. Sunil Jain, 'Lunch with BS: Parthasarathy Shome, "Democrazy" and other taxes', *Business Standard*, 21 March 2006, New Delhi.

4. Ibid.

5. Parthasarathi Shome's address to Confederation of Indian Industry Conclave, 5 October 2007.

6. Anjuli Bhargava, 'Lunch with BS: Parthasarathi Shome, On Top of the Atlantic', *Business Standard*, 20 November 2007, New Delhi.

7. Years later, in 2014, I produced *Naïve Art: Ode to the Unknown Artist*, a coffee-table volume, as a gift to my ninety-year old artist mother.

8. I continue to write on the matter even a decade later in my monthly column in the *Business Standard*. For example, see, 'Income distribution—Recent developments,' *Business Standard*, 17 October 2018, where it is argued that income distribution has not essentially improved.

EIGHT

HER MAJESTY'S REVENUE AND CUSTOMS

Before I sat down to write this chapter I pondered the matter of writing about my experiences at Her Majesty's Revenue and Customs for, after my return to India, I had covered the professional content of it in some detail in my 2012 volume, *Tax Shastra: Administrative Reforms in India, United Kingdom and Brazil,* (BS Books, *Business Standard*). I decided to try and not be repetitive in my account here, and to jog my memory on matters I had left out earlier. When I reflected on what my state of mind was at the time, I looked at an interview I had given to Shrabani Basu of *The Telegraph*, Kolkata, who was then resident in London, and is now an established author of historical novels. The interview took place in my HMRC office. I should indicate that *Financial Times*, London, had also inquired through HMRC's information office whether I would be ready to give them an interview as the news of an Indian Chief Economist at HMRC had obviously reached them. I judged that there was scant internal interest that I should do so, though I was not forbidden. I nevertheless declined them, but agreed to *The Telegraph*; that would be in the context of the Indian environment. I realised how sensitive my appointment was when, interestingly, I found an HMRC officer in the background right through that interview. I, therefore, start with relevant excerpts that perhaps reveal quite well what was going through my mind.

INITIAL STATE OF MIND

My initial state of mind, in the context of my background, was revealed in a tête-à-tête with Shrabani Basu barely three weeks after I joined

HMRC. The interview[1], first published in *The Telegraph*, Sunday, 17 February 2008, said I was the first Indian to be appointed to a senior post in the British government, and that Mr. Chidambaram had asked me if it was as prestigious as what I was doing in India. Prime Minister Manmohan Singh, who had taught me at Delhi School of Economics, needed a lot more persuasion to allow me to resign, it reported, but that I had finally managed to persuade him to let me go. Basu described aptly that, after three years in "his Pandara Park house in Lutyens's Delhi...ferried to work in an office car, Shome is... getting used to...the walking" and that I was enjoying my long walks immensely.

We sat in my suite in the HMRC building on Parliament Street, a few yards from 10 Downing Street and the Houses of Parliament. The pre-appointed offices in the UK are stark and functional, the interviewer noted. The HMRC's press officer sat in, taking notes. Basu observed that, despite my appointment being a sensitive one, even needing a special waiver from the UK Public Service Commission, I "looked very much at home".

Basu gave me credit for my roles at the IMF and NIPFP, and then for being "plucked out" by Mr. Chidambaram in 2004 to be his adviser, in which role, "Shome oversaw three budgets...value added tax and... steered...simplification of the tax process. His resignation...fuelled media speculation that he was fed up of bureaucrats...something Shome denies".

Basu was kind to report that I said this has been "misrepresented" and that, "...I come from a family of bureaucrats...worked with bureaucrats in several countries...however, specialisation is of great importance", and bringing in people "from the private sector...allows for dynamism...(in) public/private partnership." On working with P. Chidambaram, a man who can lose his cool and does not suffer fools gladly, she said Shome was diplomatic: "I worked with him closely for three years and never had a problem."

I had interacted with public finance chiefs of the UK Government, in particular, Dave Hartnett, Permanent Secretary, which led to my joining HMRC after more than three years at North Block, Basu reported. She mentioned that I had been identified as a "thought leader"...overseeing (research in) a specialised cell called Knowledge, Analysis and Intelligence (KAI), the centre for intellectual activity handling policy analysis for the UK Treasury.

After traversing my education years, Basu described how I had crisscrossed South America from Venezuela to Chile and that, barring two countries—Honduras and EL Salvador—I had worked in every country in South America to help their governments overhaul their tax structures and get the economy back on track. She commented on my fluency in Spanish, my collection of South American naïve art, and, among other attributes, Brazil awarding me the equivalent of a knighthood. In Latin America, she said, "the soft-spoken Bengali was a hero....Latin America was where his heart lay."

Extolling the man "whose handling of failing economies in developing countries is legend," when Basu asked me what I would do in the UK, I brightened up as if to say that the British tax structure also needed assistance. She emphasised that my mantra was simplicity which brought friendliness and accessibility, and concluded that, "India's loss may well be Britain's gain".[2]

ASSIMILATION INTO HMRC

On joining HMRC on 13 January 2008 as Chief Economist, I realised that I had been embedded fully in the UK Senior Civil Service (SCS Level 2) at a level just below that of Dave Hartnett, Permanent Secretary Tax. I felt a whiff of one-upmanship over India's civil service that had kept me away, had it not been for the political leadership that had offered me secretary-level positions. Now in London, Dave immediately welcomed me. Soon I also experienced the warm welcome of Gus O'Donnell, Cabinet Secretary. And I was sent off to a three-day workshop for the SCS for those who joined at the highest levels, and this preparation was immensely helpful in the three years to follow. To my amusement, it also included a lesson in how to deal with the political class. I also became a member of the exclusive board of chief economists. Interestingly, every ministry had a chief economist though in smaller ministries the rank was more junior while the title was the same. We all sat at a round table every few months to discuss an economic matter in the form of a presentation by one member, and discussed a plethora of economic challenges facing the UK at the moment. It was a crucible for learning current economic affairs even though, pretty soon, I too had to make a presentation on the UK's tax structure, likely revenue projections and recommended reforms. It was quite different from the committee of secretaries (COS) in India that was chaired by the cabinet secretary and comprised secretaries of the ministries. There was always a long official agenda to be covered and it appeared to me that the discussions were usually administrative at best and bureaucratic at worst, and occasionally an apology for a particular ministry's fiscal performance. The UK model was quite different.

HMRC was undergoing a great churning, to the extent that a department entitled 'Change' had been created. Often senior officials would go to an 'away day' where all manner of possible changes and reform would be discussed. I routinely made presentations reflecting my international experience, for Dave was never discomfited when I pointed out that a huge bureaucracy such as HMRC could learn a few lessons from emerging economies. I must say I was usually bold, probably because of, or despite, which I came to be called a 'thought leader' by the Treasurer in one of his presentations. I felt I was perceived as a senior official who turned out to be open-minded, and I felt that I could get across without too much resistance.

As this reputation grew, I was invited to make presentations in internal conferences and seminars. One that I recall well was organised by the office of the Financial Controller on 23 November 2009, on supporting business delivery, by which was meant delivery of HMRC business responsibility. I made a presentation on the effect of the credit crunch on HMRC work, for which I received the appreciation of Jon Fundrey, the Controller; it was subsequently uploaded on their Finance website. Some experiences were delightful. One such was a talk I gave to the alumni of Murray Edwards College on 14 November 2008, where the audience comprised clearly upper class, professional women. They heard me with rapt attention, and I received a thank you from Juliet Barfield, saying, "Our alumni thoroughly enjoyed your stimulating talk, which gave us a lot to think about. I for one was dying to ask many questions which time would not allow. Many thanks indeed. Best wishes." This was one example of the appreciation I continued to receive from audiences when I spoke.

I was located in Knowledge, Analysis and Intelligence (KAI) that comprised some four hundred economists, statisticians, lawyers, operations researchers and sociologists, all working cohesively in the tax formulation area. I had regular meetings with groups of them to apprise myself and give direction in technical aspects. They were highly qualified brilliant young officers. The field departments accessed KAI when they wanted to apply a particular knowledge in the field to improve their revenue intake, sometimes by solving a mystery as to what was occurring that stagnated performance. The time that KAI would need was charted in an internal time flow chart against which staff hours were allotted to check on any staff redundancy at the end of the year. I oversaw many such exercises that were conducted at the highest professional level. The same pattern was followed for the annual budget preparations and for every tax policy change—there could be one hundred and fifty of them or even higher—a detailed impact assessment statement (IAS) was prepared in a pre-determined template. The chief economist was the final signatory on the IAS as being responsible for 'quality assurance'. I possibly signed 10 percent—the most important ones—leaving the rest to my juniors. The IAS left an excellent impression on me regarding a policy change itself and its ramifications on multiple sectors of the economy and society. The signed document went to the revenue minister and was made available to Parliament.

HMRC Administrative Structure

Executive Committee

There was, however, an Executive Committee (ExCom) that was empowered to take executive decisions for the HMRC. My first realisation was that it contained few tax specialists who were one step below as department heads. In the ExCom, managers from external ministries or the private sectors had been brought in, with Dave Hartnett as an exception. I found this rather odd. The reason I mention this here is that I have always believed in specialised professions for sharp and correct decision-making, mentioning this on various occasions in India as well. In most countries that I have experienced, public bureaucracy has become quite specialised; thus the composition of the ExCom did surprise me. I myself made a technical presentation at the ExCom every so many months which had an element of bravado in its genesis.

In the UK, the HMRC or tax administration department was separated from the Treasury (TRE) or finance ministry. TRE was in charge of analysing trends and projecting revenue. I found that HMRC basically accepted this and benchmarked its revenue effort against it. As Chief Economist of HMRC, I assessed it to be my role to check on this. I found, when I took some eleven other independent projectors, that the latter's projections were invariably more conservative, sometimes significantly so. I asked a few of the KAI economists to do our own projections to crosscheck what was going on. My earlier observations were confirmed. I informed ExCom that HMRC was working with revenue projections that were too high, and that the calculated tax gap—the revenue falling short of collection—was too large. There were eyebrows raised as to how, rather, why HMRC should raise any doubts over TRE's projections. From what I gathered, expectedly, this did not go smoothly with TRE. But I had my numbers.

Staff Support

The VAT gap calculation was extremely detailed, depending on information at the micro level, and detailed to me by Mick Thackray, a brilliant statistician—but the benchmarking obviously had to be corrected. HMRC began to use my intermittent projections against the tax gap, in particular as the effort to minimise it comprised a social contract, so to speak, with Parliament. I could feel from time to time the discomfort that I generated on matters such as this, but Dave had explained clearly to me in my conversations with him from India as to what my expected role would be, and these fitted perfectly into it. Moreover he gave my work such solid support in our one-on-one meetings that I never felt intimidated. Anyway that is not in my nature. Yes I am willing to concede a point when convinced, but not under duress.

Such exercises were aplenty. My successes would have been impossible without the support of my Adviser Jon Franklin, who organised regular meetings with the multiple groups formed of the large staff, the size of which I had never supervised before. He was also excellent at summing up long technical meetings in a nutshell. He completed his Master's at Birkbeck College, University of London, no easy task in itself, but doing it while working with me without the slightest demur did impress me. Another young economist working on very innovative, almost created, areas was Jack Grigg who sought me out for time whenever he had some new idea. I always encouraged him for his fertile mind, despite occasionally hearing amused critiques from his immediate superiors. There is no space to elaborate on the numerous exercises that I supervised but I must mention that it was at HMRC that I first encountered issues in international taxation, and was briefed by another brilliant officer on a tax authority view and analysis of the Vodafone issue. At the first opportunities, I recommended Mick and Jack to the Fund's FAD which absorbed them, and later accounts from my ex-colleagues there were fantastic. No doubt Jon would also have fitted in very well at the Fund, but he was not yet ready to move at that time for personal reasons. There were so many other sharp tax officers with whom I had the pleasure of working; unfortunately it is not possible to mention them all, but let it be said that I had never come across so many bright, budding tax experts under one roof anywhere.

Stakeholder Interaction

One impressive practice was the continuing series of stakeholder meetings that were conducted by tax officers at different levels. I attended several of them to learn how they were conducted so that I could bring back that practice to India where they intensified exclusively prior to the Union Budget. The apex level stakeholder group to which Alistair Darling, Chancellor—finance minister—inducted me was the Forum for Business Taxation and Challenges of Globalisation, in which high tax officials and chief financial officers of large multinational corporations and chambers representing various sectors had the opportunity to discuss business, economic, and tax matters of the day. But they were certainly not as rambunctious as the ones that I chaired on my return to India and that I shall mention in a later chapter.

RESEARCH COMPONENTS

Research with Academia

Research has of course been of great interest to me throughout my professional life, whether in academia, at the Fund, in India in research organisations, or in government. From HMRC, I had the occasion to attend a research conference at the US Internal Revenue

Service (IRS). Several of the papers presented had been jointly produced by university professors and IRS officers. Luckily a couple of the deputies of KAI had also come along to the IRS conference; thus when we returned, I pressed for the idea of joint academia-tax official research. Thus far at HMRC, I had organised several academic lectures by outsiders on various topics in the area of taxation, which were usually held in the historic Churchill Room from whose balcony Britain's prime minister had declared victory in the Second World War, refraining from any analysis of the man. The lectures were always well attended, revealing the staff interest in research and research findings.

At the time, a massive research project on UK tax reform, the *Mirrlees Review*, was being undertaken by academia from exclusive universities. I represented HMRC but soon I realised that the papers, though of superior quality, would carry little weight within a tax administration. Nothing came of it in terms of actual policy, though I heard that it has been published as a volume. This was unlike the Meade report half a century back that did have an impact on trade and tax reform. Dave Hartnett also set up an international academic expert committee with perhaps eight tax experts from Australia, UK, US, and a couple of HMRC and TRE officials including myself, to examine tax reform in the context of the spreading global economic crisis. That also folded up after a relatively short life span for reasons primarily, in my assessment, of divergent policy views.

On my suggestion of joint research between academia and officers, some of the staff expressed doubt. I heard comments about the possible breach of confidentiality of data and I argued back that, if the US could do it, so could the UK. Jonathan Gillham was another brilliant economist who had developed a complex computable general equilibrium (CGE) model of the UK economy incorporating all manner of taxes into it so that the model was amenable to the analysis of any exogenous tax shock for the entire economy. Gillham took charge of the responsibility of setting up a laboratory of encrypted data within HMRC premises where academics could visit and carry out data modelling and analysis by mining the data generated by HMRC. There could also be useful public-private cooperation in conducting joint research. The laboratory took a few years to get going, and sometimes it seemed like we were going through an endless series of meetings, but when it finally did get going, it did so solidly.

International Research Conference

I also broached the idea of an international research conference at HMRC like at the IRS. Of course there was a lot of foot dragging in terms of the financial and staff resources it would capture. I argued that, for a start, we could do so with meagre resources and that in any event most papers would be from external academic and tax administration researchers. When I proposed it to Dave, he welcomed it, and the path to the conference was cleared. With my stiff upper lip, I had not organised even a single dinner or lunch for the participants. Dave asked me jocularly where I was planning to take the participants for a meal, and I said, "To McDonald's, out of my own pocket". He stared at me in what seemed like genuine disbelief, and immediately allocated financing for a decent meal. The conference was inaugurated by Stephen Timms, Financial Secretary (Revenue Minister) who gave a clear and thought-provoking speech on the UK economy. I usually dealt with him when called on taxation matters, and found him to be polite and open to listening. I also learnt that he had held several portfolios in previous governments, and though he was younger than Mr. Pant, he somehow reminded me of him in approach and style. In other words, Mr. Timms was easy to work with.

The two-day conference on 'Institutional Taxation Analysis', held on 21–22 September 2009, was a great success, with participants from the governments of Canada, India, UK, academia from Canada, India, Singapore, UK—Exeter, Kent, Oxford, Sussex—and several research organisations, and the tax profession. Two of my former junior colleagues from the Fund—now chiefs in tax administration—also made presentations. The sessions included time series regression on individual tax compliance, tax compliance by firms and audit policy, tax evasion, VAT Gap estimation in the UK, application of behavioural economics to policy making, evidence from microdata of the impact of a climate change levy on business, taxation and development, and several others. A band of top-notch HMRC research officers working with me manned the sessions with their own presentations or as discussants and chairs. For me it was like a dream come true. Nevertheless, I felt that in a bureaucracy such as the HMRC where financial resources were carefully accounted for through internal time and cash flow charts, even though I had organised the conference with small resources, it might get lost in the history of the institution.

Yet, by the end of November, an Institutional Tax Analysis Network was being set up with partnership with the Economic and Social Research Council (ESRC), the top research organising and funding agency of the UK government. After my return to India, using the by now predictable UK style, I received an email for registration—rather than an invitation—to the next HMRC international tax analysis conference. I noted that, and hoped that KAI would hold the conference every year and that research would also pick up through the encrypted laboratory.

While I was in HMRC, one thing that did not stop was the flow of invitations to international conferences. The variety of locale and focus was immense and I can only cite a few. The first one was the Annual General Assembly of the Centre for Inter-American Tax Administrators (CIAT) during April 20–23, 2009, in Santo Domingo, Dominican Republic, where I spoke on the challenges in modernising tax administrations. I had been quite familiar with the growing importance and influence of CIAT whose membership had spread across the globe and whose assemblies were heavily attended. Vito had sent me there as the keynote speaker at CIAT's twenty-fifth Assembly, a grand affair held in Montego Bay, Jamaica, in June 1992. That speech detailed a Latin American perspective on the trends and future direction in tax policy reform in which I statistically compared how countries in the region moved in step with one another in their tax policy changes and what should comprise the correct reform path for the future. I was Chief of Tax Policy at the Fund but relatively young; I had been aware that I could not obviously or easily influence or impress well-heeled tax administrators from across the world. Thus when I saw participants standing up to clap, I was deeply moved. It was also the beginning of a professional relationship with Mr. Hammeker of the International Bureau of Fiscal Documentation (IBFD), another well-recognised organisation based in Amsterdam with excellent library facilities, who was the repertoire for the conference. He invited me to come and spend a year at IBFD to do research at their cost, though, unfortunately, it never materialised.

Returning to 2009, I knew that after all these years my talk would go well, and it did. After all, I was also Chief Economist of HMRC. But there were a couple of snippets that were interesting and have remained with me. First, I recall that the Canadian Commissioner—the top tax official of Canada—told me during a chat that border wars could be fought not just with guns, and cited his perennial frustration with information exchange with the US. Recently, in the context of the OECD's project on tax base erosion and profit shifting (BEPS) on the means to contain multinational tax avoidance, in which inter-country exchange of MNC information is crucial, that discussion comes rushing back. I am certain that would remain a pivotal concern in the success of BEPS. The second was amusing and frustrating at the same time. There was a Chinese delegation of five, as is the case in most international fora. I had negotiated India's membership at no financial cost and the reputation factor had solved it. However, sitting at HMRC, I could not convince the relevant officer in India to join the conference, and India went unrepresented. In any event, the head of the Chinese delegation cordially requested a breakfast meeting on the tax administrations of India and UK. Accordingly we met the next day at breakfast and I briefed them on technical issues, of course taking care not to divulge any confidential or official matter. I also informed them of my familiarity with the Chinese tax system. We fixed a meeting for the next morning during which they were supposed to update me on latest developments in tax policy in China. They never showed up. On reflection, this was a behaviour pattern of the Chinese that I had encountered from my days at NIPFP when Chinese officials would be hosted to take courses in public finance, and would remain tight-lipped even about ordinary matters of China. And this pattern had continued. In my later columns, I have cautioned India about this attitude and approach of China. I concluded that, from the era around the reign of Chandragupta II, when Chinese pilgrims Fa Xian and Xuan Zang took back Buddhism from ancient Bengal, their approach has remained steadfast.

Another interesting conference was held in Bogota, Colombia, by the municipal research wing on 10 December 2009. What I found interesting was the advanced nature of contemplation of the urban officials and their eagerness to remain prepared for exigencies. Usually in Latin America any conference would elicit the presence of fellow Latin Americans from neighbouring countries. Thus there were officials from Argentina, Brazil, Chile and Mexico, all animatedly discussing new ideas and concepts. I contributed ideas on urban taxation, fees and charges including carbon tax and market-based instruments that caught their attention. Not the least, it gave me a rare opportunity to view and participate among the urban sector of Colombia, for earlier I had such an opportunity only in Sao Paolo, Brazil and Mexico City. I also accepted an invitation from the Inland Revenue Authority of Singapore, possibly to no small extent to revisit the place I had come to know quite well and appreciate for almost three years in the early 2000s.

The last, quite a different one, was a day of brainstorming organised by Shell in a French Chateau during 29–30 March 2010. I found it interesting that it focussed entirely on the future or the 2020 landscape of taxation, again for the readiness expected of an MNC of global stature. We covered the philosophical and economic outlook of the corporate tax world—the roles of countries and multilateral organisations—how prevailing tax instruments aligned with a possible future landscape, a forward look at corporate tax and tax mix, and which tax instruments could service future requirements. I found it impressive that, though it was a very small group of a dozen participants in all, they included officials from the EU, OECD, UN, US Treasury, UK HMRC (myself), Chinese tax administration, a Swedish tax expert, and a philosopher-economist. The reason I mention this small gathering is that it may be time to have such small gatherings in the light of the vastly different and possibly unanticipated global tax environment that currently prevails.

Peripatetic Visits to the Field

Returning to the bread and butter dimension so to speak, an important element of my work at HMRC comprised immersive visits to field offices. Hugh McGillivray, a superior income tax officer, was delegated to me and we scoured the length and breadth of UK, visiting seventeen offices that conducted a wide range of functions. I recall that in the tenth standard, I had learnt about Dundee producing great jam, and Aberdeen on the coast of north Scotland being the witness to the swim routes of fourteen different kinds of fishes. I had learnt about the Roman conquest of Britain and about Queen Bodicea's revolt and capture that had reminded me of our Rani of Jhansi. And of course about Stonehenge of ancient Britain, UK's cotton and steel production that had been possible on the shoulders of Indian raw materials and the near ban of Indian production through prohibitive customs tariffs through the meticulous recommendations of successive tariff commissions. We travelled through all those geographically and historically significant areas. Though now I was focussed entirely on tax policy and tax administration in the field, those early lessons did not abandon me. I brought those associations to Hugh's notice as we drove, and he appeared to smile knowingly. He was, after all, originally from Scotland.

What I learnt and recommended from those visits has been covered and presented in great detail in my *Tax Shastra* and I shall not repeat it here. What I might add is that a rather voluminous report emerged from those visits that contained many recommendations for UK's tax administration reform. That report became an agenda for ExCom, and I made a comprehensive presentation of it. There was genuine appreciation and recognition of problem areas and the need for reform. Of course reform takes its own path and speed, but the UK had already demonstrated nerves of steel in amalgamating the direct and indirect tax departments, which was a crucial reason for my accepting the job in assisting the amalgamated department to move forward. This report was my administrative contribution to that process.

I end with a vignette. I recall that at the presentation of the report, I asked that Hugh sit next to me at the ExCom table and, though the suggestion was immediately accepted, I could see some of the members shift a bit in their chairs, as if this was yet another accommodation that had to be made for this idiosyncratic chief economist. I confess I was content, but also wondered what would have happened if I asked for the same in a meeting in Kalpavriksh in North Block. I remember that in the Q&A session after a lecture I gave to incoming customs and excise officers, I told them it was more important to do one's job with respect and integrity, and that there was no need to call every superior Sir or Madam. There was pin drop silence from the front row of senior officials while, from the subsequent rows of recruits, I could hear guffaws if not thunderous applause. I challenge the Indian bureaucracy to move to first names.

The Ambiance

I should not have implied that everything was smooth and that my path was laden with rose petals at HMRC. After all, I was an alien that had suddenly landed in the lap of an advanced bureaucracy albeit in the throes of colossal change. The top officials were by and large welcoming though some were cautious. Among the deputies across departments, I perceived some were positive in outlook, and others doubtful. It was obvious there was some resentment that a complete outsider had come to occupy such a high position. But I never gave it much importance since the few superiors I had buttressed me through their clearly expressed confidence. The problem was that I also identified quite a lot of dead wood as I encountered these officials and was surprised that they continued ensconced in good positions in the British bureaucracy. Soon, however, I told myself that administration was not my responsibility, for which there were others. I, therefore, steered clear of this thorn on the way and proceeded with work by charting my own course.

Towards the end of my tenure at HMRC, I recall having a meeting with Pranab Mukherjee on 8 November in his London hotel suite regarding my return to India and on Indian tax issues. Earlier, during two visits to Delhi, I had presented two seminars organised by the Department of Economic Affairs at North Block both of which Mr. Mukherjee had attended. I noted and appreciated his saying, "Brilliant!" during the seminars and his lingering there for the entire duration which, I was informed, was not his usual practice. I was also amused to learn that there were some alarm bells that I might return there. Indeed, in London some possibilities about my going back to North Block were discussed though, in my heart of hearts, I preferred to return to full time research, perhaps on my own.

One thing was certain in my mind. Having experienced the two ensconced bureaucracies of the world—India and the UK—I had decided that, upon return to India, I would steep myself in research rather than take on a bureaucracy for a third time. Just after I had accepted the position at HMRC, DSE had offered me a professorship. But it had been too late for me to consider. I pondered my next location. Who could, however, predict fate or destiny? It was serendipity that Isher Ahluwalia called me to say that she was passing through London and requested that I meet her. She told me that ICRIER was urgently in need of an administrative head and, since she had just heard that I would be returning to India, whether I could take over ICRIER as its Chief Executive and Director. I responded that I would frankly like to conduct research and writing rather than administering another organisation. She pressed on to ask that I should join at least for a short term. As before, ultimately I could not decline her earnest plea and agreed.

In retrospect, apart from the feather in the cap for the recognition and honour it brought me, was the HMRC a good and useful experience, I ask myself. As I float over it in the swimming pool and look up at the sunlit sky and plough through my thoughts, I feel, through thick and thin, it was a unique experience indeed, one fully reflective of adventure. But I was ready to return to India. As I re-read a few of my interviews, I found one with Kanika Datta of *Business Standard* of 9 November 2010, just a couple of months prior to my return which gives a flavour of my thoughts and that state of mind. I end the chapter with excerpts.

'Return of the Taxman'[3]

The former advisor to P. Chidambaram explains why he is substituting the urban delights of London for the maddening drawbacks of Delhi.... Shome is better known to the public as the man who introduced controversial taxes under P. Chidambaram's finance ministership—the Banking Cash Transaction (BCTT) and Fringe Benefits (FBT) taxes—apart from setting the course for the reform of the indirect tax regime with the Goods and Services Tax (GST). Both FBT and BCTT have been scrapped in his absence and he is emphatically not happy—he explains why at technical length over our meal.

In 2008, Shome left his advisor's role three (sic) years before his second contract ended—and amid much speculation—for an assignment as Chief Economist of Her Majesty's Revenue and Customs in the UK. Now, with that three-year contract over, he's due back to head the influential think tank Indian Council for Research on International Economic Relations (ICRIER) from January.

He's...familiarising himself with his forthcoming responsibilities. The frequent travel doesn't faze him, nor does the prospect of relocating across continents. "Since 1995, I have moved, inter-continentally, lock, stock and barrel, seven or eight times," he tells me cheerfully. Indeed, through the course of his career, he's travelled to (many) countries and he plans to make Bhutan his (next).

... we were discussing music and his early education in Kolkata (Hindi High School) and Chennai (Don Bosco). Later at Delhi School of Economics, he was taught international finance by current Prime Minister Manmohan Singh. Was he a good teacher—and I encourage him not to say yes only for the record. Shome thinks he was one of the "three best teachers"—K L Krishna (econometrics) and A L Nagar (statistics) being the other two.

...Shome talks about his PhD in the US and how he gave up a full professorship at the American University in Washington...for the International Monetary Fund (IMF). His decision in favour of the latter was the result of a "streak of adventurism". "I felt like a novice in the IMF whereas at the university I was a Young Turk. But I realise that I plunge into adventure—if there's an opportunity to do something new I don't say no to it."

On his decision to go to the UK, I say there were two explanations for his sudden departure. One, he fell out with Chidambaram and, two, he was fed up with the bureaucrats. Which was correct? "Neither. I didn't fall out with Chidambaram at all." That's unusual, I point out. He laughs. "Many people congratulated me on working with him for so long but our relationship was very professional."

In fact, he says Chidambaram—whom he considers "super-efficient" and "dynamic"—had extended his contract by (three) years to October 2010. "I had every intention of staying but the job that the permanent secretary tax of the UK offered represented a challenge, however small, and I felt working in an embedded manner with a developed country tax administration would be a great experience". He and Chidambaram had a "hearty chat" about it and he decided to accept.

So, no problems with the bureaucracy? He scrutinises the sushi platter to avoid the squid to which he is allergic before answering elliptically. "I have come across IAS officers who are brilliant but, frankly, I think in today's day and age you need professionally-specialised people and there's not enough of them in government."

He talks about the American and Latin American models that include specialists from the professions. In government he found that "as long as my boss understood the situation and saw to it that I could function there was never any issue but I think that"—long pause—"because of our overall bureaucratic set-up politicians tend to believe that only sharpened Indian bureaucrats can face and solve complex situations, forgetting that external, experienced people can solve the same problems, probably more professionally. I don't think we can move towards a professional framework in society until and unless we do that".

....I wonder at his substituting the urban delights of London for the maddening drawbacks of Delhi. "It is strange isn't it," he replies, "but I am never unhappy here though I do tend to get unhappy abroad." His explanation is that in "aged, progressed societies" things are much more set whereas he feels happy in India "because you are continuously seeing change and the youth show that there's promise".

Although he's spent the bulk of his adult life overseas, he says he's "never quite identified with the West culturally other than literature, travel, and opera perhaps". The explanation is complex and interesting. Unlike most Indians abroad he's "quite westernised" in that he doesn't confine his social circle to "other high-quality Indians"—the "Nehru Centre crowd" he calls them. His friends are Argentinean, Chilean, Colombian, German, English...

Having travelled to all Latin American countries bar Honduras and El Salvador in his IMF days, he speaks fluent Spanish. But although he finds Latin America an "exquisite combination of West and East", he turned down citizenship offers because "ultimately, I can't give up India". One reason is its perennial "mystery and attractiveness". The other was advice from his father two days before he died that India would need Shome's generation. "That is like a blessing and a challenge but it's had an impact on me", he adds.

Tax isn't the only thing that keeps him busy. There's one tome on "modernising tax administration" in the works—but also a novel, "on the education of a personality", partly inspired by Hardy, Dickens and Lawrence, but he hasn't a publisher yet.

On books, he's effusive in his praise of Barack Obama's *Dreams from My Father* but seems less enamoured of the American dream. Reflecting a deep personal decision, Shome chose to give up his Green Card after almost 30 years. "When I went to the US embassy here to do this the young officer asked if I needed counselling. I told him I might need a lot of counselling on other things but on this one I suppose I have made up my mind!"

All evening, I've been glancing at his intriguing ring which has a stone that looks like pitted turquoise. It's called larimar, a kind of coral (quarried) (sic) near the sea, found only in Dominican Republic. He's had it since 1983. The tie, too, is interesting but very British in origin. It's from Ashford & Brooks "from where I'm told the Queen's husband and her son shop" and is covered with tiny, exquisitely embroidered weighing scales. Shome is a Libran, which is why he chose it.

We decline dessert for jasmine tea and Shome asks if we're done with the "formal" part of the dinner. So I switch off the tape recorder and the conversation gets even more interesting...

ENDNOTES

1. Shrabani Basu, 'I finally managed to persuade Dr. Singh, my former teacher, to let me go', *The Telegraph*, Sunday, 17 February 2008.
2. Ibid.
3. Kanika Datta, 'Lunch with BS: Parthasarathi Shome, Return of the taxman', *Business Standard*, 9 November 2010, New Delhi.

NINE

INDIA AGAIN
Research, Government and Committees

The trajectory of work that overtook me on my return to India in January 2011 could not have been entirely foreseen by me. I had been ready for the directorship of the Indian Council for Research on International Economic Relations (ICRIER) for, after all, I had already been director of NIPFP. But I also found the financial state of the institution to be in doldrums, and this had to be set right. It reminded me of my surprise in having to renegotiate a new MoU in Singapore over and above directing the Fund institute there. Anyhow, I took up what was required of me with gusto. We received a huge grant from the Ministry of Finance to conduct research on a large project on the Group of 20 countries. This required intense administrative work in preparing proposals and monitoring reports that demanded a lot of grinding of the teeth to forge ahead. I did it. The outcome was excellent, for I was able to publish two edited volumes—*The G20 Macroeconomic Agenda: India and the Emerging Economies* (2014) and *The G20 Development Agenda: An Indian Perspective* (2015)—from Cambridge University Press that brought together several research papers on the G20's macroeconomic and development agendas respectively. Among the several reviews, one appeared in *Choice*, a publication of the Association of College and Research Libraries, a division of the American Library Association. I excerpt from that review dated 1 February 2015, by Professor J. Bhattacharya of Iowa State University, since it provides a good gist of the objectives and outcomes of the complex endeavour:

> A subgroup of the G20, the BRIC countries—Brazil, Russia, India and China—have taken on leadership roles, signalling their increasing importance in the world economy. The (macroeconomic agenda) book edited by Shome assesses ... the G20['s] ... reform initiatives [and] discuss[es] surrounding issues such as global macroeconomic policy coordination, capital controls, the international monetary system, and the need for global structural reform. The volume is timely ... when the old economic order of Europe and the US is slowly and grudgingly yielding supremacy to a new order dominated by the BRIC countries.... Highly recommended.

I received a grant from the Foreign Office of the UK High Commission that led to a very interesting project in which I brought to the same table both tax administrators and tax practitioners in both direct and indirect tax matters. I travelled all over India to carry out a dialogue, and it resulted in another edited volume from Orient BlackSwan in 2013 titled *Indian Tax Administration: A Dialogue*, which was a harbinger of the various committees and the national commission that I would come to chair soon thereafter. Of course, *Tax Shastra: Administrative Reforms in India, United Kingdom and Brazil*, was published from BS Books, *Business Standard*, in 2012 (see Plate 27). Thus, I could get my head deep into research from which a string of publications could emerge.

Among the various conferences which I participated in, one I really enjoyed was organised in 2011 by the Fund on the global economic crisis. The discussions were wide-ranging and I found myself at odds with some of the participants including Joseph Stiglitz, but my paper attracted attention. Titled 'Fiscal Stimuli and Consolidation', it was a gist of my position that a single fiscal deficit per GDP number cannot be applied across countries to assess fiscal stimulus. This is because the fiscal multiplier depends on many characteristics of an economy including its openness, its exchange rate regime, extent of public debt per GDP, investment per GDP, and so on that had already been demonstrated by earlier authors. Thus, by taking instances of the UK and India, I illustrated with figures why an investment-oriented fiscal stimulus coupled with cutbacks in consumption-oriented government subsidies made more sense during financial crisis. I presented an analysis of the pre-announced policies of the conservative government that was elected in the UK in 2010 to illustrate voter confidence in conservatism in a government's fiscal stance. I also argued that, in fact, given its differential impacts across countries, the fiscal deficit per GDP was not the best index for measures towards economic recovery, but more direct financial indicators that should be based on potential flight capital, volatility of capital flows and stock markets, and interest rate spreads that tend to precede or were associated with financial crises. The paper was included in the conference volume, *In the Wake of the Crisis: Leading Economists Reassess Economic Policy*, edited by Olivier J. Blanchard, Chief Economist of the Fund, and co-editors David Romer, Michael Spence and Joseph Stiglitz, from the IMF and MIT Press, Cambridge, 2012. UK Cabinet Minister Oliver Letwin even wrote me a congratulatory letter after reading the paper (see Plate 28).

In a subsequent conference at the Reserve Bank of India in 2013, I again pointed to the adverse ramifications of public debt accumulation on fiscal adjustment during a financial crisis. The paper, 'Debt Accumulation in a Financial Crisis,' was published by Cambridge University Press, 2013, in *Sovereign Debt and Financial Stability*, edited by Deepak Mohanty. I recall another experience in which I was at odds with a group of mainly Oxford professors with whom I had gone on a retreat to Belaggio, Italy, in 2011 during which I differentiated the structural fiscal policies undertaken by select advanced and emerging economies. I observed a certain extent of herding towards prevailing views from which I departed. The paper, 'Rebalancing and Structural Policies—An Indian Perspective,' was subsequently published in *Oxford Review of Economic Policy* in 2012, together with the papers of others at the retreat. Among academics, in particular of the higher order, occasionally I have found that fads of the moment had to be adhered to or else a great amount of energy needed to be spent to push and maintain one's own stance. I have always picked the latter successfully though, sometimes, with considerable associated challenge.

Paradoxically, at a time when I was content doing research and managing a research organisation, mingling with the international research community, organising research conferences and stepping up the international reputation of ICRIER using my individualised approach, there was an emerging issue with India's international taxation that suddenly fell into my lap.

COMMITTEES ON GENERAL ANTI-AVOIDANCE RULES AND RETROSPECTIVE TAXATION

One afternoon I got a call from Pulok Chatterji, IAS and Principal Secretary to the Prime Minister. I was surprised since, though we had been classmates at DSE and I recalled him as friendly and sporting, somehow when I had come across him a couple of times during our official duties, he had not recognised me so to speak. Hence I too had been reticent. Now he was friendly over the phone and indicated that B. V. R. Subrahmanyam, the PM's Secretary and also an IAS Joint Secretary, would call me. As I had known Subbu, he was exceptionally clever and quick in taxation matters though we had not really corresponded during my earlier tenure at North Block. Then, in the interim, they had both gone to the Indian Government's office at the World Bank and my presumption was that they had come across my work or reputation. Now they were very friendly and, in particular, I found interactions with Subbu intellectually very satisfying and during one of which he informed me that he had completed an MSc in Economics at LSE.

This was mid-2012. Manmohan Singh was managing the Finance Ministry for a short span between the tenures of a departing Pranab Mukherjee and a returning P. Chidambaram. When Subbu and I, and Pulok and I, met, I was informed that the PM was very concerned with the vocal adverse reaction of investors—foreign and domestic—over the retroactive legislation of the government after the Supreme Court had annulled the Revenue Department's appeal against Vodafone. The retroactive amendment negated the Supreme Court's judgement line by line as if to annul it in all specificity. It was conveyed to me that I should chair a committee to impartially examine the matter of the General Anti-Avoidance Rules (GAAR) in its generality and the retrospective amendment in particular. I felt uncomfortable but, for good or bad, had also developed the reputation of accepting all government assignments. I went to see the PM and realised that he was serious about the matter and softly insisted that I should examine the issues fairly and that he had always relied on my views on tax matters, something he had also iterated some years back during our lunch prior to my departure for the UK. I had no option but to accept.

I also had continuing responsibilities at ICRIER, completing ongoing projects and books. How I took on the additional work on GAAR I am not entirely sure to this day, but I gathered power from inside myself to examine the fundamental contradictions embedded in both these emerging issues in international taxation. My right hand was Sunil Gupta, Joint Secretary in Tax Policy and Legislation (TPL) who was already well versed in the entire matter in the Indian context. Of course, I too had been illuminated on the issue while at HMRC when discussions on GAAR occurred during my three-year stay there. When I examined the Indian GAAR, it appeared to me that the most stringent of the GAARs that had been enacted across the globe had been brought under one document in the Indian GAAR. In contrast, UK had moved away from the concept of anti-avoidance to anti-abuse, or the application of rules only in extremely egregious cases. Further, such unilateral powers were handed to the assessing officer to determine and proceed against presumed avoidance by taxpayers that it would lead to unprecedented compliance burdens. Of course, being from Revenue Sunil was, by and large, imbued with the government view; yet he was open-minded and we had many a useful discussion, eventually arriving at via media on several points.

One matter we clarified was the essential distinction between tax mitigation, tax avoidance and tax evasion, three concepts that the government's position had confused and that, over the years, I had also found to be in a confused state in some corners of the tax world. Tax evasion was illegal and forbidden. Tax mitigation was legal and any good tax adviser would inform his clients on the legally acceptable mitigation of his contribution to the exchequer. It was tax avoidance that was the seat of the problem in that, while it was strictly legal, it might not reflect the intention of the law. Note that tax avoidance by its very nature is confusing for it may simply not be feasible to read the mind or interpret the intention of government legislation. Nevertheless, neither is it impossible to identify egregious tax avoidance verging on tax evasion when multiple transactions through a circuitous route of tax havens are designed merely to avoid tax. This would be tax abuse, and the UK legislated against it. India's framework on the other hand was too all-enveloping and one that could crush the feasibility of tax compliance, business decision-making and foreign and domestic investment.

For example, the 2010 DTC Bill contained a provision stating that an arrangement which resulted in any tax benefit would be presumed to have been entered into for the main purpose of obtaining the tax benefit, unless the taxpayer proved otherwise. It was in the 2012 Finance Bill but was not brought into the Income Tax Act (ITA). However, there was another section in the 2010 Direct Tax Code (DTC) Bill that was brought into the ITA. It provided that an arrangement would be presumed, unless proved to the contrary by the taxpayer, to have been entered into for the main purpose of obtaining a tax benefit if the main purpose of a step in, or part of, the arrangement was to obtain a tax benefit, notwithstanding the fact that the main purpose of the whole arrangement was not to obtain a tax benefit. The expert committee on GAAR found this to provide no guidance for the taxpayer as to how he was to prove what he was being required to prove. Under the circumstances, tax compliance was being rendered impossible.

Accordingly the expert committee completed the report in less than one quarter, by September 2012, since PM wanted to know the findings as quickly as possible. I did not consult him before writing the recommendations since it was an independent expert committee, of which the revered Shri K. Rangachary was also a member. A chartered accountant by training with a reputation of being fiercely independent, he had been chairman of both the Central Board of Direct Taxes (CBDT) and Insurance Regulatory and Development Authority of India (IRDAI). When he congratulated me, I knew I had been on the right track. The GAAR committee recommended an overarching principle that GAAR should be applicable only in cases of abusive, contrived and artificial arrangements. However, this recommendation was not reflected adequately in the government's Press Release of 14 January 2013, or in subsequent amendments brought in the ITA through the 2013 Finance Act. The Press Release did elaborate that, where a part of the arrangement was an impermissible avoidance agreement, GAAR would be restricted to the tax consequence of that part which was impermissible, and not to the whole arrangement. While this was a small victory for the committee, it was not reflected in the 2013 Finance Act. Thus a conflict between the Press Release and the ITA emerged. These discussions continued with CBDT during 2013 when I went back to North Block in 2013. Those discussions will be forever embedded in my memory.

Nevertheless, I did not anticipate the immediate global impact of the GAAR report. Emails reiterating "thought leader", "rock star of tax" and other oxymorons from my international acquaintances became a regular feature and I could not keep pace with the media coverage. Yet what I attempted, and possibly did, was to clarify issues, identified anti-avoidance measures with a reining in of the possibility of unfair ploughing of taxpayers, and limiting the time period within which a GAAR investigation must be completed. A fundamental message in all this was the primacy of investment and economic growth over the taxman, yet providing him with all instruments to judge fairly and under the guidance of superiors. Later I found even the Delhi High Court referring to the committee's views and recommendations in its judgements and felt fully satisfied with it. And subsequently reference to it was made in significant detail in professional books on taxation, perhaps the latest being, *The Interaction of Domestic GAAR with Tax Treaties*, by Vikram Chand from Lausanne University in Switzerland, a copy of which I just received from the author in March 2018. So its study continues.

I maintained that the posture of GAAR should cater to the context of investment in all my media interviews. In a chat with Supriya Srinate of *ET Now* dated 17 July 2012, when I was beginning the committee's work, I emphasised that our corporate tax needed to be globally comparable because capital is mobile. Economists, chartered accountants, policymakers, industrialists and foreign investors who are in India are major stakeholders in the know-how of foreign investment, I further said, and that GAAR should not distort business decisions. Not only business dailies such as *Business Standard*, *The Financial Express*, *BusinessLine*, *Financial Chronicle* and *Mint* covered the establishment of the expert committee in some detail, but I also found *The Times of India*, *Hindustan Times*, *The Indian Express* and other regional dailies such as *The Telegraph* of Calcutta and *The Hindu* of Chennai doing the same. That is when the matter came to the attention of even my almost ninety year old mother, who read the eventual report meticulously and asked me all sorts of questions. In the meanwhile, the papers continued to report on the process of stakeholder consultations—'Shome panel on GAAR sets in motion consultation process' (*The Hindu*, 27 July 2012); GAAR talks to be intensified etc.—thus keeping the pressure up on the committee.

The good thing about the GAAR report was that Manmohan Singh was still Finance Minister and Pulok and Subbu were still very much in charge at PMO (see Plate 29). They wanted the report to be put out in the public domain as having been accepted by government. The committee's recommendations have been analysed the world over in such detail that I shall not revisit them here. However, a few points are worth mentioning. One was the recommendation to apply GAAR from 2016–17. Even though it appeared that it was being postponed for half a decade, I felt that investments already in the process should be protected and grandfathered, and it was equally important that tax officers be trained not to convert GAAR into a revenue generating device; after all, I had been witness to routine transfer pricing adjustments out of line with global practice. Eventually, GAAR indeed came into being in 2017.

There were general accolades from the media and many others from the major business dailies. Quoting from among papers on 2–3 September 2012, *Hindustan Times* said that the recommendations of the GAAR committee "have come as a breath of fresh air. They demonstrate that even at this late stage, a course correction is possible that can revive the country's investment activity".[1]

The Economic Times editorial of 3 September 2012, 'Parthasarathy Shome panel's recommendations on GAAR make sense, on the whole', however, stood out in my assessment. Amusingly pointing out that the sound of GAAR "evokes a picture of the tax department as a truculent dog straining at the leash", its opinion was that the recommendation to postpone GAAR to 2016–17 would enable "holistic reform of taxation". It further said that the recommendations to: stop taxing capital gains from sale of listed securities, have a threshold income for any application of GAAR, include a negative list of matters to be kept outside the application of GAAR, create a five-member panel to approve the invocation of GAAR by majority vote, and have three of the five members from outside the tax department "all make eminent sense". Stressing the need for complete clarity that GAAR be applied only in cases of abusive, contrived and artificial arrangements, the editorial emphasised the hoped for conduct of officers who administered GAAR, and agreed that sufficient time was required to frame rules and train tax personnel. The postponement of GAAR and the expert panel's stance should, therefore, be seen as a pragmatic response to investor qualms about how a GAAR-empowered tax department needed to prepare for it over a three-year period in terms of framing proper rules and training personnel. Perhaps its most attention drawing conclusion was that the GAAR committee pointed towards the need for preparing tax proposals over the medium term, rather than in one fiscal year, and that such planning should assist India in collaborating with tax authorities globally and, thus, "capture the value that globalised business ... occludes from tax jurisdictions"[2].

All reviews did not shower rose petals, however. *Business Standard*'s editorial 'Don't delay GAAR' dated 4 September 2012 found "questionable" the matter of delaying GAAR's introduction, the lack of emphasis on the Mauritius route of foreign investment, as well as the removal of the short term capital gains tax on listed securities but, nevertheless, favoured the levying of the Securities Transaction Tax (STT)[3]. I had been so used to this daily's positive review of my work that this editorial jolted me a bit though, soon, its subsequent reviews generally resumed their positive stance.

To explain, the committee's brief was also extended to include the role and reform of certain taxes. Accordingly, in its report it also recommended that "the government should abolish the tax on gains arising from transfer of listed securities, whether in the nature of capital gains or business income....In order to make the proposed tax neutral, the government may consider to increase the rate of STT appropriately". The STT rate at the time was 0.1 percent, and a slight increase would not have distorted businesses while it could fetch some revenue. It has always struck me how the business community tends to react negatively when any aspect of taxation hits them irrespective of whether another new aspect benefits them. And this happened immediately. To quote from various papers: 'Tax issue hits securitisation market hard' (*The Indian Express*, 3 September 2012); "But increase in STT to substitute tax on capital gains will increase transactions cost in India"[4] (*The Hindu BusinessLine*, 2 September 2012); 'Shome panel report could hit broking firms' (*The Hindu BusinessLine*, 2 September 2012) and so on.

Dr. Manmohan Singh still continuing as Finance Minister, with Pulok and Subbu in charge at PMO, they wanted the report to be put out in public as having been accepted by government. Mr. Chidambaram soon took over the Finance Ministry once again and gave it to CBDT for examination. If the government had already accepted the report, I did not fully comprehend the role of another examination by the same body whose first draft on the matter had been set aside after which my committee had been formed at the Prime Minister's behest. This is an example of some practices in Raisina Hill that continue to confound me. Be that as it may, I had to appear in the meetings that PC called to discuss the recommendations of the committee. At the end of the report, the committee had presented more than thirty detailed examples of cases in which GAAR should or should not be applied. Sadly I heard it said that the examples were unnecessary since it would all be learnt from field experience. I would not comment more on those meetings.

As the work on GAAR terminated, work on retrospective taxation commenced. Like in the case of GAAR, I found myself in disagreement with the position the government had taken on this crucial matter. I tried to convince officers, some of whom had worked under me in my earlier tenure in North Block, of the folly of introducing retrospective amendments to tax law in the way it had been done in the context of the Vodafone case. My explanation was simple. I distinguished risk from uncertainty. A business can be expected to take a decision to invest in reflection of his attitude towards risk—averse, neutral or preferred—but this is impossible if in time t+1 he is told by the government—the tax department—that the investment that he had made in time t based on the tax law at time t—actually had not existed; instead he is informed in t+1 that the law in t had actually been different. The validity of risk taking is thereby vitiated and uncertainty in business decisions takes hold. That is what the retrospectivity in changing that particular tax law had done.

My chairing the committee on retrospective taxation appeared to generate a lot of speculation regarding the committee's recommendations but my mind was clear in the context of existing legislation at the time of investment. The committee accordingly submitted its report at the end of October. It recommended prospective taxation. A spate of media coverage followed on this most sensitive issue that had consumed the foreign investor community. Might the tax department have felt that if retrospective amendments were disallowed, they would be burdened with a lot of refunds?

To conclude, the matter was not just one-sided, however. It was also true that the tax department had cautioned Vodafone, the buyer, that it should withhold tax on its purchase of assets from Hutchison, the seller of assets based in India, since tax liability might occur, and that it should at least set those monies aside for eventual tax payment if any. However, withholding was not carried out and monies were not set aside in a protected account since Vodafone was of the opinion that it was not liable to pay tax on the deal that was entirely an 'indirect' transfer of assets from one multinational to another that was taking place in a third, external jurisdiction. And it so happened that, after traversing the judicial system, Vodafone did win the case against Revenue at the Supreme Court. Boomeranging that judgement was incorrect under prevailing law and it was done at the cost of great uncertainty in business decisions and investment.

That being said, it must be recognised that the focus of the entire issue has been erroneously targeted. It is not prospectivity in taxation that is the culprit but the inability to tax indirect transfers. The entire matter of not taxing indirect transfers is a myth designed for tax avoidance and underwritten by Western jurisdictions that the Base Erosion and Profit Shifting (BEPS) project of the Organisation for Economic Co-operation and Development (OECD) is finally attempting to confront. Thus, as per the 'source principle' of taxation that suggests collection of revenue in the jurisdiction where income is generated from an asset, India should have collected and possessed the revenue in this particular case. Unfortunately it went about the matter retrospectively that cannot be justified if a criterion of transparency of intentions is applied. Thus it is crucial that the matter be revisited in a new Direct Tax Code in which indirect transfers should not be excused from source taxation, however, with full and a sufficiently long period of grandfathering.

This period of my immersions in taxation had been professionally fulfilling no doubt but, at the same time, I was looking forward to returning to research in areas that I had felt I must complete in my professional lifetime. Ernst and Young, one of the global 'Big Four' tax advisory firms had named me 'Tax Luminary', which enabled me to indulge in some globe-trotting, giving lectures on my conception of tax reform, receiving feedback and getting to write that final book for students as I had promised my mother. The epitome of all that seemed to end in a beautiful poem by Anish Thacker, a young staff member of Ernst and Young, that went like this:

A Tax Professional's World

Section, sub-section, rule, explanation, proviso,
We live with these day in and day out.
Tribunal and court decisions we randomly quote,
For social occasions, we are counted out.

Welcome to our world – the world of Tax!
One of frequent intellectual meandering,
Where throughout the year we seldom relax
And ordinary words are given a complex meaning.

Transfer pricing, indirect transfers, GAAR
Take up most of our working day,
When better halves call us at times late by far
All that we do is shoo them away!

Safe harbours, APAs and repatriation strategies
Are our current fair weather friends
Tax litigation however keeps going on for ages
And decisions reported nowadays seldom make sense.

Income-tax confused even the great Einstein
Who found it the most difficult to understand
We tax professionals yet, ceaselessly keep at it
Hoping things just don't go out of hand!

Yes, this is our world – a vexed one for many,
For us, it's more than our home
For we are used to the constant tyranny –
And all sections appear to lead to Shome!

And I looked forward to resuming those activities. But, upon returning to ICRIER, FM called me on my mobile from his and asked me to show up in his office. I did. He asked me to come in as his adviser once again, this time as Minister of State. I said, could I think and get back. He responded, at this time I should be standing with the technical aspects of the government's public finance policy. Very politely I insisted that I would get back to him. On my way home, I convinced myself that I should stick to research, and sent him a text message indicating that I would do any work on committees looking at selective aspects while continuing my independent research. He called back almost immediately and asked me to revisit his office. I did. I recall a twenty-minute conversation. It contained confidential exchange about several matters including the course of one's career, which I appreciated but shall refrain from elaborating. I agreed to return after finishing my work at ICRIER. After all, I had never had any professional quarrel or reason not to work with him. On 7 December 2012, *The Economic Times*, *The Financial Express*, *Business Standard* and several other dailies reported, 'Tax expert Shome joins Team FM as Adviser, again'; 'Shome is new adviser to Finance Minister'; 'Shome back in Finance Ministry as adviser' and so on. I re-entered North Block on 31 December 2012 (see Plates 30 and 31).

DIRECT TAX CODE AGAIN—FUTURE INCOME TAX REFORM

The first main task that FM assigned me was a re-examination of the DTC. The DTC that I had worked on prior to leaving for the UK had undergone modifications and uploaded for comments in 2010. Comments were incorporated to the extent that, in my view, it now looked close to the existing ITA itself. That version had then been sent to the Parliamentary Finance Committee (PFC), chaired by Shri Yashwant Sinha. My responsibility was to assess their comments and recommend to FM to incorporate or reject them. Examining the entire DTC once again was not a simple affair. CBDT was examining the PFC's comments though, in our meetings with FM, I realised that there was a high likelihood of returning even closer to the ITA. Even highly intelligent tax officers tend to take a Revenue stance in such situations since they are simply not trained to look at taxation's macroeconomic effects, as some of them honestly admitted to me. Indeed, some indicated it would be contrary to their responsibility to move from the revenue objective to macroeconomic concerns. I respected that view but knew I had to chart out an independent course if I were to meet FM's expectations.

I informed FM that I would like to work with a few brilliant young officers who had the ITA under total control and who would be able to guide me in the pros and cons of changing the ITA in its minutest detail. FM gave me full freedom to select the officers. I found three whom I shall mention for their brilliance: Sandeep Bandhu, Pankaj Jindal, and Navneet Manohar. Navneet had already been assigned as my officer on special duty (OSD) and whose work I had found to be impeccable. The three of them together showed me the way to traverse the ITA once again and in a new light while keeping the PFC's suggestions fully on the slate.

I feel there is not much point in revisiting the recommendations of the DTC, which I had been asked by FM to rework with the three colleagues, though it may be useful to recount some issues that linger after the 2009, 2010 and 2014 versions, especially since it is being examined once again. Essentially, in the final analysis, the DTC should revert to the 2009 version with slight modifications.

During all of 2007, I had the opportunity to work on the initial 2009 (DTC09) version. Upon my return from HMRC, it was clear to me that the 2010 version (DTC10) that had emerged after stakeholder and tax administration inputs was a pared down version resembling the ITA itself rather than DTC09 as I indicated above. Nevertheless, having gone to the PFC, DTC10 had received major initial suggestions, and rightfully so. The task to examine the PFC recommendations and imbue meaningfulness into DTC10 was completed over 2013–14. Thus, when considered in its entirety, the work on DTC had stretched over 2007–14. The final draft—say DTC14—had cleared all ministries but was not taken to cabinet.

The new, or current, government first indicated unwillingness to reconsider the DTC, a decision I lamented. Government is now revisiting the DTC. Thus there is some usefulness in listing selected recommendations of DTC09 and DTC10 and comparing the two, so that the direction of the newest version comprises meaningful reform. I will desist from DTC14 since, first, it technically did not appear for stakeholder discussion (though it must be available on file); second, the currently ongoing exercise should possess the possibility to reconsider DTC09 that DTC14 did not have the luxury of doing; and, third, analysing three earlier DTC versions would comprise an overdone dish.

Tax Treatment of Retirement Savings

DTC10 was similar to ITA except for marginal differences. Provident Fund was treated in one as EpEE, with partial exemption (Ep) in the investment/contribution stage, then the interest earned would be exempt (E), followed by retirement income which was also exempt (E). However, in the other, it was EpEEp in that some forms/parts of the withdrawal were taxed. Thus DTC10 reverted to differentiate across savings instruments which any structural tax reform should obviate.

In DTC09, all savings including Provident Fund were subject to EpET. The contribution to retirement was exempt (Ep) only if deposited in a Retirement Benefits Account with an intermediary, exempt (E) during accrual, and taxed on withdrawal (T) to compensate for exemption during the previous two phases of the participant's life cycle. Treatment of retirement benefits in DTC10, however, was similar to that in ITA where retirement benefits were exempt up to prescribed limits.

Ideally, DTC09 should be reverted to if a balanced treatment of taxation of savings is contemplated in the reformed DTC.

Taxation of Capital Gains as Ordinary Income

DTC09 included capital gains in total income and applied the marginal income tax rate. For capital assets held for more than one year, cost of acquisition/improvement would be indexed. Any capital loss would be carried forward to subsequent years for set off against capital gains.

DTC09 would abolish Securities Transaction Tax (STT). Capital gains from transfer of equity would become a part of ordinary income. DTC10 retained STT and proposed a special scheme for capital gains computation for STT charged transactions. Different calculations were then provided for listed equity shares held for more/less than one year on the basis of a scaling down formula. Variations were stipulated for non-STT paid capital gains. Again, it was similar to the ITA structure.

Clearly DTC09 was superior and should be reverted to. Further, it would be better not to distort markets with even low STT rates at a wide range for various types of transactions.

Capital Gains Savings Scheme

DTC09 proposed the Capital Gains Savings Scheme (CGSS), deposits into which would be tax-free until withdrawn. DTC10 withdrew this 'rollover' scheme while maintaining two other rollover schemes in agricultural land and residential house that were available in ITA and DTC09.

The CGSS should be reinstated as it appeared in DTC09 reflecting its structural reform characteristic of encouraging savings.

Minimum Alternate Tax

DTC09 had proposed a minimum alternate tax (MAT) with reference to the value of gross assets. DTC10 reverted to MAT on the basis of book profits as in ITA, increased the rate from 18.5 percent to 20 percent, and extended the carry forward period from 10 to 15 years. It was termed Book Profits Tax.

The DTC09 gross assets-based MAT should be reconsidered while removing hurdles such as cascading in work in progress (WIP) which is not a productive asset, carving out pass-through entities, the parent-subsidiary structure, and ensuring compatibility with double taxation avoidance agreements (DTAAs). The rate should be worked out carefully, based on a presumed return to capital and the corporate income tax rate, and be capped at 1.5 percent of gross assets.

Taxation of Non-Profit Organisations

In DTC09, the tax liability of a non-profit organisation (NPO) was 15 percent of the 'surplus plus capital gains on transfer of any investment/financial asset'. There was no scope of setting apart any sum for future use. DTC10 reverted to comparability with ITA in several respects including exemption for investment or deposits in specified modes for up to three years.

In DTC10, an exemption of one lakh was provided; income above that would be subject to 15 percent tax. These were close to ITA in the sense that NPOs under ITA set apart 15 percent for an indefinite period (the remaining 85 percent also allowed to be set apart for five years on the basis of an application to the concerned Assessing Officer, AO). DTC09 had mitigated the concern with AO examining assessment records of five to six years. This advantage was removed in DTC10.

Thus taxation of NPOs should reflect DTC09, however, with a new provision that an NPO may deposit 15 percent for future use, reflecting the need to differentiate what is ongoing current expenditure from clustered capital expenditure. It must be recognised that NPOs continue to play a crucial role in the development of India in areas where governments have been unable to provide adequate socio-economic services. Challenging NPOs with heavy-handed taxation or putting up non-tax barriers against them comprise mistaken policy. Rather, the good ones must be treated with care while the bad ones identified, examined, and action taken as needed. A cookie cutter approach should be avoided for it is certain to lead to the disappearance of NPO-provided essential services directed to the needy and vulnerable.

Wealth Tax

DTC09 proposed charging wealth tax on all assets, including financial assets. The law was structured to be simple and implementable. A high threshold of Rs 50 crore and a low tax rate of 0.25 percent were proposed. DTC10 provisions were aligned to the existing Wealth Tax Act with a few additions of some financial assets located outside India. Wealth Tax was subsequently abolished.

In a country like India—where 0.001 percent of the top wealth cohorts are enjoying the most rapid increase in wealth concentration in the entire world—a tax on wealth is imperative for equity. If appropriately conceptualised and implemented, it should also generate revenue. Net wealth definition of DTC09 should be reinstated, ensuring that all assets—real and financial—are included, keeping the tax rate at 0.25 percent between Rs 50–100 crore, and 0.5 percent above Rs 100 crore. The tax rate should be kept very low so that the wealth tax is successful in terms of both compliance and revenue collection.

Taxation of House Property Income—Presumption and Exemption—and Interest Deduction

DTC09 proposed taking gross rent as the higher of contractual rent or presumptive rent (calculated at 6 percent per annum of the rateable value fixed by the local authority or the cost of construction of the property). In DTC10, gross rent was the actual rent received or receivable and not taken on presumptive basis. ITA uses the concept of notional rent.

The ITA (i) exempts one owner-occupied residence from income tax; (ii) taxes second and higher numbers of owned residences; and (iii) allows deduction of interest in case of the first, exempting self-occupied property up to Rs 2 lakh. This results in an obvious double deduction. It also implies an inequitable structure of income and wealth taxation of real property ownership. Exempting one self-occupied house irrespective of value subsidises extremely high-income and high-wealth owners, while taxing middle income owners who may acquire additional properties later in the earning cycle. Further, aspect (iii) unjustifiably allows deduction of interest on a large residence though not on a second small residence.

Hence it is suggested to introduce a monetary threshold above which a self-occupied residence would be subject to (presumptive) income tax. This should be appropriately high, say Rs 5 crore. Second, interest paid on the exempted portion of self-occupied property should not be deductible to avoid the mentioned double deduction. Even if not self-occupied, interest deduction should be allowed up to Rs 2 lakh, with inflation adjustment over time.

Wealth tax (which has presently been abolished) should separately exclude Rs 5 crore from calculation of the wealth tax base to ensure consistency between income tax and wealth tax.

Change in the Income Tax Rate Structure

International indexes are revealing that there is a wider dispersion in the distribution of income today. Therefore the prevailing rate structure implies that effective progressivity in income tax has declined. Increase in the share of consumption tax with the introduction of a widely based GST would reduce effective progressivity even more. Therefore, any new DTC should introduce new rates of 35 percent and 40 percent for brackets of Rs 1–3 crore and above Rs 3 crore respectively. Presently, even a rate of 45 percent above Rs 6 crore is justified. This will not be internationally incomparable.

First, that there would be a flight of professionals appears to be invalid since comparable countries have higher rates than India. And, second, any reaction from those who would bear rates of 35, 40 and

45 percent of unfair burden should be addressed through enhanced tax administration efforts to improve tax compliance and expand taxpayer numbers—especially the self-employed—while eschewing a strategy of search and seizure. Only then the handful of individuals who declare taxable income of Rs 1 crore could be increased.

Separating Employees from the Self-Employed

In order to bring in the self-employed more successfully into the tax net, the self-employed could be separated out from the salaried. Currently in India, both the salaried and self-employed are subjected to the same rate structure. Offering a preferable rate structure to the self-employed such as individual proprietors may be considered in light of the higher risks involved in earning income from business compared to salary income.

A counter argument could be that the self-employed are already preferred since they are taxed on net profit while employees are taxed on gross salary; but note that standard deduction has just been restored. Note further that many self-employed have recently come under the GST regime as services are now being additionally taxed at the level of states. And even though the tax is designed to be passed on to final consumers, the self-employed often do not perceive it the way tax experts do. Further, in the GST introductory stage, their compliance costs have been significant.

Minimise Compliance Costs

In both GST and income tax, the perception persists of an increase in compliance costs, for example, recent requirements to submit balance sheet information by relatively small income earners. There is an overriding consideration regarding right to privacy. Without specifically attributing their actions to the European Convention on Human Rights, European tax administrations operate in accordance with it, possibly under the presumption that any disclosure of information could comprise prima facie breach of that right. In India, even if the disclosure demand is retained, disclosure should be demonstrated to be necessary and not routine or disproportionate, in particular for smaller economic agents.

To conclude, there are many other innovation aspects in DTC09 such as those pertaining to the financial sector that should be retained. And the BCTT should be reinstated reflecting the soft landing of demonetisation.

OTHER AREAS OF WORK

The weight of work never ceased, such is the pressure of North Block. Just like during my earlier North Block years when I assisted FM in the formulation of his tax proposals for the Union Budget, I did so during this period as well, though the focus was primarily on structural reform—DTC and GST. Nonetheless, FM asked my view on several other issues and asked me to solve taxpayer complaints. I will take one example here to illustrate the intricacy of issues that would develop on a regular basis.

Commodities Transaction Tax

A bit of a background is called for. In the Finance Act of 2008, a new Commodities Transaction Tax (CTT) was to be levied on the transactions of specified taxable commodities. However, the provisions of the 2008 Finance Act were amended in the 2009 Finance Act (No.2), and the CTT never came into existence. The reintroduction of the CTT would bring parity between securities transaction and commodities markets which had been blamed for instability in commodity prices. In this context, FM asked me to analyse commodity market transactions to test the feasibility of reviving a tax on commodities transactions. This primarily emanated from two considerations: first, bringing parity between securities transactions and commodity transactions by imposing a tax similar to the STT; and second, curbing the financialisation of commodities markets.

When I discussed the matter with stakeholders, representatives from commodities exchanges argued strongly against any such levy, stating that exchange-traded commodity derivatives were basically a risk management platform for hedging against adverse price movements. They also expressed that, while stock market participants solely stressed profits from soaring share values, commodity market players operated with the twin objective of risk management at micro and price discovery at macro level. It was a thin-margin business since commodities were already taxed to the tune of almost 12 percent in the form of Mandi tax, value-added tax, excise duty, cess, handling costs and warehousing charges before they were placed on the trading platform. Thus, tax on commodity derivatives along the lines of the one for the stock market could potentially drag down the transactions level, according to them.

The data, however, indicated a different story to me. Actual delivery based transactions in Indian commodity markets were quite small. As per data available on the website of Multi Commodity Exchange of India Ltd (MCX), which was one of the four commodity exchanges approved by Government to deal in commodity derivatives in an electronic trading environment, the total value of commodity transactions during 2012 were to the tune of Rs.1,48,90,596 crore. Transactions through MCX constituted almost 85 percent of the commodity transactions through commodity exchanges. The overall value of delivery-based transactions—in which actual delivery occurred—was Rs.6050 crore or 0.0406 percent of total transactions. Further, almost all of the delivery-based transactions took place only in a few commodities such as gold, silver, cardamom, cotton, mentha oil, and sugar.

Our analysis revealed that, for non-agricultural products other than gold and silver, virtually no transaction resulted in actual delivery. Therefore, clearly, most persons who participated in the exchange were not involved with physical trading of the commodity. This pointed to the financialisation of commodity markets in India, and I saw no reason not to impose a CTT in India in pursuance of neutrality with the STT.

At the time, STT was being charged at differentiated rates. It was 0.025 percent of the value of transactions for non-delivery based sale of equity shares or unit of equity transactions. The rate was 0.1 percent of the value for delivery-based transactions. It was 0.17 percent for sale of an option or futures in securities and 0.125 percent for sale of an option when the option was exercised. For sale of a unit of an equity-oriented mutual fund the rate was 0.25 percent and, for the sale of unutilised equity shares under an offer of sale, it was 0.2 percent.

To add to the complexity, the rates of tax of STT for non-delivery based transactions were 0.025 percent and 0.017 percent. On the commodities side, almost the entire transactions through commodities exchanges were non-delivery based. Thus the potential revenue that could be generated from a CTT at rates similar to STT, would range between Rs 2,500–3,500 crores, not an insignificant figure.

Accordingly, in the 2013–14 Union Budget, CTT was re-introduced, however, only for non-agricultural commodity futures at the rate of 0.01 percent (which was the rate on equity futures). Along with it, transactions in commodity derivatives were interpreted to be non-speculative; hence, for traders in the commodity derivative segment, any losses arising from such transactions could be set off against income from any other source (similar provisions were already applicable for securities market transactions).

A separate provision for CTT was made in the 2013 Finance Act and associated rules were notified in June, with effect from 1 July. The notification listed 23 agricultural commodities that were exempt from CTT. However, in February 2015 a revised list of 61 exempt commodities was notified including certain commodities where trading was currently not taking place, thus paring down its scope.

Tax Forum

An even wider ranging activity emerged at FM's behest during the last year of his tenure. Unanticipated by me, in July 2013 he announced that I would chair a Tax Forum for the exchange of views between industry groups and Government on tax related issues, in simpler terms, where stakeholders would present their immediate tax policy conflicts and administration obstacles, and I would have to hear them and solve their problems. This came as a bolt from the blue since I was already deeply involved with reviewing the DTC. I had no choice but to take it up of course.

I was supported by officers of the CBDT and CBEC at senior and junior levels. We heard the views of industry groups and associations, while it also provided us an opportunity to explain to them the Government's stand on tax related matters. My main challenge was to keep taxpayers from overindulgence or exaggeration in making a point and, at the same time, urging or perhaps commandeering officers to listen to their problems analytically. To ensure this, I did not entertain the grievances of any individual taxpayer. In order to have structured and meaningful discussions, I provided a template for all representations into which all tax issues or tax disputes would have to be categorised and fitted. This resulted in surprisingly high efficiency in problem-solving, and the word got around. More and more chambers began to send in requests to meet. In this sense, India is bottomless and, at some point, FM asked me to draw the line for the work on DTC also had to be completed.

The Tax Forum held 18 meetings during August–September 2013. It discussed issues related to direct taxes as well as indirect taxes concerning an industry group or sector. During the two-month period, the Forum met every Wednesday with representatives from the information technology sector, manufacturing sector, infrastructure sector, the services sector including insurance and reinsurance, financial services, furnace and foundry, export sector, and emerging issues in international taxation. This exposure to the private sector, in particular chartered accountants and advocates, had an indirect benefit in that I perceived talent and where it lay.

The Tax Forum identified 29 issues in direct taxes and 47 issues in indirect taxes that merited removal of obstacles and the need for clarifications or amendment of procedures. These issues were sent to the respective Boards for further examination. FM discussed them with the two Boards and took final decisions to remove difficulties faced by taxpayers. Several circulars and notifications were issued by CBDT and CBEC pursuant to those decisions. Some others were in the process of being issued when Parliamentary elections took place in May 2014. Matters that required changes in law were expected to be addressed in the forthcoming Union Budget. However, lamentably, I found that despite agreement, on certain matters those changes did not subsequently occur. This is where the lack of follow-up by a tax administration assumes great importance in dashing the hopes of a compliant taxpayer who is attempting to act as per rules and law.

Nevertheless, the Tax Forum's consultations brought to the notice of Government a tax related issue or dispute at a preliminary stage, resulting in its resolution much before it could snowball into a greater difficulty for the taxpayer. FM studied every recommendation prior to elections and took a view that was recorded or a circular issued. True, I had pressed him to complete the work so that no stakeholder would remain dissatisfied that a decision pertaining to his profession or trade was left undecided. It certainly helped taxpayers in resolving several longstanding issues, both in direct and indirect taxes. On 12 May 2014, I wrote to FM, "With the Tax Forum meeting today, the Forum process I complete. I summarise below the process and outcome..." etc. FM called me, all smiles and indicated, "I have completed your Forum work." I too smiled and responded, "Sir, it was *your* Forum and your reputation. Thank you for taking the time to complete it." And a Press Release on completion of Tax Forum work followed.

TAX ADMINISTRATION REFORM COMMISSION

Towards the end of 2012, the Prime Minister asked me a couple of times what could be done to improve India's tax administration to improve the taxpayer's confidence. I have always maintained that the success of tax administration the world over is a handshake with two palms or a double-edged sword. Cooperation is crucial for it to be successful. I explained where I believed the fault lines lay in the Indian tax administration. Quicker than I could anticipate, Subbu called me to indicate that PM would like a full-fledged commission—as opposed to a committee or task force or working group—at the national level for tax administration reform, and that he planned to talk to FM about it. I volunteered a few names who might chair the work. Soon the matter came to FM, who called me and indicated PM's wish to me. What immediately occurred in North Block bureaucracy I would not like to mention for it would not serve any purpose. Suffice it to say that the matter dragged on from every corner, until FM took the matter in his own hands. At his request, I gave him the names I had in mind. He smiled and responded that I should chair it. Frankly, I did not welcome it, for how many times would I push through my ideas for reform—and now in tax administration—in the Indian environment? After all, I had only human abilities. I expressed doubts on my chairing the commission, but FM explained that this would be the first time that a full-fledged commission would be formed for the reform of India's tax administration and that, like PM, he too felt that I should chair it. I changed my attitude and retreated from his office, looking forward to the work. FM worked on a draft announcement that was soon out.

Here I was the Chairman of India's Tax Administration Reform Commission (TARC), but I was not given to see the drafts of the terms of reference. Despite being a national commission, it was not given any control over its budget. That followed with the impossibility of finding office space or being allocated some. Finally I went to FM and told him the problem. He asked how much space was required. I had it all worked out already. He told me to find the space; allocating it would be his problem. The senior bureaucrats with power over allocating space were travelling abroad at that time, which I did not know. It was serendipity that I came to know of it from officials of that country itself, one with which I had been familiar for decades. Officials there expressed amused surprise that I had not gone along, leave alone not known, about the visit of the Indian bureaucrats. That kind of attitude was unheard of in that part of the world to my knowledge. Nevertheless, it gave some of the younger officers the freedom to inform me where space was available. I ran to FM and informed him. He allocated the space in faraway Saket and, though I would have to travel back and forth between North Block and Saket, I jumped to accept it. One of the high officials who had been an obstacle during the process retired soon after, and visited my office to seek blessings in the next phase of being a grandparent. Thankfully I found within myself the necessary forgiveness and I genuinely gave the person my blessings. Why do I relate this experience—because, while staying away from most such episodes, it is perhaps also important to convey at least some of the obstacles that loom relentlessly in the face of an outsider, unless one tends to agree totally and go along with the bureaucracy. This, of course, has never been possible for me, known as I have been as a change agent, thought leader and so on. Yes, it has been uphill, but people have been known to climb steeper mountains.

The TARC is the longest report that I have penned or chaired. It had the benefit of excellent senior members in whose selection FM took keen interest and it was done entirely by the two of us rather than by bureaucrats. It was my idea to bring in stalwarts from the private sector together with the government sector of course, and FM readily agreed. Thus we had two ex-chairmen of CBDT and CBEC, two ex-members of the same, and two recently retired CFOs from private sector multinationals of impeccable reputation. In the metros, the Commission held meetings with the highest officials in the departments themselves as well as with quasi-government organisations and learnt of the multiple constraints related to efficient tax functioning. It travelled to the far corners seeking to hold free and fair discussions and learn from them. It met the private sector through chambers rather than individually. It went to ports and land border posts of India to check field practices. At the same time, lessons learnt were constantly jotted down and expanded upon as it went along. It must be said that the Commission also had the benefit of several 'support groups' comprising chartered accountants and advocates in specialised areas together with selected top notch officers whose suggestions buttressed the formulation of its final recommendations.

I shall not review the recommendations of TARC here for that would be too voluminous and time-consuming, but mentioning a handful would be useful. First, we reiterated the urgency, as had been recommended by previous committees, in removing the post of Revenue Secretary reflecting the decrease in the need over time of administrative experience and, rather, the need to emphasise and bring in professional expertise at the highest level of Revenue. Second, we recommended the amalgamation of CBDT and CBEC into one department as was the prevailing practice all over the world. Only that would eliminate duplication of work, attract and consolidate information on taxpayers in a legitimate and efficient way rather than being based on fishing for information. Third, we identified as crucial the treatment of taxpayers as 'customers' reflecting global practice, and began the report with that aspect. Fourth, we emphasised empowering officers to speak for the department *pari passu* with locating accountability for a decision until an issue was resolved. Accordingly, we indicated that specialisation in a subject matter should be encouraged. Fifth, we strongly recommended that, before a tax policy change, an 'impact assessment' on the economy and social sectors be carried out and provided full details on how to go about doing it. Accordingly, we recommended an expansion of technical staff from about fifteen to two hundred and fifty.

Suffice it to say that TARC's recommendations were formulated in two stages. The new government had come in in May 2014. Since TARC had been formed under the previous government, I perceived it as my duty to visit Mr. Arun Jaitley, the new Finance Minister, to ask if TARC should continue or wrap up immediately. I found him to be receptive for the first thing he said was that an ambassador—I shall desist from saying who except to indicate that the person was exalted—had visited him just before me and had indicated to him that unless the Indian tax administration was reined in and made more efficient, India would continue to have problems with foreign investment. The ambassador had also told him to look carefully into the already published GAAR report, and that the investment community was looking forward to the forthcoming TARC report. Mr. Jaitley told me that tax terrorism had to be curbed and indicated that TARC should continue and complete its work within the allotted time. He also said that the Commission should come by to meet him when the first set of recommendations was ready.

Commission members were keen that TARC should publish its report. Its members were so senior that, with all due respect to them, I kept silent on the matter for, reflecting my years of experience with that many countries, I respected confidentiality totally. When the first set of recommendations was ready, I brought in the members to meet Mr. Jaitley, a meeting which lasted fairly long. I summarised the thrust while each member took sufficient time to inform him about his or her area of focus. Having finished, as we got up and went towards the door, I turned back and went to him. I asked if we should put up the report on the Finance Ministry's website. He said, of course. I pursued the point and cautioned that some of the recommendations were strong and might not be popular with the bureaucracy. He responded without hesitation that it was an expert report and it should be shared. At that point, he reminded me of K. C. Pant whom I had met fifteen years back. I left relieved and informed the members; some of them looked at me carefully, possibly realising that I had kept the matter of publishing the report from them and under my chest until the minister gave the go ahead. I had won the day with them. We uploaded the report on the Ministry website on 16 June 2014.

I was awestruck by the media reaction on 16–18 June 2014, and cite a few. 'Taxman heal thyself: Reforming tax administration is integral to creating a welcoming investment environment' (Editorial, *The Times of India*, 18 June 2014); 'cause I'm the taxman: Shome panel suggests sweeping reforms' (Editorial, *The Financial Express*, 16 June

2014); 'Abolish Revenue Secretary post, merge CBDT, CBEC, broaden PAN reach: Parthasarathi Shome panel' (*The Indian Express*, 16 June 2014); 'Avoid retro tax law as a principle: Shome panel' (*The Hindu BusinessLine*, 16 June 2014); 'Abolish Revenue Secretary Post; merge CBDT, CBEC, says Tax Administration Reform Commission' (*The Economic Times*, 16 June 2014); 'Government panel calls for overhaul of tax regime' (*Mint*, 17 June 2014); 'Avoid retrospective amendments: Shome' (*The Hindu*, 17 June 2014); 'Abolish revenue secretary post, says Shome panel' (*The Financial Express*, 17 June 2014); 'Abolish post of revenue secy: Shome panel' (*Business Standard*, 17 June 2014); 'Stop more-revenue-anyhow policy: Shome' (*Business Standard*, 18 June 2014); 'Panel outlines tax rejig route' (*The Telegraph—Business*, 17 June 2014). The spate continued on 19 June, with more insight into the details of what TARC had said: 'Avoid refund delays, treat taxpayers as customers: Tax panel to revenue dept' (*The Financial Express*, 19 June 2014); 'Shome panel recommends radical overhaul of tax structure' (*The Economic Times*, 20 June 2014) and so on. On 2 July 2014, *The Financial Express* wrote an incisive editorial titled, 'Worsening tax terror—CAG auditing transfer pricing cases a bad idea', in which it elaborated on some of the statistical evidence that TARC had provided on the low percentage of disputes that the tax department ultimately wins in the judiciary and various solutions to the problem that TARC had provided.

TARC submitted its second report on 26 September 2014 and, on 27 September, the Ministry of Finance's Press Information Bureau issued a long statement on its recommendations. Media coverage was once again comprehensive. Between 27–29 September 2014, they took up the recommendations on the Customs Department with particular emphasis, as we had heard several complaints on both sides, from importers, exporters and officers: 'More proactive role for customs: TARC' (*The Asian Age*, 27 September 2014); 'CBEC should develop a vision, strategic plan for Customs department: TARC' (*The Hindu BusinessLine*, 27 September 2014); 'Use technology to detect fraud, tax panel tells Customs' (*Business Standard*, 27 September 2014), and so on. Thus the needed reforms in that department had caught their attention.

In early December 2014, TARC submitted its third and final report in which it brought back some old ideas that had been dumped after poor reaction from the public. One was the BCTT and the other was the FBT. While *The Hindu*, *Mint* and *Business Standard*—'tough tax pills'—reported and analysed the TARC recommendations in good detail on 3 December 2014, editorials in both *The Financial Express* and *The Economic Times* on 4 December 2014 disagreed with bringing back the BCTT and FBT. After enumerating several good recommendations, *The Financial Express* said that there were some problems with the TARC recommendations such as bringing back the FBT and the BCTT. FBT had been a source of harassment; also "...it is not clear why a tax needs to be levied in order for the taxman to be able to track ATM transactions", but it continued on 5 December 2014 with another editorial entitled, 'Restarting the tax durbar' on TARC's acceptable recommendations in its judgment. *The Economic Times* was more sweeping in its critique with an editorial titled, 'Shome Panel Disappoints—Adopt GST instead of reviving BCTT, FBT'. Clearly, the daily had made a U-turn on TARC recommendations between July–September and December 2014.

Finally, I should mention some of the many generous articles by tax experts on the three TARC reports that I found to be well informed and usually quite incisive. It is not possible to mention them all but the ones I took particular note of were by Sudhir Kapadia (*The Financial Express*, 24 June 2014), Mukesh Butani (*The Financial Express*, 26 June 2014), Satya Poddar and Shalini Mathur (*Business Standard*, 1 July 2014), Santosh Tiwari (*The Financial Express*, 4 September 2014), Girish Vanvari (*The Financial Express*, 6 December 2014), Gautam Nayak (*Mint*, 11 December 2014), Santosh Tiwari (*The Financial Express*, 5 December 2014), and Gokul Chaudhri (*The Financial Express*, 16 February 2015). It appears that articles in *The Financial Express* caught my attention somewhat more than other dailies though, of course, this could just reflect the information chain I was faced with at the time.

Before I move on to the next issue, I must acknowledge the calls I received while I was in my TARC office in Saket from Mr. P. K. Mishra, the new Principal Secretary to the new PM. He generally wanted to know five measures or ten steps that they should take in the immediate run to sharpen tax policy and administration. I always responded the same day or the next, reflecting the importance of the matter and my unfailing interest in reform. I also had to visit his office on occasion to discuss particular crucial issues he had in mind. This culminated in my participation in a pre-Budget meeting that the PM, as Chairman of Niti Ayog, called before the 2015 Union budget. A dozen economists were called, and the PM indicated that he had called to hear and learn from them. I was the fourth to speak. I started by explaining the difference between risk and uncertainty as perceived by potential investors, and that risk could be handled by investors reflecting their attitude towards risk, but not uncertainty which they could not assess or model. I emphasised that uncertainty was very much continuing at the time, almost a year after the government had assumed office. The PM was listening intently. As I differentiated uncertainty from risk, he took out his notebook and began taking notes. That visibly changed the hearing from those around him. I made ten recommendations on immediate tax reform for the Budget. I found many of them in the Budget speech in one form or another. I completed the work on TARC soon thereafter and, reflecting an earlier decision, moved out of Delhi in pursuit of research.

GOODS AND SERVICES TAX

Before I returned to North Block, I was invited by Yashwant Sinha, Chairman of the Lok Sabha's Standing Committee on Finance, to appear before it to give my independent opinion on the GST on 13 July 2012. It should be available in the Parliamentary records and I do not see the need to comment on it further. Suffice it to say that I was content to appear before the Committee where I tried my level best to convince the members about the need and efficacy of introducing a GST in India for cleaning up indirect taxation and facilitating business operations. As we completed the session and emerged for lunch, Mr. Sinha said to me, Partho, you did a good job in taking my colleagues a long way to accept the GST. Needless to say, I was delighted to hear his comment. However, I was sceptical that the GST could be introduced prior to the 2014 Parliamentary elections if adequate preparation by taxpayer and tax administration was to be given heed. This was reported on 30 July 2012 by *The Economic Times* quite comprehensively. And Sijbren Cnossen, an internationally well-known Dutch professor in the field of indirect taxation, made scathing presentations on India's proposed GST in February and August 2012 in Indian and international conferences that did not help the GST cause in international academic or business circles.

After I re-entered North Block at the end of the same year, I nevertheless found that work on the GST was well on its way. FM asked me to help out to the extent I could while keeping in mind the work demands on the DTC. Accordingly I kept my close attention on the DTC, though I could not get away from the GST as FM would ask me questions on technical matters for which I needed to be totally on board. For example, he asked whether there was any need to continue the regime of 'Declared Goods', a special category of goods on which the Centre imposed its rate structure when those goods were traded among states, and I had to provide a detailed analysis and comments. There were several minute items which I shall desist from describing. At the macro level, a Constitutional Amendment was required for the GST since the taxes assigned to the two levels of government in the Constitution by India's founding fathers were going to be fundamentally altered. The Committee had provided comments on the draft Bill. FM asked me to comment on that as well. Thankfully both DTC and GST aspects were pleasurable work, though the associated bureaucracy was not.

The work on the Constitutional Amendment was completed, but Manmohan Singh made an unanticipated announcement that the GST would have to await the next government. Indeed it did. But the GST structure that was eventually put in place veered significantly from an ideal GST. One year has now passed after the GST was introduced on 1 July 2017. I have provided excerpts below from an interview of mine with S. Rajendran of The Hindu Centre for Politics and Public Policy that appeared on 19 May 2017, just prior to the 1 July introduction of the GST, which revealed my continuing doubts regarding its structure, tax compliance and implementation.

'Goods and Services Tax may not really be the biggest tax reform'[5]

"If the proposed GST structure was closer to the ideal, it would comprise fundamental tax reform. If, however, one examines the proposed structure of the GST, it becomes difficult to view it as one of the biggest tax reforms since independence. In earlier periods, in 1996-97, the income tax structure was fundamentally altered with a significant cutback in the rate structure to 30, 20 and 10 per cent, which encouraged work effort and improved revenue intake. A decade later, the value added tax (VAT) was introduced at the level of the States as a prime example of Centre-State fiscal cooperation. This radically altered the earlier State-level Sales Taxes. Again, revenue intake shot up while providing impetus to business.

"In that context, if one is calling the new tax a GST, it should not have differentiated between goods and services; yet that differentiation will continue as before with concomitant adverse impact on litigation. Second, an administrative requirement will make it essential for inter-State dealers to register in every State they trade in. This goes against the common market principle that GST was supposed to usher in. Importantly, third, it also means that a trader can be picked up for audit in any of these States thus making tax compliance difficult if not impossible for taxpayers. Fourth, the Centre and the States have brought under their respective control the same taxpayers even at lower turnover levels thus implying an increased compliance burden on taxpayers with tax administrations at both levels to deal with. Thus the various tax administrations—horizontally across States and vertically between the Centre and States—are increasing their power with little perceptible increase in their accountability."

"...Petroleum and electricity are essential inputs in the supply—production and distribution—chain. By keeping these out, both upstream and downstream cascading will occur....First ... the [non-GST] tax paid cannot be credited out by businesses when they buy and use petroleum products. Second, petroleum being outside GST, petroleum companies themselves—since they are excluded from GST—are unlikely to get any credit for the GST that they will have paid on their own inputs. Thus petroleum companies will add the tax they will pay on inputs into their product price; and businesses that purchase petroleum will build in the tax they pay on their petroleum input into the sale price of their product. Thus there will be double cascading." [The same will occur for electricity.]

"...If one considers the exclusion of real estate from GST and all other inputs and exemptions, some estimates show an exclusion of 60 per cent of GDP from the GST base. If we ignore real estate, we could perhaps work with a figure between 40-50 per cent. In any event, a large portion of GDP is being excluded.... Ideally there should be two rates [of GST]—a general rate and a lower rate for popular consumption items. We are moving away from it. I can imagine that the States disagreed and finally the Centre agreed. But the Centre's resolve should not have been compromised merely for the sake of having a GST."

"...Even today, by and large, foreign investors continue to be dissatisfied with Indian tax administration practices at the field level. This needs to change so that business confidence returns. GST will be an important test to check if the corner has been turned and the business community experiences a perceptible improvement in the ease of paying taxes. The tax authorities both at the central and state levels have to be given the opportunity to work on this and achieve success."

"...Unfortunately, corruption flows through the veins and arteries of India as reported relentlessly by both Indians and foreigners. I have maintained that corruption is a double-edged sword; it cannot occur from one side only. The acquiescence of the general public to corruption in order to take the short cut has vitiated society. That has enabled corruption. As corruption spreads, it becomes more acceptable, thus fuelling the fire even further. Fearfully, the most powerful are most corrupt, its obverse side being the spread of extreme poverty. Poverty has become a political tool and we Indians shamelessly accept it as inevitable. Foreign well-wishers cannot comprehend this aspect of our society though they may love India just like we do."

"...I believe that the GST by itself will have little impact on corruption. We have an impeccable ability to subvert procedures. Even a measure such as demonetisation was being successfully subverted immediately after it was set in motion. Nevertheless, inasmuch as computerised processes 'successfully' replace many face-to-face transactions under the GST, corruption should be checked somewhat within this narrow sphere. That would comprise a good beginning. But a comprehensive solution to corruption lies elsewhere."

[In terms of fiscal federalism,]..."my question is whether all the time and resources spent to decide matters between the Centre and States can be justified in the form of improvements for businesses, their productivity, the impact on GDP, on resultant tax revenue, and comparability and benchmarking of India with the rest of the world. Or are we going to be unable to change the truncated, autarkic economic environment that we essentially have irrespective of the colour of administrations that come and go. If the GST can assist in garnering foreign and domestic investment and generate economic growth while containing inflation, it would have gone a long way. I hope so, despite the many faultlines in its structure and probable gaps in its administration."

[Nevertheless I was pleasantly surprised that during GST's first year, the tax department did a good job in making serious attempts at a smooth transition and implementation. This I elaborated in *Business Standard* a year later on 18 July and 15 August 2018.]

[In the area of income tax,] "A Direct Tax Code (DTC) had been carefully developed and completed in 2009, revised in 2010, finalised in 2013, examined by the Parliamentary Committee on Finance whose comments were addressed meticulously, was cleared by line Ministries, and ready to go to Cabinet in 2015, got delayed, and then general elections took place. The incoming policymakers declared that the DTC would be set aside since most matters therein had already been addressed." [Though, in an apparent change of mind, it was indeed taken up again.]

[One area that needs attention is]..."tax incentives where investments protect the rich from high tax rates. Inequity is built into the tax structure, another example being the exemption of one residence irrespective of its value while a lower middle class person has to pay presumptive tax on even a small second home that may have been acquired towards the end of a professional career. And changes in the colour of successive administrations have not resulted in corrective steps in such aspects of the Income Tax law. Thus claims of equity within the income tax structure are unfounded."

It is hoped that the ongoing examination of the DTC will revisit the 2009 DTC and undertake the measures proposed in it.

MIXING WORK WITH PLEASURE

I would not like to conclude this chapter with the impression that it was all work and work alone. Thus in 2013, it was serendipity that I found myself at the site of several religious celebrations. These included spending Buddha Purnima in Benaras sitting on a boat, watching the extraordinarily beautiful dancing fire-play of the *arati* in a rendition of devotional songs with the full moon rising behind me on the Ganga; spending Vinayak Chaturthi in Mumbai, visiting the most popular Ganesha *pandal*s and witnessing human devotion at its most acute; spending Durga Puja in Kolkata and being fortunate enough to visit the most artistic, prize-winning *pratima* and accompanying decorations in the north, south and central parts of the city on three consecutive days while being part of a committee of international judges; and sitting from 6 am to 6 pm right across from the *ratha*s on Rath Yatra day in Puri, and scurrying to give a tug at the ropes pulling the chariots heavenwards. At the same time I was welcomed at Haji Ali in Mumbai in contemplation, and found myself with friends on Christmas Day in Mexico City at one of Catholicism's holiest shrines—the cathedral dedicated to the Virgin of Guadalupe who, goes the legend, had appeared to an American Indian. It was thus an incredibly rich and adventurous year, much needed to balance the relentless demands that emerged continually from my professional responsibilities. And such visits continue to this day across India and the world, globetrotter as I remain.

Why? The only response I can manage is that these impulses are inexplicable yet not unusual. Ramakrishna Paramahamsa and Vivekananda had both concluded that the outcome of all religions is the same, going even beyond religion itself. Ramakrishna had in fact lived as a Christian and a Muslim for some periods of his life just to see if he could feel any difference, but found none. Seeing that hookahs at his home were identified separately for guests of different castes and faiths, Narendra—the young Vivekananda—tried them out and concluded, "I see no difference". And to those who nevertheless differentiated, Ramakrishna said, "You should be a devotee, but why should you, therefore, be a fool?"[6] Thus, in the current era, those who propound Vivekananda to the exclusivity of Hinduism need to educate themselves and initiate a course correction.

ENDNOTES

1. Dhirendra Kumar, 'Tasty GAARnish for an unpalatable dish', *Hindustan Times*, 2 September 2012, New Delhi.
2. *ET* Bureau, 'Parthasarathy Shome panel's recommendations on GAAR make sense, on the whole', *The Economic Times*, 3 September 2012.

3. 'Don't delay GAAR: Do it properly—but do it now', *Business Standard*, 4 September 2012, New Delhi.

4. K. R. Srivats, 'Hike STT levy to offset capital gains tax abolition: Shome panel', *The Hindu BusinessLine*, 2 September 2012, New Delhi.

5. S. Rajendran, 'Goods and Services Tax may not really be the biggest tax reform: Parthasarathi Shome', The Hindu Centre for Politics and Public Policy, 19 May 2017.

6. See Chaturvedi Badrinath, *Swami Vivekananda: The Living Vedanta* (New Delhi: Penguin Books, 2006), Chapter 2, 22–30.

TEN

MOVING FORWARD

As I completed my tenure at TARC, I made haste to complete ongoing volumes. Indeed, that activity has not ceased to this day. Hence I seek the indulgence of the reader to let me place a couple of illustrations before them.

MY WRITING CONTINUES

Tax Compendium

I gathered and revitalised a collection of my research papers, some co-authored and some my own, written over the last four decades almost. Going back to them, I was myself a bit taken aback as to their continuing relevance over such a long period to students and policymakers alike. *Taxation Principles and Applications: A Compendium* was published by Lexis Nexis in 2014 and inaugurated at a gala function in New Delhi organised by D. S. Rawat, Secretary General of Assocham (see Plate 32). It contained thirty-eight chapters under eight sections comprising an overview; incidence and distribution effects of taxation; efficiency effects of taxation; VAT, GST and customs tariffs; innovations in taxation; national and regional experiences; tax administration; and concluding with highlights of tax design. There were excellent reviews of the book in major business dailies and magazines. Unfortunately there is little space to quote from all of them here. Therefore, I shall quote only from two reviews. The first is from the 8 April 2017 issue of the *Economic & Political Weekly* by Pinaki Chakraborty, professor at the National Institute of

Public Finance and Policy (NIPFP), which was full of insights. And the second is from the January–June 2014 edition of the Delhi School of Economics journal *Indian Economic Review*, by Pulin Nayak, professor at DSE, which pointed out the most relevant aspects of the book.

In his 952-word review titled, 'Evaluating Taxation Systems and Policies', Professor Chakraborty says the book is a

> comprehensive collection of ... fascinating papers ... meant for scholars, teachers, graduate students and policymakers ... a rare balance of theory and application of policy analysed in the context of specific sub-continental regions ... would greatly help tax administrators and practitioners ... particularly in ... developing countries ... eloquently elaborates on critical discussions and empirical evidence relating to the incidence, equity and parity effects of taxation ... a most significant contribution in tax policy and tax administration ... [reflecting] the author's vast experience in managing tax policy issues globally ... Shome is 'truly one of the leading international tax thinkers'.[1]

In his even longer 1378-word review, Professor Nayak comments,

> The compendium includes papers on virtually all major issues in ... taxation, viz., theory, policy, administration and actual practice. ... going back to Kautilya's '*Arthashastra*' ... 'A wise Chancellor is one who collects revenue so as to increase income and reduce expenditure. He shall take remedial measures if income diminishes and expenditure increases' [Kautilya wrote,] ... emphasiz[ing] the importance of the internal management of the tax system ... The author writes with great clarity and brings to bear his mastery over theoretical issues as well as his extensive experience as a high profile international tax policy maker. The volume could be profitably used as basic reading material in post graduate courses in public finance anywhere in the world. ... tax administrators and policy makers would do well to carefully go through this comprehensive, well researched and up to date tract.[2]

Sixty Critical Commentaries

A second volume of collected papers of a very different nature arose almost accidentally as requests increased from different directions to republish some of my columns in business dailies. Consequently I selected sixty of my monthly columns written exclusively for *Business Standard* between 2009 and 2016 on various topics covering the macroeconomy, fiscal policy, general taxation matters, income tax, indirect tax, international economic relations, socio-economic policy, political economy, and the newest emerging concerns in India. The volume, *Development and Taxation: Sixty Critical Commentaries*, was published by Academic Foundation in 2017 and was separately released in all the metros (see Plate 33). I have a penchant for using statistical tables and graphs to illustrate even my newspaper columns, and I was informed that the collection has been quite useful for illustrating economic puzzles in the classroom. Nothing gives me greater pleasure than to be told that my work has been, is, or will be, useful to students.

MOVE TO BANGALORE

The genesis of my move to Bangalore was an informal conversation I had with Mohandas Pai while sipping a cappuccino at the American Café at India Habitat Centre, New Delhi, in 2013. He had lamented that there was no real base for research on the newly emerging area of international taxation in Bangalore, and whether I would lead the path to establish one. Frankly, I had earlier explored Kolkata and Chennai, though nothing had come of it. Some good professional friends from Mumbai insisted that Mumbai being the centre for the practice of international taxation, I should go there. But my connection with Mohan from the days when we were together in the empowered committee for computerisation of the tax departments at North Block, and his never failing presence to keep in touch with me during my years at HMRC, clinched my decision. I agreed to move to Bangalore.

Thus we set up the International Tax Research and Analysis Foundation (ITRAF) in Bangalore. I found that some of the bright accountants and lawyers who had participated in the Tax Forum meetings in North Block were residents of Bangalore—they were all practising professionals; but Mohan and I focussed on those who were keen on research, and our group came into being in 2015 with much fanfare. We refrained from its ballooning into something unmanageable. Instead, my vision was, in this electronic age, a research entity that would encourage and attract research from all corners of India and abroad. The model I developed was of the submission of research proposals by any interested researchers and the completion of their work after being vetted, subject, of course, to quality control. The experiment has worked and we have brought out two edited volumes on emerging issues in international taxation in India as well as on the crucial area of corporate tax base erosion through profit shifting (BEPS) across international tax jurisdictions by multinational corporations. Both volumes have been published from Wolters Kluwer in 2016 and 2017—the first two years of ITRAF's existence—by authors who have included academicians, lawyers, accountants and tax administrators. All in all, ITRAF has turned out to be a one-of-a-kind vehicle for research in a specialised field, and its output is in high demand. A third volume from Oakbridge is just out.

Even as I move forward on my research on taxation, an aspect I have observed is that economists have, by and large, ring-fenced themselves so to speak from the area of international taxation even though I consider their participation to be important. Indeed, one of the gaps in the prevailing taxation literature is the dearth of intellectual thought and research emanating in a comparable manner from related professional fields that affect various stages of the taxation process. This process comprises the formulation of tax policy, often by economists, the interpretation of the intention and the writing of tax law by lawyers, the calculation of tax to be paid based on the specifics of the law determined and recommended by accountants and tax advisers, and the collection and examination of tax received by tax administrators from taxpayers. All these aspects are intrinsically inter-related.

To fill this gap to a small extent, I was successful in bringing together barristers, chartered accountants, tax administrators, though only a couple of practising policy economists, including myself, on a single platform on the research contained in *BEPS: The Global Taxation Agenda*, one of the volumes mentioned above. The volume provides a good example of how different professions with a common research orientation can be drawn together to produce a scholarly work whose whole is larger than the sum of its individual parts. Of course, the challenges involved in bringing together such a diverse set of active professionals to contribute even on a theme of common professional interest should not be underestimated.

MOVE TO LONDON

To bridge the gap in the medium to long term, however, there has to be a fundamental change in how academic economists approach the teaching of taxation and to attempt to introduce international taxation to students at an early stage of their learning. Recognising the urgency of this, I have ensconced myself in the Law Department at LSE as a Visiting Fellow to understand and assess the teaching of taxation law and its relevance and incorporation in the teaching of the economics of taxation. This pondering and educating myself represents one step up in the amalgamation of taxation as a composite field of learning from the economist's corner that would encompass to some degree at least tax law, tax calculation and tax administration. That is my endeavour of the moment.

Another benefit of London has been reconnecting with academics here. I must mention Lord Meghnad Desai, voracious and versatile scholar of not only economics but also a vast range of Hindu epics, and more importantly, my teacher from the DSE days, as well as Philip Baker, Oxford professor and Queen's Counsel whose acquaintance I had made in India while at North Block and who has been crucial in not only my understanding a little more of the legal tenets of taxation but has also been immensely helpful in my settling into London. And, London being at the crossroads of international research, I have been introduced to American and Latin American scholars including Dr. Eduardo Baistrocchi at LSE. Discussions with them on ongoing international research are both insightful and pleasurable. And, of course, LSE remains a living crucible of lively discussions and eye-opening deconstruction of not only the prevailing knowledge and principles of taxation but also of many other areas of concern such as the degenerated global condition of income and wealth distribution. I am enjoying this period immensely.

As I end, I would like to touch upon my deep concerns regarding the current winds blowing in every which direction to dismember the understandings behind the concept of tax reform, as I have recently expressed in my paper at the LSE, 'Contours and Conflicts in Tax Design: Principles and International Practice', LSE Law, Society and Economy, Working Paper 11, 2018. Tax design is said to be based on certain principles comprising efficiency of resource allocation despite taxation's distortionary effects, maintenance or encouragement of equity among taxpayers, and assisting in macroeconomic stabilisation. Other safeguards are a tax system's revenue productivity, clarity of taxation law, ease of tax compliance, and facilitation of tax administration. Common experience reveals, however, that no tax structure complies with these criteria all at once.

The term reform is variously used by authors and across tax professions—economists, legal experts, accountants, administrators—their emphasis varying significantly. Bridging these gaps remains a crucial challenge. Empirical evidence also suggests that when a new administration takes over, it puts its own stamp on tax policy, egged on by lobbyists who were adversely affected in earlier change cycles. And, with the internationalisation of taxation, a country's tax structure gets affected by developments in political or trading blocs.

In my paper, I pointed towards vacillations and drifts in the way tax changes occur. Consumption taxes (VAT/GST), production taxes such as excises, environment taxes, user charges, direct taxes including income and wealth taxes, and their component taxes on dividends, capital gains, cash-flow, presumptive bases, minimum tax payments, and emerging factors in international taxation are taken up.

In conclusion, the effects of taxes go beyond narrow economic aspects. Legal, accountancy or administrative aspects carry important implications. The glass wall between tax economics and tax law or accountancy, and between tax economics and tax administration, if removed, would generate an awareness with beneficial crossover effects. Then tax reform can be discussed on the same plane and be implemented with comparable understandings.

Thus do I bow out with a preoccupation in mind.

ENDNOTES

1. Pinaki Chakraborty, 'Evaluating Taxation Systems and Policies', *Economic & Political Weekly* 52(14): 39–40, 8 April 2017.

2. Pulin B. Nayak, *Indian Economic Review* 49(1): 143–145, January–June 2014.

EPILOGUE

This has been a professional memoire that has focussed primarily on my higher education and professional journeys through continents and decades. However, it has been my conviction based on experience that one's life—and, therefore, profession—is the sum total of one's childhood and youth that form the foundation of the future years, as may be gleaned from *The Inner World* by Sudhir Kakar, author and psychiatrist:

> The old nature vs nurture, heredity vs environment, controversy boils down....to an acknowledgement of every individual's dual heritage: our biological-physical endowment indelibly embellished by the culture of the particular society which surrounds us from the beginning of life, enveloping us like the very air we breathe and without which we do not grow into viable human beings.[1]

Mine is the same. Since I am constrained, however, from delving into an account of my childhood in the confines of these pages, I have decided to recall just a few scenes from both childhood and adulthood that have had a profound impact on me and my later life.

The first was my father's departure from the house of his father when I was seventeen. It was an indelible lesson that everything in life was ephemeral, for the flat we moved into was relatively small and the children were instructed to take as few possessions as possible. Apart from some of my mother's inheritances at her wedding, including much loved porcelain figurines from England, Japan and China, all of which had an attraction as I grew up, left behind were grand utensils of yesteryear made of white and dark marble, brass and silver. But my consternation was in abandoning my meticulously organised textbooks and exercise books from primary school onwards, thanks to my mother's orderliness from which I too had learnt. I could take along only a handful and still recall the texts and search for them on websites, such can be the damning ramifications of memory. My grandfather, great grandmother and my father died over the next three years. It was heartrending to see a ninety-five year old mother slumped over the corpse of her eldest, seventy-six year old son. I recall my great grandmother telling me in Sylheti that, with the departure of my mother, Lakshmi had flown out of the house. My grandfather continued to have an influence on my academic resolve for, though I stood fifth in the university in Madras Matriculation—thus becoming a National Scholar—and third in Calcutta University in my Pre-University Science exams—thus becoming state scholar—when I went to touch his feet as was the custom those days, both times he insufficiently accepted my *pranam* and indicated that my effort and, along with it the outcome, had not been complete. So I tried harder. When I stood first in my Bachelor's Honours degree at Calcutta University, he was not alive.

The second was witnessing my father breathe his last, after suffering in a 'nursing home' for a fortnight, when I was twenty-one. Among the many things he would say, as long as his physical condition allowed him to, there were two I would like to mention. First, he advised me never to buy a property for, once one entered the property, his peace of mind flew out. I had sensed my mother's discomfiture at his statement, but had smiled despite not fully comprehending its meaning or relevance. But it left an imperceptible and life-long impact on me for I can never be an absentee landlord; if I have bought property when located in a city in India or abroad, I have always gotten rid of it at departure, though I have had to usually do so when the housing market had been on the ebb. This behaviour and attitude appears to fully reflect my father's foreboding. Second, prior to sinking into a coma, the news arrived that I had stood first in Delhi University in MA Previous, the first year master's exam. When I informed my father, he was visibly glad; yet he told me that my generation would be needed to build India and that, even if I went abroad for further study, I should return to serve India. This has been an ever-lasting consideration in my life choices professionally. This was the father who taught me values that have remained steadfast.

He accompanied me to every university exam and saw to it that I was served coconut water during breaks and backed me up during exam recesses when I looked nervous. He took me on cross-country journeys to experience India, and they have remained etched in my memory. His manner of educating me was indeed quite unique.

The third most gruelling experience was to witness my mother's last breath in hospital when her final insistent wish was to die at home. The wiles of modern medicine withheld me from taking her home for the greed of keeping a ninety year old alive at any cost and the weakness that withheld me from making a decision. Ultimately, strong as she was in personality, it appeared that she had given up on me, yet I could not respond to her wish. That pain has been so harrowing and ceaseless that I have been surprised that a person approaching seventy could experience such intensity in emotions even as modern medicine teaches that, with age, emotion-generating brain cells die and are not replaced. Today, from experience, I feel that science may be correct, and yet it may be nonsensical to combine scientific fact with the workings of the heart.

It is difficult today to assess my mother's contributions in their fullness for there were so many aspects to it. On the one hand she could be indulgent but often she was strict. In adulthood, when I jocularly accused her of having been strict, she responded by saying that one of every two parents had to be strict when the other was indulgent. I entered Don Bosco's in Madras in Class VI, and recall standing first in class in every exam. I was given a 'double promotion', but my mother did not allow it as she felt I should not miss out any step in my education and should assimilate learning fully along the way. Many years earlier, she herself had received double promotion at the Brahmo Girls' School in Calcutta and, though she continued to excel in core subjects, and in arts and sports, her comprehension in mathematics suffered. I recall being grateful at her decision for, had I received double promotion, I would have lost my friends whom I had nurtured that first year in Madras after losing my friends in Hindi High in Calcutta. I had also learnt to be in a Catholic school and recite, *Our Father who Art in Heaven*, switching from *Saraswati Vandana*—it was ironic that earlier in Calcutta, Hindi High had been specifically selected over St. Xavier's at my father's insistence, but in Madras the only option had been a Catholic school.

At Don Bosco's, there were some strange practices. The first was that students had to sit according to their 'rank' in class, the top students starting in the last row, and the line winding up like a snake with the weakest performers in the front row right under the careful eyes of old-style teachers most of whom were practiced in using their palms across a lagging student's face. The second practice of note was that students were awarded 'cards' after every major exam, yellow 'progress cards' for having moved up ten ranks, white 'honorary cards' for the first three ranks in every section of a grade, and a red 'merit card' for the first student among all sections of the grade. It so happened that I received the merit card in every exam. Just before the half-yearly exam in Class VIII, my mother said to me that I should concentrate on studies. I was a bit surprised that she should say that and indicated that she could rest assured that I would receive the merit card as usual. She responded that, that might be true for the moment, but commented whether I had noticed that the difference in marks between me and the next first boy in another section had been decreasing in the last few exams. I was so amazed to realise that she had been silently keeping abreast of such minute details of my performance and dissecting them that my eyes widened and my jaw dropped as I looked at her incredulously. She simply turned and walked towards the door.

I also recall that at quite an early age, I had an aversion to touching certain things. My mother told me, *lajja, ghrina, bhoy—teen thakte noy.* She told me to repel shyness, aversion and fear for these three would reduce one to nothing. Whether or not I have mastered all three elements, this has certainly been the highest lesson I have learnt in life.

In the same vein, even in her eighties, she would read every writing with which I was associated including the GAAR and retrospective taxation reports, Planning Commission reports, and even parts of the TARC report. While I could hear her sighs of appreciation and disbelief, she would also cross-question me and ask me to explain certain concepts. Her preoccupation, right from my IMF days, was if my policy recommendations affected the middle class adversely. I used to joke with her that she was the only eighty year old woman in the world who knew so much about the by-lanes of taxation. She would smile and, invoking me, give a motherly reply. Yet, as my reading and writing intensified, including a book on art dedicated to her, today I realise that I gave her less and less time at a moment that I should have immersed her with all my time. This was the mother I lost and in a manner I abhor to this day. Though, surrounded by her family, everyone fed her drops of *gangajal* as her last breaths were leaving her, to my last day I will continue to feel that her passing did not happen the way it should have. Just after she had passed away in hospital, on her bed at home, we found a poem written in her hand:

‘নীরব’

নীরব হইতে বড় হয়েছে বাসনা
নীরবে সাধিব আমি সকল সাধনা
নীরবে করিব সদা হরিগুনগান
নীরবে করিব হৃদে হরিরূপ ধ্যান ।
সংসারে কত কিছু দুঃখ আর ভয়
নীরবে সহিয়া যেন করি সব জয় ।
জীবনের কাজ সব নীরবে বুঝিব
প্রাণ দিয়ে সদা তাহা নীরবে সাধিব ।
যখন আসিবে দেব তব আবাহন
নীরবে তোমার কাছে করিব গমন ।
অতি ভয়ংকর সেই মৃত্যুর যাতনা
তুমি থাক প্রাণে আর রবেনা ভাবনা
তব পদে নিবেদন ওহে দয়াময়
নীরবে আমার যেন সব শেষ হয় ।

Silence

From silence has crested my desire
In silence shall I perform all service
In silence shall I sing the praises of Hari
In silence shall I call Hari from my heart.
Life carries so much sorrow and fear
In silence may I bear and overcome.
In silence may I understand life’s work
And in silence may I undertake them.
When Your call comes, Oh! Almighty
In silence shall I depart to you.
Though excruciating be the pain of this death
With you in my heart, there is no fear.
I surrender to your feet Kind Lord!
May my end occur in silence.

Returning to childhood, among a thousand memories, three small events have never faded from my mind's eye. The first was an encounter with Jawaharlal Nehru when I was eleven. He was visiting Madras, and we had been invited to afternoon tea with him. Of course my mother had fitted the children with the best from our wardrobes. The gate at the Governor's house led to a long tree-lined drive filled with deer. The wait for the Prime Minister was short. As he appeared, we rose and sat down with him. He talked with my parents as if they had known one another very well. Eventually he looked at us children and smiled. He asked me, "Have you learnt Tamil?" I could see my father's consternation. Reflexively I responded, "*Vanakkam*". Nehru's smile widened and he asked me to approach him. I did. He took out the red rose from his lapel and fixed it on me. Then he turned me around and sat me close to him as he continued to chat. As we left I could see my father's pride in his pan-India son in the making. Indeed in another five years, as I left school, I could speak colloquial Tamil acceptably and my father occasionally referred to me as "Tamil" of which I was quite proud. Slowly the language receded, though even today I can manage an inadequate Tamil in an emergency.

The second event took place the same year when Queen Elizabeth and the Duke of Edinburgh visited Madras in 1961. From school we had gone to Pantheon Road, a block away from Casa Major Road where my school was located, and stood in line, some with the Indian Tricolour and others with the Union Jack, to wave when the Queen passed by. Eventually, the Queen, all smiles and waving her hand gently, slowly drove past standing in an open car with the Duke standing by her side. As I recall, she wore a bright pink dress and made a huge impression. As my parents left for her reception that evening, I asked my mother if I could come along. She smiled and said, perhaps one day I would meet her. Late in 2017, I was judged to be a person of 'exceptional talent' under the approval of an anonymous British Academy. I jocularly asked, "Do I get to meet the Queen?"

The third was the visit of Anita Bose, Netaji Subhash Bose's German daughter, to Madras. The ovation the young woman with her father's face and apple cheeks received as she drove past the boulevards was stupendous. My father accompanied her. That evening there was a grand reception on our terrace for which I saw my mother herself prepare her famous fish croquets and cakes. The terrace was jammed.

I witnessed the entrance of Shri Rajagopalachari, India's former Governor General, and also Shri Kamaraj, then Chief Minister. Many years later I learnt that the two generally did not meet; nevertheless they were there together that day to celebrate one of the chapters of India's independence movement. As an adult, I reconnected with Anita and, during one of her visits to Delhi, she informed Amit Mitra (the current Finance Minister of West Bengal), who invited me to a small dinner at his home with some of the extended Bose family. It was an evening I enjoyed. And even today, as uncles and aunts in the extended family have come in contact, the evening get-togethers organised by them on my short visits to Kolkata are most pleasurable.

But all early memories are not fun and frolic. There was an event in early adulthood that stabbed like a dagger through my heart. This was the passing of my maternal grandmother. I was abroad and just could not make it to her deathbed. I received several calls imploring that, in those last days of her life, she was mistaking everyone for me, saying I would certainly come to see her. I could not. I dedicated one of my books to her. Instead of describing why she was so important to me, let me just quote from the Preface of *Development and Taxation*, Academic Foundation, 2017.

> I dedicate the volume to Niharika Guha, my grandmother. Married at fourteen and widowed at twenty-five, she was dedicated to my education, taught me my first songs on her organ, and also fables and epics. She ensured my material and cerebral sustenance by providing not only top-notch tutors but also my first tennis racquet and guitar. I am proud to dedicate these writings to a classical Indian woman.

Like my mother, my grandmother had also attended Brahmo Girls', but her education had been cut short by an early marriage and then widowhood. But that never limited her onward intellectual progress or domestic care until her last breath for those who surrounded her in the joint family in which she lived.

Galactic experiences and moments in life come while reading something completely unanticipated or while learning from teachers. I have been most fortunate in having brilliant, caring and demanding teachers throughout my life. Those episodes are too numerous and comprise the contents of another volume. Therefore, for their immeasurable contributions, I have dedicated this professional memoire to my teachers.

ENDNOTES

1. Sudhir Kakar, *The Inner World: A Psycho-analytic Study of Childhood and Society in India* (Oxford University Press, 1981).

INDEX

Abraham, Mr. Pylee, *xiii*
academic achievements
  awards, 8
  early childhood and education, 1–2
  PhD thesis, 6–8
Adviser to Finance Minister, 150, 154–155
  on anomalies in tax structure, 169
  on automation of tax departments, 177–180
  on Banking Cash Transaction Tax (BCTT), 169–171, 202
  committees and responsibilities, 180–182
  on Fringe Benefits Tax (FBT), 172–175, 202
  Goods and Services Tax proposed (2006–07), 163–165, 202
  introduction of VAT structure, 155–162
  on large taxpayer units (LTUs), 175–177
  proposed changes in tax incentive calculation, 165–166
  on Right to Information (RTI) Act, 180
  on Special Economic Zones (SEZ) Act, 166
Agarwal, Pawan, 123
Aguirre, Carlos, 23, 93
Ahluwalia, Isher, 133, 201
Ahluwalia, Montek Singh, 140–141
Alma Ata, 81, 83, 85–86
American Institute of Indian Studies (AIIS), 16
Andorra, 89–90
Aranguren, Mario, 44
Argentina, 128, 133–134, 139, 198
  exchange rate, 47
  tax administration and policy, 47
  tax reforms, 49–50
  tax to GDP ratio, 47
  VAT structure, 47–48
Ashra, Sunil, 134, 136
Asian Crisis of 1997–98, 132
Atchabahian, Adolfo, 55
Atkinson, Tony, 16
Atkinson's Inequality Index, 119
Atuk, 62, 64
Australia, 128

Bagchi, Amaresh, 122, 125–127
Bagchi, P., *xiii*
Baistrocchi, Eduardo, 246
Baker, Philip, 246
Bandhu, Sandeep, 219
Banerjee, Deepak, 9
Banerjee, Ruben, *xiii*
Banerji, Nikhil, 155

Bangladesh, 96–100, 147
Bardhan, Pranab, 137
Barfield, Juliet, 191
Basque Region, 90–91
Basu, Kamal, 65
Basu, Kaushik, 16, 137
Basu, Shrabani, 188–190
Batra, Anurag, *xiii*
Batra, Ravi, 4, 7–8
Batra, Ravindra, *xiii*, 4, 6
Bejia, 66
Belgium, 107
Beytia, J. M., 50
Beytia, Manuel, 55
Beza, Ted, 27–28, 30–31
Bhargava, Anjuli, 12, 153, 168–169, 184
Bhattacharya, B. B., 10
Bhattacharya, J., 206
Bhaumik, Sumon, 125
Bhushan, Shri Phani, *xiii*
Bilbao Garai, Juan Miguel, 90
Biswas, Miss, *xiii*
Blanchard, Olivier J., 208
Bogota, 63–64, 113
Bolivia, 110, 133
  tax system, 113
Bose, Anita, 253–254
Bose, Netaji Subhas Chandra, 96, 145
Botero, 66
Botswana, 72–76
Bouche, Father Camille, 65
Brazil, 113, 128, 133–134, 190, 198
  financial transaction tax (FTT), 170
  information technology (IT) usage in tax administration, 39–40
  tax incentives, 38–39
  tax pressure on companies, 49
  tax revenue collection, 35
  tax to GDP ratio, 35
  VAT structure, 36–38, 162
Brown, Gordon, 183
Browne, Christopher, 98
Brunton, Paul, 155
Bulganin, 86
Butani, Mukesh, 234

Cambodia, 147
Camdessus, Mr., 104, 112
Canada, 128
careers
  Adviser to Finance Minister, 150, 154–162
  as Chief Economist in Her Majesty's Revenue and Customs (HMRC). *see* Chief Economist in HMRC
  as a consultant at World Bank, 15
  as Director of NIPFP, 69, 115, 123–128
  at IMF. *see* IMF years
  as permanent invitee in Trade and Economic Relations Committee (TERC), 180
  as RBI Chair Professor at ICRIER, 133–139
  chairing Tax Forum, 227–229
  teaching at TAU, 9–13
  Visiting Fellow at Australian National University (ANU), 17–18
  Visiting Fellow at DSE, 16
  Visiting Fellow at LSE, 17, 246
Caro, Dr. Soraya, 46
Carrizosa, Miguel, 61
Casimir, 66
Cavallo, Domingo, 46–47
Ceaucescu, President, 87
Centre for Inter-American Tax Administrations (CIAT), 112, 197
Chairman of Tax Administration Reform Commission (TARC), 175, 229–235, 251
chairing Tax Forum, 227–229

chairmanship of tax policy working group, 128–131, 139–145
innovations in taxation, 130
integrated VAT structure, 144
lectures on tax policy, 131
medium-term measures, 129–130
recommendations for indirect taxes, 143
state-level VAT structure, 130, 144
tariff policy reforms, 129
Tenth Plan tax policy and administration, 139–145
views on dividend distribution tax, 143
Chakraborty, Pinaki, 242
Chakravarty, Manas, 135
Chakravarty, Soumen, 125
Chakravarty, Sukhamoy, 10–12, 16, 18
Chand, Sheetal, 111
Chandra, Sarat, 186
Chatterjee, Mrs., *xiii*
Chatterji, Pulok, 209, 213–214
Chaudhary, Rohitash, *xiii*
Chaudhri, Gokul, 234
Chaudhuri, Mrinal Datta, *xiii*, 10
Chaudhury, Eva Datta, 10
Chaudhury, Mr., 97, 99
Chaudhury, Pyarilal Shome, 99
Chavez, Hugo, 149
Chelliah, Raja, 37, 127
Chidambaram, P., 38, 93, 125, 127–128, 136–138, 149–175, 189, 202–203, 209, 215
Chief Economist in HMRC, 182–184
Executive Committee (ExCom), 192–193, 200
international research conferences, 196–199
Knowledge, Analysis and Intelligence (KAI) cell, 189, 191–192
research with academia, 194–195
staff support, 193–194
stakeholder meetings, 194
visits to field offices, 199–200
Chile, 107, 198
tax administration, 53
VAT evasion, 53
China, 100–103, 133, 147, 198
Chowdhury, Debasish Roy, 135
Clinton, Bill, 113
Cnossen, Sijbren, 235
Coefficient of Human Inequality (CHI), 119
Colombia, 133
Colombian tax reforms, 42–46
tax administration measures, 44
VAT reforms, 43
'Commander of the Order of the Southern Cross', *xv*, *xvi*, 25, 69–70
conferences on taxation trends, 112–114
Corden, Max, 17–18
corporation income tax, 6
Costa Rica, 108
large taxpayer unit (LTU), 51–52
tax administration, 50–51
tax reforms, 51–52
VAT structure, 50–51
Cram Notes, 67–68
Crane, Catalina, 46
Czechoslovakia, 107

Darling, Alistair, 183
Dasgupta, Ajit, *xiii*, 9
Dasgupta, Asim, 139, 159
Datta, Dipti Bhushan, *xiii*, 9
Datta, Kanika, 202
David, 74–76
Dayuma, 54, 66
Denmark, 107
Dernburg, Tom, 12–13
Desai, Ashok, 135, 153
Desai, Lord Meghnad, *xiii*, 2, 246
Dey, Nikhil, 180
Dickens, Charles, 17, 204

Director of ICRIER, 206
analysis of General Anti-Avoidance Rules (GAAR), 209–218, 251
Director of NIPFP, 69, 115
Central State Tax (CST) reforms, 126
committee work, 126–128
research and administration, 123–125
Dong, Mao Tse, 102
Dunn, David, 44
Dutta, Bhaskar, 125

Economic Commission for Latin America and the Caribbean (ECLAC), 53
Economist Programme (EP), 22
Ecuador, tax reforms in, 54–55
Eichengreen, Jerry, 132
Elena, 87
Elizabeth, Queen, 253
Empowered Committee (EC) of India, 38
Empowered Committee of State Finance Ministers, 156–160
Enhanced Structural Adjustment Facility (ESAF), 97–98, 111, 133
Escolano, Julio, 54
Ethiopia, 107
Eva, 11

Fajgenbaum, Jose, 30, 40
Fernandez, Arturo, 35
Fernandez, Roque, 47, 49
Figliuoli, Lorenzo, 35
Fiscal Responsibility and Budget Management (FRBM Act, 2003), 181
France, 107
Franklin, Jon, 193
Fundrey, Jon, 191

Gandhi, Mohandas Karamchand, 64
Gandhi, Rajiv, 121
Gandhi, Ved Prakash, 76, 94
Gatti, Rev. Fr., *xiii*
Georgescu, Florin, 88
Ghana, 111
Ghosh, A. K., 125
Ghosh, Amitav, 186
Gillham, Jonathan, 195
Gold, Joseph, 107
Gomez-Sabaini, J. C., 50
Goods and Services Tax (GST), 163–165, 202, 235–239
Goods and Services Tax (GST) Council, 38
Gorcea, Eugeniu C., 88
Grigg, Jack, 193
Guajardo, Ildefonso, 58
Guatemala, 60–61
Guldotti, Pablo, 49
Gupta, Ashok, 139
Gutierrez, Ricardo, 47
Guyasamin, 54

Hadar, Joseph, *xiii*, 6
Haindl, Erik, 35, 42, 53, 63, 90
Hammeker, Mr., 197
Harberger, Arnold C., 6–7, 42
Hartnett, Dave, 182, 189, 192–193, 195
Hazra, Indrajit, *xiii*
Henkin, Louis, 110
Hife, Emanuel, 43
Hill, C. P., 28
Hommes, Rudolf, 45–46

IMF years
African experience, 72–79
ambassador to Singapore, 145–147
Andorra, 89–90
Argentina, 46–50
Asian experience, 93–103
Bangladesh, 96–100
Basque Region, 90–91
Brazil, 34–42, 190
Chile, 53–54

China, 100–103
Colombia, 42–46, 62, 66, 199
Costa Rica, 50–52
discomforting issues, 31–32
Dominican Republic, 27–29, 31, 33
early missions, 23–33
Ecuador, 54–55
as Fiscal Affairs Department (FAD) economist, 30–31
Guatemala, 60–61
honors, 25, 40, 69–71, 190
Ireland, 91–92
Italy, 92–93
Kazakhstan, 81–87
mission's finding on VAT, 77–78
Nicaragua, 57–59
Paraguay, 61–62
Peru, 55–57
publications during, 23
Romania, 87–89
Spanish language learning, 25–26, 28
teach tax policy, 80
terms of reference (TOR) in consultation, 35
Thailand, 93–94
Turkey, 94–96
Venezuela, 29–31, 33
India, 107, 147
centre-state relations, 128
Friendship Treaty with the Soviet Union, 86
government's poverty alleviation efforts, 118–119
HDI ranking, 119
Inequality-Adjusted HDI (IHDI), 119
Integrated Rural Development Programme (IRDP), 118
Long Term Fiscal Policy (LFP), 115–116
modified VAT (MODVAT) structure, 116
multidimensional poverty, 120
poverty situation, 117–122
reform of tax structure, 115–117
resettlement in, 101
tax revenue to GDP ratio, 116
tax to GDP ratio, 219
VAT introduction, 38
Indian Tax Administration Reform Commission (TARC), 57
India's Fiscal Matters, 134
Indonesia, 147
International Bureau of Fiscal Documentation (IBFD), 197
International Tax Research and Analysis Foundation (ITRAF), 244–245
international trade theory, 6–7
Ireland, 91–92, 132
Israel, 132
Italy, 92–93
Ito, Takashito, 114

Jain, Sunil, 167–168
Jaitley, Arun, 232
Jalan, Dr. Bimal, 129
Jana, Prahlad, *xiii*, 9
Japan, 147
Jeanne S. Mattersdorf Award, 8
Jindal, Pankaj, 219
Jones, Ronald, *xiii*, 3, 6
Joseph, Mr., *xiii*
Joseph, Mr. Manuel, *xiii*
Josette, 12
Joshi, Dharmakirti, 135

Kakar, Sudhir, 248
Kalmanovitz, Salomon, 44
Kamaraj, Shri, 254
Kapadia, Sudhir, 234
Kaplan, Professor Joe, *xiii*, 2–5
Kapoor, Raj, 85
Karnik, Kiran, 177
Kasbekar, S. R., 135
Kathma Diyar Vergisi, 94–95

Kazakhstan, 81–87
state budget deficit, 82
tax reforms, 82–83
Kemp, Jack, 112
Khatkhate, Deena, 135
Kher, Jayant, 135
Khusro, A. M., *xiii*, 10
Kiguel, Miguel, 49
Kondratiuk, Pedro, 42
Krishna, Elizabeth, *xiii*, 10
Krishna, K. L., *xiii*, 10, 203
Krishna, S. M., 138
Krueger, Anne, 114, 151–152
Kumar, B. V., 125
Kumar, Dharma, *xiii*, 10

Lahiri, Jhumpa, 186
Lakshmi, 249
Lalita, 11
Lambarri Gomez, Carlos, 90
Lee, Hsien Loong, 145
lending policies of IMF, 104–110
European Recovery Programme (ERP) financing, 108
illustrations, 108–109
Intensified Collaborative Approach (ICA), 105–107
purchase and repurchase policies, 109
Use of Fund Resources (UFR) policy, 109
Lerda, Juan Carlos, 53
Letwin, Oliver, *xvii*, 208
Liem, Yvonne, 67
Lipton, David, 27
Livingstone, Lyndsey, 68
Lourderaj, Mr., *xiii*

Machado, Vera, 40–41
Maciel, Everardo, 40, 49
Mahaprabhu, Shri Chaitanya, 99
Majumdar, Shyamal, *xiii*
Majumdar, Tapas, *xiii*, 9–10
Malan, Pedro, 49
Malaysia, 132, 147
Manohar, Navneet, 219
Markle, Meghan, 80
Marques Moreira, Marcilio, 36
Mathur, Shalini, 234
Mattos Filho, Ary Oswaldo, 36
McGillivray, Hugh, 199
media interviews, 135, 162
Business Standard, 167–168, 184–186, 202–205, 239
The Economic Times, 173, 175, 212–213
Hindu BusinessLine, 182
The Telegraph, 188–189
Mellon, Father, *xiii*, 25
Mendez, Estuardo, 60
Mendez, Rudolf, 52
Merino, Aida E., 54
Mexican taxation, 112
Mexico, 109, 133, 198
Mieszkowski, 7
Miranda, Mr., *xiii*
Mishra, P. K., 234
Mitra, Amit, 127, 254
Modi, Arbind, 131, 140
Modi, Narendra, 165
Mohanty, Deepak, 208
Moily, Veerappa, 138
Moreno Leguizamon, Dr. Carlos J., 124
Morris, Cynthia, 12
Mozambique, 111
Mrinal, 11
Mukherjee, Anjan (Anjanda), 3
Mukherjee, Nivedita, 153
Mukherjee, Pranab, 201, 209
Mukherjee, Shri Sadananda, *xiii*
Mukhopadhyay, Hiranya, 125
Mukhopadhyay, Sukumar, 123, 139
Munoz, Roger, 51
Musgrave, Richard A., 6
Muten, Leif, 58
Myint, Hla, 16

Nabanita, 11
naïve art, 41–42, 54, 60, 66, 185, 190
  Ecuadorian, 54
  Guatemalan, 60
Naïve Art: Ode to the Unknown Artist, 41
Nagar, A. L., *xiii*, 10, 203
Nath, Dwarka, *xiii*
Nath, Miss, *xiii*
National Informatics Centre (NIC), 160
National Rural Employment Programme (NREP), 118
Nayak, Gautam, 234
Nayak, Pulin, 16, 243
Nazarbayev, President, 81, 84
Nepal, 133
the Netherlands, 107–109
Nicaragua, 57–59
  hyperinflation, effect of, 57
  tax evasion, 57, 59
  tax reforms, 57–59
  tax to GDP ratio, 57
Nilima, 96
Norregaard, John, 68
Norway, 108

Obama, Barack, 204
O'Donnell, Gus, 190
Ordonez de Molina, Ana, 60
Ortega, Daniel, 57
Otero, Susan, 68

Pai, Mohandas, 177, 244
Palestine, 132
Pant, K. C., 140–141, 232
Paraguay, 61–62, 133, 139
Parande, Yashodhan, 179
Pattanaik, Prashant, 3–4
Penner, Rudolph, *xiii*, 5
Peru, 55–57, 110
  hyperinflation, effect of, 55
  tax reforms, 55–57
  tax to GDP ratio, 55
Pessino, Carola, 49
Piketty, Thomas, 141
Pisa, Julio, 44
Poddar, Satya, 234
poverty alleviation programme, Fund-assisted, 110–112
Prasad, Rajendra, 96
publications
  BEPS: The Global Taxation Agenda (2016, Wolters Kluwer), 245
  'Contours and Conflicts in Tax Design: Principles and International Practice' (2018, London School of Economics Law Working Paper 11), 246
  'Debt Accumulation in a Financial Crisis' (2013, in Mohanty ed., Cambridge University Press), 208
  Development and Taxation: Sixty Critical Commentaries (2017, Academic Foundation), 243–244
  The G20 Development Agenda: An Indian Perspective (2015, Cambridge University Press), 206
  The G20 Macroeconomic Agenda: India and the Emerging Economies (2014, Cambridge University Press), 206
  Indian Tax Administration: A Dialogue (2013, Orient BlackSwan), 207
  'Rebalancing and Structural Policies—An Indian Perspective' (2012, *Oxford Review of Economic Policy*), 208
  Taxation Principles and Applications: A Compendium (2014, Lexis Nexis), 23, 242

Tax Shastra: Administrative Reforms in India, United Kingdom and Brazil (2012, BS Books), 188, 200, 207
work on Mexican value added tax, in *National Tax Journal* (1988), 23

Raha, A. K., 179
Rajagopalachari, Shri, 254
Rajendran, S., 236
Rajmal, Shri, 135
Rakshit, Mihir, *xiii*, 9
Ramachandran, Mr., *xiii*
Ramanathan, Sellapan (Nathan), 145
Rangachary, K., 211
Rangarajan, Dr., 123
Rao, Mr. Subba, *xiii*
Ravi, Narasimhan, *xiii*
Rawat, D. S., 242
Ray, Gautam, 131, 166
RBI Chair Professor at ICRIER, 133–139
adviser to Government of West Bengal, 139
adviser to Madhya Pradesh government, 136–137
analysis of Indian fiscal federalism, 133–136
member of Karnataka Tax Reforms Commission, 138–139
recommendations of direct tax code, 218–225
income tax structure changes, 223–224
proposed Capital Gains Savings Scheme (CGSS), 220–221
proposed changes in compliance costs, 224–225
proposed minimum alternate tax (MAT), 221
proposed wealth tax, 222
reintroduction of Commodities Transaction Tax (CTT), 225–227
taxation of capital gains, 220
taxation of house property income, 222–223
taxation of non-profit organisations, 221–222
taxation of salaried and self-employed, 224
tax treatment of retirement savings, 219–220
Restrepo Salazar, Juan Camilo, 46
Robins, Harold, 149
Rodrigo, Guillermo, 49
Rodriguez, Dr. Jorge Alberto, 49
Rodriguez, Jorge Armando, 44
Romania, 87–89
Romer, David, 208
Ronald, 41
Roy, Arundhuti, 186
Runudi, 3
Rural Labour Employment Guarantee Programme (RLEGP), 118
Russell, William, *xiii*
Rwanda, 131–132

Sanchez, Carlos, 47
Schenone, Osvaldo, 42–43, 54, 63–64, 89, 133
Schmidt-Hebbel, Klaus, 53
Schulthess, Walter, 47
Sen, Amartya, 10–11, 16
Sen, Nabendu, *xiii*, 9
Sengupta, Dr. Arjun, 128
Sengupta, Nitish, 153
Seth, Vikram, 186
Sharma, Roopa, *xiii*
Shome, Paresh Lal, 96–97
Shome properties, 99
Singapore, 132
Singh, Digvijay, 136–137
Singh, Dr. Manmohan, *xiii*, 37, 128, 153, 183, 189, 209, 214, 236
Singh, Kanwarjit, 123

Singh, V. P., 121
Sinha, Yashwant, 140, 235
Social Dimensions of Adjustment (SDA), 111
Soto, Alan Saborio, 52
South Africa, 76–79
Southern Methodist University (SMU), 4–6
Spahn, Paul Bernd, 35, 63, 90–91, 123, 133
Spence, Michael, 208
Sri Lanka, 147
Srinate, Supriya, 212
Srivastava, D. K., 140
stabilisation programmes, 105
Stern, Nick, 5
Stiglitz, Joseph, 207–208
Stotsky, Janet, 67
Structural Adjustment Facility (SAF), 98, 111
sub-prime crisis, 181
Subrahmanyam, B. V. R., 209, 213–214, 229
Sundaram, K., 10
Sutradhar, 173–174

Tacchi, Carlos, 47
Tagore, Rabindranath, 186
Tanzi, Vito, *xiii*, 12, 20–22, 25–26, 31, 33, 35–36, 39, 41–42, 46, 48, 50, 53–54, 56, 78, 83, 112, 125, 128, 133–134
Tata Consultancy Services (TCS), 160–161
tax avoidance, 210
tax base erosion and profit shifting (BEPS), 198, 216
tax evasion, 210
tax incentives, 15
tax mitigation, 210
Tendulkar, Suresh, *xiii*
Tendulkar, Vijay, 10
Thacker, Anish, 217
Thackray, Mick, 193
Thailand, 147
Tiwari, Santosh, 234
Toro, Juan, 53
Turkey, 94–96, 108

Ullah, Aman, *xiii*, 7, 10–11
Ulster, 132
University of Rochester, 2–5
Use of Fund Resources (UFR)-related economic programme, 26

Vallejos, Victor M., 44
value added tax (VAT), 29
Vanvari, Girish, 234
Venezuela, 149
Viswanathan, Renuka, 138
Vodafone issue, 194, 215–216

Wachtel, Howard, 9, 12, 15, 22
Western Hemisphere Department (WHD) country programme, 27
Wisman, Jon, 12
Woldemariam, Assi, 68

Yew, Lee Kwan, 146

Zabel, *xiii*
Zee, Howell, 67
Zinn, Howard, 28